D1609856

WILLIAM THE LION

WILLIAM THE LION
1143–1214

Kingship and Culture

D.D.R. Owen

TUCKWELL PRESS

For Berit

First published in 1997 by
Tuckwell Press Ltd
The Mill House
Phantassie
East Linton
East Lothian EH40 3DG
Scotland

Copyright © D.D.R. Owen 1997

All rights reserved
ISBN 1 86232 005 5

The publisher gratefully acknowledges subsidy
of the Scottish Arts Council for the publication
of this book

British Library Cataloguing-in-Publication Data
A Catalogue record for this book
is available on request from
the British Library

Typeset by Hewer Text Composition Services, Edinburgh
Printed and bound by Cromwell Press, Melksham, Wiltshire

Contents

Illustrations

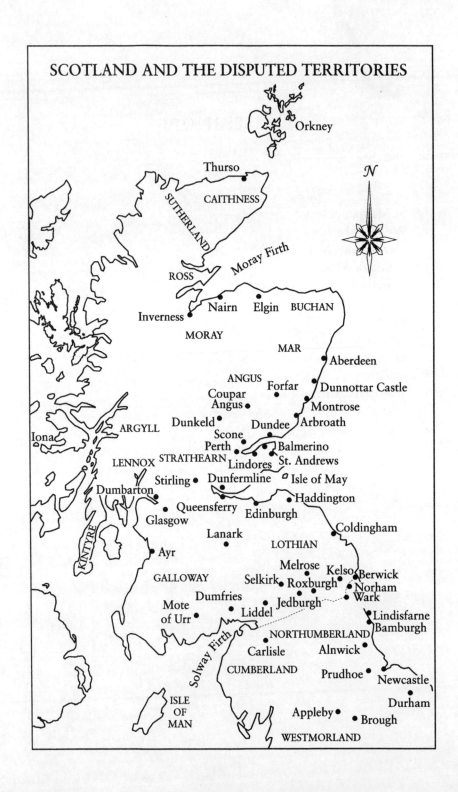

SCOTLAND AND THE DISPUTED TERRITORIES

Orkney

N

Thurso

SUTHERLAND

CAITHNESS

Moray Firth

ROSS

Nairn Elgin BUCHAN

Inverness

MORAY

MAR

Aberdeen

ANGUS Forfar Dunnottar Castle

Coupar
Angus Montrose

Dunkeld Dundee Arbroath

Scone

ARGYLL

Iona

Perth Balmerino

STRATHEARN Lindores St. Andrews

LENNOX

Stirling Dunfermline Isle of May

Dumbarton

Queensferry Haddington

Glasgow Edinburgh

Lanark Coldingham

LOTHIAN

KINTYRE

Ayr

Melrose Kelso
Berwick

GALLOWAY Selkirk Roxburgh Norham

Dumfries Wark

Mote Liddel Jedburgh

of Urr Lindisfarne
Bamburgh

Solway Firth

NORTHUMBERLAND

Carlisle Alnwick

CUMBERLAND

Prudhoe Newcastle

ISLE
OF
MAN Durham

Appleby Brough

WESTMORLAND

N

Durham •

• Whitby

Richmond •

York •

Chester •   Nottingham •

WALES

• Yarmouth

Northampton •   Huntingdon •

Woodstock •

• Oxford

Bristol •   Windsor •   • London   Canterbury •

Glastonbury •   • Bruges

Salisbury •   Winchester •   Dover •   Dunkirk

Southampton •   • Calais   FLANDERS

CORNWALL   • Portsmouth

• Arras

PICARDY

ENGLISH CHANNEL

Beauvais •   CHAMPAGNE

Cherbourg •

Rouen •

• Caen   • Paris

• Falaise

Chartres •

NORMANDY   • Troyes

Mont-Saint-   • Le Mans

BRITTANY   Michel

MAINE   • Tours

Angers •   TOURAINE

Fontevrault •   • Chinon

ANJOU   Mirebeau •   • Poitiers

POITOU

AQUITAINE   • Limoges

• Périgueux

SCOTLAND'S
SOUTHERN
CONNECTIONS

• Toulouse

Preface

Our conversation had turned to the role of Scotland in Europe when I mentioned to my acquaintance the dominant French influence on the kingdom of William the Lion. His shocked reaction was hardly, I felt, in the spirit of the 'auld alliance'. They'd certainly, he went on, never taught him anything like that at school. And come to think of it, he hadn't been told about much at all before Bannockburn. Indeed for him Scottish history of the years around 1200 was as remote as the fabled accounts of William's contemporary Gengis Khan. When I pointed out that a mere ten octogenarians joining hands down the centuries would link the Lion's days to our own, he conceded that there might have been a worrying gap in his education. Perhaps he should try to repair it. So where should be begin?

As there was no accessible biography of independent Scotland's longest-reigning monarch, I wondered if I might be of some service to my friend and others like him by providing an account of William's reign set within its broader historical and cultural context. No historian myself, I approached the task with an interest roused by my researches into such contemporary literature bearing on Scotland as had escaped the depredations of time. Of crucial importance was a hitherto sadly neglected work, a spirited and witty romance composed by one of William's subjects for the entertainment of his courtiers. I had become convinced that, although on the geographical perimeter of Europe, Scotland had made a significant contribution to the cultural flowering that goes by the name of the Twelfth-Century Renaissance. Of this my friend had declared himself open to persuasion.

The present study, then, has a dual purpose. Leaning heavily on the scholarship of historians past and present, I shall piece together the story of William's reign as it spanned that exciting period in European history which saw the high point of feudal chivalry and crusading endeavour under the ascendancy of the rival dynasties of the ambitious Plantagenets and the French Capetians. At the same time I shall present my account against the background of a developing Scottish society which, while cherishing its native traditions, was open to the wider European scene, on which it left its own distinctive mark. My hope is that the two aspects of my study will prove mutually illuminating and help to draw the reader closer to this fascinating period in Scotland's history.

The Notes have been kept to a minimum. For further information, see especially the works asterisked in the Select Bibliography.

Acknowledgements

My first debt of gratitude is to that chance acquaintance whose name escapes me but whose self-confessed ignorance persuaded me of the need for a study along these lines. My attempt to be of some service to those in his position has profited from the advice of numerous colleagues, but especially from the shrewd comments passed on my text by David Dorward and W.W. Scott. I must also express my thanks for all the help cheerfully provided by the staff of the St Andrews University Library and not least by my wife Berit.

D.D.R.O.

The Family of William the Lion
(abridged)

Kenneth I (MacAlpin)
c. 843–58

Malcolm III (Canmore)
1057–93

m. (1) Ingibiorg   m. (2) Margaret

Donald III (Bane)
1093–7

Duncan II
(1094)

Matilda (or Edith:
m. Henry I
of England)

Mary

Edgar
1097–1107

Matilda
(m. Stephen
of England)

Alexander I
1107–24

David I
1124–53
m. Maud (Matilda)

Earl Henry
d. 1152

Malcolm IV
1153–65

William (The Lion)
1165–1214
m. Ermengarde

David
Earl of Huntingdon

Alexander II
1214–49

(daughters who
m. English nobles)

ONE

Ancestry and Early Life

In 1165 William succeeded to the throne as twenty-seventh in the tangled line of Scottish kings commonly reckoned to have been inaugurated over three hundred years earlier by Kenneth MacAlpin. He, as Kenneth I, is credited with being the first to rule over both Picts and Scots, whose fortunes had by then become bafflingly interwoven. Before him, the country had been settled and often disputed by several different peoples, of whom the first we can identify were the Celtic-speaking Picts. They held varying regions of modern Scotland in the face of pressure from the south by the Romans and, after their departure, by the invading Angles of Northumbria. Meanwhile, in the south-west, the extensive territory of Strathclyde, which originally included Cumbria and stretched as far as Dumbarton in the north, was an independent kingdom, the home of Britons, near-relatives of the Welsh. It was possibly with their collusion that the Scots, speakers of a different form of Celtic known to us as Gaelic, left their native Ireland by the end of the fifth century and established in Kintyre and Argyll their own kingdom of Dalriada; and this they progressively expanded, largely at the expense of the Picts. An important encroachment on their territory occurred at the hands of the Vikings or Norsemen, who, from the end of the eighth century, followed up their raiding activities by occupying the western isles and a good deal of the seaboard as well as Shetland, Orkney, Caithness, Sutherland and part of Ross.

After these centuries of turmoil, much of which is left obscure by the often conflicting evidence of the annals, the advent of Kenneth MacAlpin in about 843 provides a welcome starting point for what we may think of as Scottish history, if not the history of Scotland. Here at least is a name to put at the head of a genealogical table. Of warrior and probably royal stock from Dalriada and conceivably with some Pictish blood, he was the first to figure as king of both Picts and Gaels in the jumbled testimony of the royal lists. The characteristically Pictish tradition of matrilinear succession gave way to the more familiar European preference for the male line; and though not every subsequent move in the passing down of the kingship can be fully explained (might may sometimes have prevailed over right among the claimants), there is no doubt that Kenneth was the distant ancestor of William the Lion. But we shall jump some eighteen intervening reigns and take up the story again with William's great-grandfather, Malcolm III, who died half a century before his birth, but whose memory must have been very much alive among his elders. Known to his contemporaries as 'Canmore' (the Gaelic 'Ceann Mor' meaning literally 'Great Head'), he more than anyone turned Scotland's face away from the vicious domestic feuding exploited in Shakespeare's *Macbeth* and towards the wider horizons south of its borders. Not that Malcolm's own path to the kingship was a peaceful one. The system of succession as it had evolved encouraged the more impatient aspirants to the throne to dispose prematurely of any current occupant; and only after the slaying of Macbeth and his stepson Lulach was Malcolm's title secured in 1058.

At that time Scotland's south-eastern border may have been notionally on the Tweed. But the whole area between the Forth and the Humber with its large Anglo-Saxon population was not securely held by either the Scottish or the English crown, each nursing ambitions to control the earldom of Northumbria with its rich cultural inheritance and great strategic value. To the west, Cumbria was similarly open to dispute, despite pledges traded between the Scottish and English kings, with aid being promised by the former to the latter. A visit by Malcolm in 1059 to the court of Edward the Confessor resolved nothing, but was followed by a Scottish raid into Northumbria while its earl was on pilgrimage in Rome. This was only one episode in the general turmoil that foreshadowed the collapse of the Anglo-Saxon dynasty. It is possible that Malcolm, who at that time was married to Ingibiorg, daughter of the Viking earl of Orkney, had a finger in a Norse invasion of Northumbria in 1066. Although this was quelled by the new king Harold, it deflected his attention from the Norman threat which was promptly realised on the field at Hastings with Harold's own defeat and death and the accession of King William to the English throne.

The Conquest confronted Malcolm with a new set of circumstances. A cousin of his was vested with Northumbria by William; but matters there remained temptingly unstable. In 1068 Edgar Atheling, scion of the defunct Anglo-Saxon royal house, took refuge at the Scottish court together with his mother and sisters, Margaret and Christina; and they were joined by others opposed to the Conqueror. Whether or not with

Malcolm's connivance, Edgar and his supporters then attempted to seize Northumbria, but only to be harshly thwarted by William. Shortly afterwards, Malcolm himself conducted a brutal but equally abortive campaign, launching an assault on the earldom from the west by way of his lands in Cumberland. A perhaps biased chronicler tells how it resulted in many English captives being hauled north into slavery.

At about this time Malcolm, whose first wife Ingibiorg had somehow left the scene, replaced her with Edgar's sister Margaret, to whom we shall return. Suffice it here to note that he thus allied himself to the old royal house of England. The Conqueror, evidently alert to the danger this posed for him, proceeded to march into Scotland with naval support, crossed the Forth, and confronted Malcolm by the Tay at Abernethy. His move ended peacefully, with Malcolm pledging allegiance to William and making over hostages, probably including Duncan, his son by Ingibiorg. That was in 1072. For seven years Malcolm must have smarted under this humiliation; but then, with William warring in Normandy against his own son Robert, he broke his pact and once again went ravaging Northumberland as far as the Tyne. This provoked a vicious revolt by the Northumbrians, which prompted William to despatch Robert, with whom he was now reconciled, to lead an army into Scotland. There in 1080 he received Malcolm's renewed submission at Falkirk; and on his return he founded a New Castle upon the Tyne.

So matters stood for another decade until, with the Conqueror's successor William Rufus preoccupied like his father in Normandy, Malcolm once more invaded Northumbria. Again his ambitions came to nothing; for William's response was prompt and effective. With his brother Robert, he pursued the Scottish king as he retreated with his spoils of war, came up with him in Lothian, and forced the yoke of homage upon his shoulders as before. To make matters worse, in the following year, Rufus took over Cumberland as far as the Solway and built a castle at Carlisle. As well as its garrison, he introduced large numbers of settlers into the newly restored town and its environs. This brings us to 1092. A year later, an attempt by Malcolm to treat with Rufus in Gloucester having proved fruitless, he returned to Scotland, mustered an army, and made one last incursion into Northumbria. This time the earl was ready for him. A trap was sprung near the river Aln; and there Malcolm perished along with his eldest son. Three days later, on 16 November 1093, his mortally sick wife Margaret followed him to the grave. Obsessed as he had been with extending his rule to the south, Malcolm had been forced to give best to the might of the Norman inheritors of England.

With the focusing of his interest on and beyond his southern borders (though doubtless still keeping a wary eye on his lands to the north), he had largely turned his back on his Gaelic inheritance. Regrettable though the cultural loss may have been, politically Scotland's claim to be a truly European power would strengthen in the following centuries. It is supposed that the youthful Malcolm had spent Macbeth's stormy reign in Northumbria under the protection of its earl, Siward; and that could partially explain his hankering after the lordship of the northern English territories. This Anglo-Saxon connection was then reinforced by his marriage to the princess Margaret; and it might be argued that the new family ties provided a more worthy incentive for his later forays beyond the Tweed.

Margaret, granddaughter of King Edmund 'Ironside', is believed to have been born in Hungary in the mid-1040s. She is renowned above all for her deep piety, which was praised by her contemporaries and formally recognised by her canonisation in 1250, some thirty-six years after the death of her great-grandson William the Lion. Throughout her reign as queen, she showed, it seems, an intense interest in ecclesiastical affairs, and this at a time when the traditions of the ancient Celtic church had not yet been fully accommodated with those of Rome.

Christianity appears to have been introduced into south-west Scotland during late Roman times or soon after by the ministration of British missionaries, among whom was the shadowy Saint Ninian. They and their successors spread the faith among the Scots of Dalriada and undertook the progressive conversion of the southern Picts. Another of their number was Saint Kentigern, affectionately known as Saint Mungo ('dearest friend'), who is credited with the founding of the church at Glasgow. Better documented is the life of Saint Columba, who left his native Ireland in 563 to found the monastic community on Iona. Gradually Christianity supplanted the old pagan rites throughout the Scottish mainland and the Northern Isles, fostered in a scattering of humble churches and the isolated cells of anchorites, many only remembered through place names, if at all.

By the seventh century, the Celtic church had become established in Lindisfarne on the Northumbrian coast and extended its influence as far south as the Thames. But then, confronted by the variant traditions of the church of Rome (notably regarding the calculation of the date of Easter), it began its slow retreat. A significant event was the synod convened at Whitby in 664, at which the Roman usage found general favour. With the turning of the tide, the characteristically loose monastic organisation of the Celtic church lost ground to the tighter structure preferred by Rome, with the bishops responsible for their designated territories and constituent parishes. Having been raised in the Roman tradition, Queen Margaret brought her own influence to bear on this gradual process, or reform as some would see it, which never had a final resolution. Even in the days of William the Lion, disputes rooted in the conflict of traditions were still liable to arise from time to time.

We can imagine William being intrigued by the life of his distinguished ancestress, an account of which has survived for posterity in the glowing Latin prose of her confessor who, though he only signed himself 'T', is normally identified with Turgot, one-time monk at Durham and later Bishop of St Andrews.* He dedicates his work to Margaret's daughter Matilda, then queen of England after her marriage to Henry I in 1100, saying that he bows to her request to undertake it in view of his particularly intimate relations with her mother. Despite his eulogistic style and with possible reservations concerning certain doctrinal points he mentions, we have no reason to doubt his word on Margaret's general character and practices.

From childhood, he tells us, she had led a strict life, applying her remarkable memory to the study of devotional texts. Her marriage to Malcolm was the result more of the persuasion of her friends than of any personal inclination to the life of a queen. Her great piety did not prevent her from being a pleasant conversationalist as well as ready with wise advice on matters of state. Generous to religious foundations, she chose to build at the place of her marriage (Dunfermline) a splendid church dedicated to the Holy Trinity, to which she made rich benefactions, as also to the church at St Andrews. Her own chamber she turned into a workshop, where noble ladies in her service busied themselves with the making of rich clerical vestments.

Though of an equable temperament, she was capable of great sternness and severity, which made her both loved and feared by her close associates. She had her children strictly brought up, ordering them to be whipped when they misbehaved and well instructed in Christian

* *Life of St Margaret Queen of Scotland* by Turgot, tr. William Forbes-Leith.

principles. Her husband himself dreaded giving her offence; and it was through her insistence that he was attentive to the exercise of justice, mercy, almsgiving, and his religious duties.

She did much to enrich the kingdom, encouraging merchants to bring in precious wares from various countries. In particular she introduced more colourful dress and ornaments and encouraged new, elegant fashions, insisting on the smartness of the royal entourage and that a large body of retainers should accompany the king on his travels. At the same time, she brightened the royal palace with silver and gold. All this was done not out of a love of vain pomp, but to enhance the royal dignity. Her own humility remained unaffected; and indeed she required Turgot not to be sparing with his rebukes, should she merit them.

Turgot then mentions her reform of Scottish ecclesiastical practices, recalling in particular a three-day council at which she was supported by a few of her friends. In the debates, Malcolm, who spoke English as fluently as his own tongue (Gaelic), acted as interpreter for both sides. Decisions were taken on a number of reforms: the keeping of Lent according to Roman tradition; the obligation to take the Sacrament at Easter; the dropping of 'barbarous rites' (unspecified) from the celebration of Mass; the prohibition of worldly activities on the Lord's Day; the banning of marriage between a man and his stepmother or the widow of his deceased brother.

Margaret's devotion to prayer and fasting is stressed: it was even to lead to her grave infirmity. So charitable and concerned with the needs of the poor was she that on occasion she actually purloined the king's own property to give it to the needy. Her compassion extended to the liberation of many English captives who were kept in slavery in the kingdom. She held hermits in particular veneration and used to visit them in person. Pilgrims too were the objects of her charity; and for those bound for the shrine at St Andrews she established lodgings on both sides of the Forth, providing them with servants and ships to carry them free of toll (the Queensferry passage was so named in her memory).

The period of Lent and the forty days before Christmas she observed with the utmost rigour. Daily she washed the feet of six paupers and personally fed nine infant orphans. Another three hundred of the needy were served with food in the royal hall; and of these she herself waited on two dozen, whom she then supported throughout the entire year. Her own fasting was not without personal cost, however, for it induced acute stomach pains from which, says Turgot, she suffered throughout her life.

He tells of one incident which was considered a miracle at the time. A book of Gospels, which she had had beautifully adorned, was accidentally dropped into a ford by the person who had charge of it on a journey. Some time later it was found lying open at the bottom of the stream virtually undamaged by the water. In this Turgot believed he saw the hand of the Lord.

Just before her last, fatal, illness, she realised that she had not long to live and took her farewell of the faithful cleric, begging him to care for her children and instruct them in pious humility. Her last hours were described to him by another beloved priest, who was present. It was three days after the death of her husband that her son Edgar arrived with that tragic news. Finding her so close to her own end, he was at first reluctant to reveal it. She, however, guessed what he had to tell and, thanking God for the penance of this further sorrow, gave up her soul to Christ. Turgot was among those who brought her body to the church she had founded in Dunfermline (the place of her death is not mentioned, though later accounts speak of Edinburgh); and there it was laid to rest opposite the high altar. (After her canonisation it would be placed in a precious shrine and reinterred with that of her husband beside the altar.)

We must assume that the picture of Margaret thus painted by Turgot for her own daughter was a reasonably close likeness. Her extreme piety cannot be in doubt; but whether or not her early inclinations were to retreat from the world, we are left with the impression of a woman of formidable will prepared to confront public affairs in her own way without shirking the responsibilities her marriage laid upon her. Herself a princess by birth, she was determined to maintain and even enhance the dignity of the Scottish crown. At the same time, she did her best to ensure that her husband was worthy of it. Not only her subjects but Malcolm himself, we are assured, held her in awe; and her counsels did not fall on deaf ears. She was concerned that Scotland should move with the times in secular as well as religious matters; and despite her own frugal ways, she had at heart its prosperity and the welfare of its religious institutions. As regards the latter, her especial care was for the church at Dunfermline, founded by her as a Benedictine priory, but eventually raised to the status of abbey in 1128. She is also said to have restored the monastery on Iona.

Her considerable influence over Malcolm, as is often pointed out, is reflected in the Saxon names given to the first four of their six sons: Edward after her father, Edgar after her brother, and Edmund and Ethelred after her grandfather and great-grandfather respectively. Malcolm, with his English preoccupations, may have needed little persuading in the matter. On the other hand, the depth of his commitment to his wife's high ideals in both secular and religious matters can only be guessed. The image posterity has formed of him may well have gained some lustre from her reflected glory.

The violent death in 1093 of both Malcolm and Edward, his eldest son by Margaret, put the stability of the kingdom at risk. A resurgence in Celtic feeling accompanied the accession of Malcolm's brother, Donald 'Bane' ('the Fair'). His right to the throne was then disputed by Duncan, Malcolm's son by Ingibiorg, who had spent many years as hostage at the court of the Conqueror and his son Rufus and was now living there of his own free will, remote from his Celtic roots. With the active support of his Anglo-Norman hosts, he marched to Scotland and seized the throne. Six months later, however, he came to a bloody end; and Donald resumed his reign, which then continued until his ousting by the combined efforts of Edgar Atheling and Rufus. He was replaced by Edgar, the second son of Malcolm and Margaret and nephew of the Atheling. Thenceforth Scotland's destiny was irrevocably linked to that of England and its Norman rulers.

Edgar reigned from 1097 to 1107, but as vassal of the English crown; and when Henry I, on his accession in 1100, married his sister Matilda (also known as Edith), Anglo-Scottish relations were further cemented. Edgar, who had remained wifeless, was succeeded by a fifth brother who, as Alexander I, occupied the throne until 1124. Although he took as his wife an illegitimate daughter of Henry I, they had no children; so he was followed as king by David, the youngest of Malcolm's sons.

As David had earlier been endowed with much of Lothian, Teviotdale and Strathclyde, Alexander's own interests seem to have had their focus within what was then thought of as Scotland proper, that is the lands north of the Forth. A particular concern for him was the establishment of the royal authority over the Scottish church without interference from England. Matters came to a head when he chose Turgot, his mother's faithful confessor, as the first non-Celtic bishop of St Andrews. The point at issue was the right of the archbishop of York, as metropolitan of the province to which Scotland belonged, to undertake the consecration.

This went against the grain with Alexander; and although Turgot eventually withdrew to Wearmouth in Northumbria, where he spent his last days, the dispute over York's authority was far from resolved. It was to rumble on through the reign of David I and, as we shall see, reached crisis point in that of William the Lion.

Under Malcolm Canmore and his older sons, then, Scotland had been finding its destined orientation in political, religious and social matters; but it was David's reign that did most to set the stage on which his grandson William was to play his lengthy part. Born in the early 1080s, David accompanied his sister Matilda to the English court, where she was to reign as Henry's queen. There, quite apart from the honour paid him as the queen's brother, he seems to have won general approval. He may have campaigned with Henry in Normandy and was certainly entrusted with some official duties within the kingdom. Then, in 1113 or possibly the following year, Henry found for him a wife of some substance though not in the first flush of youth. This was Maud (or Matilda), grand-niece of the Conqueror and widow of Simon de Senlis, from whom she had inherited an earldom in the shires of Huntingdon, Northampton, Bedford and Cambridge along with other lands all of which now passed to David. By this time he had also secured possession of the lands bequeathed to him in southern Scotland; so to all intents and purposes he had the status of one of Henry's barons when, in 1124, Alexander died without issue and he succeeded to the Scottish throne.

It was under David I that feudalism took firm root in Scotland, largely replacing the looser 'tribal' organisation of Celtic society and kingship, though never fully accepted in the remoter areas. Having evolved among the Franks and taken shape in Capetian France, feudalism, in its ideal form, was a system of government based on the twin principles of secure land tenure and the maintenance of loyal relationships between individuals. The land that constituted the fief was held by the tenant or vassal from his lord in exchange for service on his part and the assurance of the lord's protection in return. The service involved an important military commitment, commonly expressed in terms of knight-service for specified periods, as well as financial aid when needed. Among the lord's rights was that to arrange the marriage of a vassal's male heir, if a minor, and of a female heiress of any age. The mutual obligations were confirmed by a formal act of homage and pledging of faith, often on holy relics, thus incorporating a religious sanction. At the head of the so-called feudal triangle was the king, subject only to God; and beneath him were his barons, who exercised authority over any lesser vassals they might have, while at the base the peasants tended the land for their masters and themselves enjoyed some rights of their own.

This was the social structure, largely patterned on the English model, that became established, with some local variations, in twelfth-century Scotland. While the supreme secular authority was vested in the king, he placed much reliance on his high officials, who appear frequently as witnesses in surviving royal charters. Although the duties of most of them were in the first instance centred within the royal court, their domestic function broadened to encompass affairs of state as the new system of government was progressively consolidated and adapted to Scottish conditions.

Next to the king in prestige and influence was his chancellor. Appointed from the clerical ranks, he was responsible for the drawing up and keeping of records as well as being available to the monarch for consultation and advice. He presided over the 'royal chapel', a team of trained officials which, as well as chaplains to the king's person and family, included clerks and scribes and even, it seems, a royal physician or two. This was the 'civil service' of the day, often used by talented men of ambition as a convenient path to a bishopric.

Then there was the royal chamberlain, one of the barons in regular attendance at court, where his special concern was the royal finances. Under him served members of the lesser nobility, to whom were assigned specific duties. The doorwards (or ushers), for instance, were primarily responsible for ensuring the king's security. The general management of the household was in the hands of the stewards (seneschals), who were also of noble rank. Under Malcolm IV, their office became hereditary and gave its name to the family from which the royal line of Stewarts (or Stuarts) emerged in the fourteenth century.

Although the king would not necessarily have had every member of the royal household at his constant beck and call, he would normally have been attended by a substantial number of them as he moved from place to place. For his life was to a large extent peripatetic: he no doubt favoured certain residences, but Scotland had as yet no permanent capital (Edinburgh would only be fully recognised as such in the sixteenth century), and he would hold court wherever he was drawn by matters of state or, when the opportunity arose, by the aristocratic addiction to the hunt. When more serious business was afoot, he would need to keep in close touch with another of his chief officers, the royal constable; for on him he relied for the mustering of his military forces, normally with the cooperation of the earls, on whom he could call for contingents of men to serve in his campaigns.

There was also the administration of justice to be taken care of; and this was the responsibility of the justiciars, a small number of leading nobles, each wielding the royal authority over one of the main regions of the kingdom. On a more local level the law was dispensed by sheriffs, who might themselves have been of noble birth. While the king's men enforced, to the best of their ability, the rule of justice on the secular level, there were matters over which the church claimed jurisdiction. So, with a certain amount of give and take, the ecclesiastical courts acted outside the royal system in the common cause of maintaining order and a just peace throughout the land.

The religious institutions were the spiritual cement of the feudal structure. Even the hermits, dwelling apart from society, acted as living examples of the devotional life, whilst the priests serving in churches preached and taught the laity their duties towards God and man. Others who renounced the commerce of the world by choosing to live within closed communities, exemplified, at least in theory, the possibility of social harmony based on religious principles. Following the example of his pious mother, David I was to show a more than conventional commitment to the church and its servants.

Even before becoming king he had demonstrated this by making endowments in his English lands; and as lord of Strathclyde he had enriched the see of Glasgow. Thereafter, he played a vital role in encouraging the monastic movement in Scotland. As we saw, Saint Columba had early established a community of Celtic monks on Iona; but monasticism as we know it was, like the feudal system, a transplant from France under the aegis of the Anglo-Normans. Benedictines were early arrivals, and it was some of their number that Queen Margaret called from Canterbury to found the priory at Dunfermline. This David raised to the dignity of abbey; yet the original order was to make little progress in Scotland. David's interest was engaged more by the Tironensians, who followed a reformed version of their rule. In 1113, four years after that order's creation at Tiron near Chartres and eleven before his accession, he brought some of its monks from their home establishment to Selkirk, then, on becoming king, transferred them to a new abbey at Kelso. In 1116 he had himself made a devotional journey to Tiron. He also favoured the Augustinians who, though living in a community, were not cloistered but, as canons, served within their local districts. Under his supervision some of these canons were fetched from England to found Holyrood Abbey at Edinburgh, whilst others were called from France to Jedburgh; and an Augustinian priory was installed alongside the Celtic (Culdee) community at St Andrews. As well as these and other foundations, four houses were created for the more aloof Cistercians, notably the abbeys at Melrose and Newbattle: their strict austerity seems to have held an especial appeal for David. Towards the end of his reign his constable, Hugh de Moreville, settled a group of Premonstratensian canons at Dryburgh, where their abbey followed an originally Augustinian rule now showing a strong Cistercian influence. David was thus, directly or indirectly, responsible for a large influx of French and Anglo-Norman religious, who were to have an important influence on the cultural as well as spiritual life of his country.

While he has received much praise for the liberality shown by himself and various of his barons to the church and its servants, he has also been criticised by other generations for being over-generous in his provision of great tracts of the best land for their use and revenues for their upkeep. This, it was felt, had led to the relative impoverishment of the crown as the wealth of the new religious institutions grew. But there were great gains as well as losses. Among the intangible rewards for the benefactors was the assumption and, usually, stipulation that in these foundations prayers would be offered in perpetuity for the salvation of their souls and those of their family. On the more practical level, the lands they had made over would be well tended and fine buildings would be erected on them, which would provide lodging for travellers, rich and poor alike, and places of refuge for those who needed it. The communities would encourage skilled craftsmen of all kinds and, from their own number, men of literacy and often learning as well as scribes to pass on pious and other texts in carefully worked manuscripts. They provided the scholarly base for the growth of a significant Scottish culture, which, though it was heavily indebted to that of the French and Anglo-Normans, found on occasion its own voice, as will be seen. Whereas the texts copied and studied by the monks were largely standard pious works, it may be mentioned that the Augustinians in particular had a reputation for being receptive to secular as well as religious literature; and they may have had a hand in making some of it known in Scotland.

These civilising influences which David encouraged throughout his long reign were strengthened by the relatively peaceful conditions that prevailed within his kingdom. It could be argued that the main trouble he encountered was largely self-inflicted, as it stemmed from his meddling in affairs beyond his borders, namely the squabble over the English succession in anticipation of the death of Henry I. The rival candidates were firstly Henry's daughter and David's niece Matilda, known as 'the Empress' since she was by this time the widow of the German emperor, and secondly Stephen of Blois, husband of another of David's nieces. Henry had come to favour Matilda; and David, in his role of leading English baron, was the first to swear support for her. However, by the time of Henry's death late in 1135 she had found a second husband, the Plantagenet Geoffrey of Anjou; and the English lords lost no time in settling Stephen on the throne.

David's reaction was to occupy Cumberland and Northumbria and lay siege to Durham, whither Stephen proceeded post-haste and tried to negotiate a peace. The agreement they patched up brought no solution satisfactory to David; so early in 1138 he launched a ferocious attack on Northumbria, to which he had tried to press a claim on behalf of his own son Henry. Stephen countered with an equally vicious attack into Lothian; but, undeterred, David led another motley force into English territory. This time, however, he had outreached himself; and his army was routed at the so-called Battle of the Standard near Northallerton in Yorkshire. Yet even this defeat was not decisive, largely because Matilda's supporters were on the warpath in the south; and David renewed his operations. Stephen tried to buy him off by handing over much of Northumbria to his son Henry, as earl. Then, although the new earl joined Stephen in his struggle against Matilda, when she appeared to gain the upper hand David hurried to her side. Once more, however, his move was ill-judged; for at Winchester they were outmanoeuvred, and David fled back to his northern lands. This was in the autumn of 1141.

That was the end of David's adventuring on English soil. It had brought him both loss and profit: the loss of his earldom of Huntingdon and Northampton, forfeited to Stephen, but the gain for his son of that of Northumbria. Henry had also received Carlisle, which was David's favourite residence. There he was to die in 1153, though his body would be taken to lie beside those of his mother and brothers in Dunfermline Abbey. Four years before this, Carlisle had been the scene of a significant ceremony. For within its walls David had conferred

the order of knighthood on another Henry, the sixteen-year-old son
of Geoffrey Plantagenet and the Empress. And it was he who, on
the death of Stephen in 1154, was to be crowned King of England as
Henry II.

To his successors David bequeathed a kingdom largely subjected to
a foreign aristocracy under royal control alongside, and often intermar-
rying with, its native earls. There were still, of course, parts of modern
Scotland which did not recognise his authority: in Galloway it was far
from secure; the Western Isles were under Norwegian suzerainty and
Argyll and Kintyre virtually autonomous; rebellion brewed in highland
Moray and Ross, whilst the royal hold on Caithness was insecure. One
way of defending the marginal regions was to grant lands there to
some of the newcomers. These new settlers, Anglo-Normans as well
as natives of other French regions including Flanders, were for the most
part unfieffed knights of noble extraction eager to further their careers in
Scotland; others were men of substance who might already own property
in England. Once installed on the estates granted to them, they built
their own castles, not yet of stone but wooden structures set on mottes,
natural or artificial mounds. They had close relations with the various
religious institutions, which provided not only spiritual and cultural
support but general economic benefits too, especially in the matter of
the management of the extensive ecclesiastical properties. The country's
economy was further strengthened by the creation and development of
the burghs, sited at strategic trading-points and generally under the
protection of the nearby castle. The encouragement of merchants from
near and far promoted the development of commercial routes and the
strengthening of communications with the Continent as well as England.
Moreover, the establishment of royal mints and a Scottish coinage was a
token of a healthy and stable economy. David left his kingdom in good
internal shape.

When he died in 1153, he was succeeded not by his son Henry,
earl of Northumbria, who had himself died the previous year, but
by Malcolm, the eldest of his three grandsons. A mere eleven years
old on his accession, Malcolm IV 'the Maiden' (so called because of
his life-long reluctance to take a wife), was perhaps a year senior to
William, whilst his other brother David was born only in 1152 after
his father's death. Let us look, then, at the family background of these
three brothers with all its European ramifications.

As we have seen, they and their three, or perhaps four, sisters could trace their line back to the Conqueror through their father. They could do the same through their mother Ada; for she was the daughter of the Norman earl of Surrey William de Warenne (or Varenne), who also counted the Conqueror among his kinsmen. For good measure, she was as well the great-granddaughter of the Capetian Henry I of France. Ada de Warenne (the name persists as the modern Warren or Warrand) was married to Henry, newly earl of Northumbria, in 1139. After his death, she remained the first lady of the Scottish court, and so in touch with affairs of state, during the reign of Malcolm and the early years of that of William, neither being married in her lifetime, until, having retired to her dower lands in Haddington and Crail (Fife), she died in 1178. Of her daughters one married Florence, the count of Holland, and another Conan, duke of Brittany. Following the royal tradition, she made generous benefactions to religious houses in England and in Scotland, where she founded a Cistercian nunnery at Haddington. Often associated with her sons in the witnessing of charters, she had, we must assume, their interests very much at heart and doubtless exerted a significant influence on their lives.

After the death of their father, the two elder boys, who had probably spent their early years largely under their mother's wing, were suddenly thrust into public life. Their grandfather David at once had Malcolm conducted by Duncan, the earl of Fife, round the Scottish regions and presented as his designated heir. He then personally took young William to Newcastle upon Tyne for recognition by his future subjects as Earl of Northumbria. The following year, 1153, he himself died, and Malcolm was escorted to Scone for his inauguration as the new king.

Scone, near Perth, was the traditional place for the ceremony, having been chosen by the Romans for the site of one of their camps before the Picts gave it this special significance. We cannot be sure of the exact ritual involved; but elements of it probably originated in an ancient Indo-European fertility cult before being adopted by the Celts. The king was seated on the Stone of Destiny, then enrobed and presented with the symbols of his authority. It is unlikely that at this period a crown was used, despite the fact that some Scottish monarchs do appear crowned on their seals, and Malcolm himself is thus represented in a miniature in the 1159 charter of Kelso Abbey. References by later chroniclers to a crowning are probably anachronistic. But whatever its precise nature, the ceremony, accompanied by full Christian rites, would have been steeped in a solemn mystery that must have made a deep impression on the youthful Malcolm and, if he was in attendance, his brother William.

Malcolm was still only twelve and reliant on his leading barons as well as his mother when a long shadow was cast over his kingdom by the accession to the English throne of the dynamic Henry II, himself no more than twenty-one. Whereas Scotland had achieved a relative stability while England was torn by internal divisions, the situation was now at least partly reversed, with England adopting a firm and aggressive stance, whilst Scotland with its boy-king was in a vulnerable position. Some of his subjects, it seems, were reluctant to see Malcolm paying homage to Henry for Cumberland and Westmorland, William being his own vassal for Northumbria. The relations between the two countries were to become a dominant factor in the affairs of Malcolm and his successors.

Even before Henry's arrival on the throne, other threats had to be faced. Norse sagas tell of the sacking of Aberdeen by the marauding king of Norway; but be that as it may, the kingdom was put in more serious peril by the challenge of Somerled, the Norse-Celtic lord of Argyll. Early in 1154, a year of famine in Scotland, Somerled rebelled with his nephews against his royal overlord. Whatever immediate designs he may have had were thwarted; and one of his nephews was captured and sent to the king's stronghold of Roxburgh to be held with his father, who had long languished there as a result of an unsuccessful struggle against David. So Somerled turned his attentions to the Western Isles, which by 1158 he had wrested from the Norse king of Man. Thereafter he made his peace with Malcolm for a time, only to resume hostilities in 1164, when he arrived with an army to launch an assault against Glasgow. That was his final fling, as he was defeated and killed near Renfrew.

Long before the recalcitrant Somerled had met his end, King Henry showed his hand as regards his policy towards his northern neighbour. Ruler now of an empire that stretched from his wife Eleanor's homeland of Aquitaine to the Scottish border, he was not attracted by the prospect of a robust, independent Scotland whose friendship was less than assured, particularly in view of its kings' pretensions to large tracts of English land. Before his knighting in Carlisle, the young Henry Plantagenet had actually himself pledged to his great-uncle David I that should he become king he would confirm him in possession of the whole of the earldom of Northumbria. Now, as Henry II, he was no longer prepared to suffer such a loss to his own realm.) So, on his way to deal with problems in Wales and presumably at his own request, he met with Malcolm to rearrange matters. The business was concluded in July 1157 at Chester, whither they may have travelled together from Peak Castle in Derbyshire. The upshot was the resignation by the Scottish king of all his northern English lands, namely Northumbria, Cumberland and Westmorland, in exchange for the earldom of Huntingdon, which King David had earlier lost.)

This seems a poor, if prudent, bargain for Malcolm; but it must have been a harsh blow to the self-esteem of his brother William as he saw his rights to Northumbria suddenly vanish. Was the fourteen-year-old's resentment directed, we wonder, against his brother? Or did he feel more bitter towards the arrogant Plantagenet, to whom Malcolm now owed allegiance for Huntingdon? Resentment there certainly was, as William's later behaviour would show; and Henry's gesture in soon granting him the lordship of Tynedale, a large region of upper Northumberland, did little to ease the hurt. According to certain chroniclers, the two kings met again at Carlisle early the next year; and there, it is said, Henry conferred knighthood on William, but not on Malcolm on account of some ill feeling between them.) Both boys were learning the hard way that it is not always easy to accommodate pride with politics.

In 1159 Henry may have used his authority as Malcolm's feudal superior in respect of his English lands to call for his support in a foreign venture. Seeing a chance to revive his wife Eleanor's claim to Toulouse, he planned a campaign to that effect and in March summoned his vassals to rally to his cause. A few weeks later, Malcolm held court in Roxburgh; and there, in the presence of his mother and brothers and many of the mighty of the land, he granted Kelso Abbey its charter. It is likely that he also used this occasion to make arrangements for his journey south together with some of his nobles. From a remark credited much later to William it is supposed that he was also in his brother's company. Malcolm may have needed little or no persuasion from Henry to join in this chivalric adventure; and for William the new knight, if such he was, it would have been an exciting and formative experience.

The Scottish party crossed the Channel on 16 June and eight days later joined Henry in Poitiers. With his assembled army, they moved south to Périgueux; and that is where, at the hands of King Henry, Malcolm achieved his ambition of receiving knighthood.) As regards the knighting of William, there is an alternative and perhaps more plausible tradition that he too received the accolade at Périgueux, not Carlisle, and that it was bestowed not by Henry but by his own newly honoured brother. Whatever the truth, the earlier rift between the two kings had plainly been healed. Now all was ready for their march against Toulouse. They were not, however, destined to taste victory. After a protracted siege of the city, King Louis of France appeared on the scene in support of his brother-in-law the Count of Toulouse. Reluctant to take arms against Louis, who was his feudal superior, Henry renounced his enterprise and headed back to Normandy by way of Limoges with the Scots in his train. Malcolm seems to have been in no hurry to leave his company, for he did not return to Scotland until early the following year. It is very probable that the brothers attended his Christmas court in Falaise, which was graced by the presence of Queen Eleanor. Perhaps there was talk of the forthcoming marriage of their sister Margaret to Duke Conan of Brittany, and even the suggestion that Malcolm might marry Conan's sister Constance, though that alliance never took place. In any case, the boys would during their travels have had a taste of both active chivalry on the grand scale and also of the rich courtly life of the Plantagenets.

If William was still in his brother's company when he returned to Scotland in 1160, he would have become involved in another siege, this time as one of the defenders. For we are told in the *Melrose Chronicle*[*] that when Malcolm reached the city of Perth, he was besieged there by six of his earls who, strongly disapproving of his quitting the kingdom for a lengthy expedition to Toulouse, had it in mind to capture him. Fergus, the lord of Galloway, was presumably a leader of the revolt, as it was only put down after Malcolm and his loyal vassals had raised the siege and made three separate punitive forays into Galloway. The humbled Fergus was forced to relinquish his lands to his two sons and himself took the habit of a canon in Holyrood Abbey. It may well be that young William played some part in these turbulent events and witnessed other disturbances during his brother's reign. Some sources speak of a short-lived uprising in Moray; and we have seen how Somerled met his end in 1164 in the course of a raid up the Clyde. As well as the procedures of peaceful government (we have over a dozen of Malcolm's

---

[*] See *The Chronicle of Melrose* under the year 1160 (Stevenson's translation names King William in error for Malcolm).

acts in which he is named as witness), William was learning salutary lessons regarding the need to preserve the security of the realm.

We know that in 1163 he accompanied Malcolm, probably by way of Carlisle, to Henry II's court at Woodstock near Oxford. There, on 1 July, the Scottish king, along with the newly tamed Welsh leaders, paid formal homage to Henry and/or to his son the Young Henry (the chroniclers differ). As confirmation of his peace with England, Malcolm left behind as hostage his other brother David, now eleven years old. Among those in attendance at the court was Thomas Becket, who had been consecrated Archbishop of Canterbury the previous year. He was a man towards whom William was to give evidence of great admiration and reverence. It was probably on their way home that Malcolm was laid low at Doncaster by a severe illness. Although he recovered on that occasion, one can imagine William reflecting on mortality and his own position as the present heir to Scotland's throne.

Malcolm, in fact, never seems to have been restored to complete health. He did continue to deal with the normal affairs of state, though with diminishing zeal. In 1162 he had broadened his family connections by arranging the marriage of his sister Ada to Count Florence of Holland, who came to fetch her from his court. And if he kept his family's interests at heart, he certainly remained true to its devotion to pious works when, two years later, he brought monks from Melrose to found the Cistercian abbey of Coupar Angus in Perthshire and liberally endowed it with land and revenues. In the summer of 1165 an unconfirmed rumour reached the ears of the learned John of Salisbury that Malcolm had tried to reconcile Henry II with the fugitive Thomas Becket. But if true, that would have been one of his last initiatives. According to the fourteenth-century chronicler Fordun, his interest in the things of this world waned so much towards the end of his reign that his subjects were uneasy and he made William 'custodian of the kingdom'. On 9 December 1165 he died at Jedburgh, leaving behind a reputation for gentleness and piety. His brother was probably present and one of those who accompanied his body for burial with his ancestors in Dunfermline Abbey. It was on Christmas Eve that the inauguration of the new King of Scotland took place at Scone according to the ancient rites; and so began the reign of William I, the 'lion of justice' as Fordun was to call him.

TWO

Cultural Background

When William came to the throne he had, for a twenty-two-year-old, a remarkably wide experience of the world and its ways. He was now faced with the problem of governing his kingdom and asserting its place in Europe. Internally he would have to try to control the tensions that existed within an ethnically mixed and widely scattered population of perhaps half a million. He would also need to balance the authority of the state against that of the church, with the Becket affair in England providing an ominous warning of the dangers of failure. How prepared was he to meet his daunting obligations?

As a boy, William de Warenne (as he was styled in some charters before his accession) would have learned a great deal about family matters from his elders: from his father the earl of Northumbria, and perhaps even more from his wise grandfather David. He would have picked up more still from his own observation as he watched at close range the events of his brother's reign unfold, travelling in his company in Scotland and England and then, as an adolescent, across the Channel in Normandy and beyond as far as the sunny skies of Poitiers and Toulouse. From his early years he had the benefit of his mother's feminine and more distinctly Norman view of things, widening the perspectives of his developing awareness of public affairs.

Ada would have overseen his education as a young child. Inculcating the polite manners desired if not always observed in the noble courts, she would also have instilled into him the rudiments of the Christian faith and its observance according to the principles of the good Queen Margaret. Such instruction as he received in reading and writing would probably have come from a court chaplain or other priest, who might have given him a smattering of Latin. Literacy, though, cannot be taken for granted in a young nobleman of the period. More certain is that as he grew up he would have been trained with other boys, and not necessarily in the royal household, in the more exclusively male pursuits of armed combat, hawking and hunting. His less vigorous pastimes could have included backgammon and chess, as well as the social graces of song and dance.

Storytelling had an important place in the life of the medieval aristocracy. Not only did it help to pass long evenings when the days drew in, but it served too as a vehicle for the preservation of age-old traditions, a reminder of the listener's inheritance, of principles of conduct and such other moral lessons as might be drawn from the tales. Professional storytellers would ply their trade from court to court. Some of them would be native Scots, no doubt offering legends from the ancient Celtic past performed (for they were performers more than simple raconteurs) in Gaelic when appropriate, but in French for most of the new nobility. But the majority of these spinners of tales, like their wares, knew no boundaries; and many of them would have followed their patrons from England or even on occasion from the Continent, or so it has been claimed, though firm evidence is lacking. We may be sure that young William's ears would not have been closed when, with the tables cleared after a meal, a visiting *jongleur*, to use the French term, took his fiddle and stepped forward to declaim to its accompaniment some stirring fiction couched in inspiring verse.

Not that the professionals would have had a monopoly of all the tales there were to be told. William was surely impressed, as he sat at his father's or grandfather's knee, by accounts, suitably embellished, of the deeds of his ancestors: stories of blood and thunder, triumph and treason from the times of the early Scottish kings; accounts of grim tussles with Vikings and Saxons; of how the notorious Macbeth had usurped the throne of David's own grandfather a decade or two before William's other forebear the Conqueror had seized the English crown and later swept into Scotland to impose his authority there. That was in the days of Malcolm Canmore, whose hit-and-run escapades could have been the subject of other anecdotes. But more suitable for young ears was the life-story of Malcolm's queen and William's great-grandmother, the saintly Margaret, about whose memory legends must already have been growing, although she was not to be canonised in his lifetime. If stories of Queen Margaret would have come more appropriately from his mother's lips, William's father, earl of Northumbria, might have captured his interest with tales of that much-disputed territory, preparing already the ground for his future ambitions. And how his young blood would have been stirred by recollections of that solemn ceremony in Carlisle, when his grandfather had conferred the order of chivalry on Henry, future king of England! His mother Ada might also have nurtured his taste for chivalric deeds by telling him stories of her own ancestors and patrimonies in England and Normandy and even further afield: how, for instance, her father had himself fallen into the hands of the Turks when he took part in the disastrous Second Crusade.

As related within the royal court, all this would inevitably have been an 'edited' version of the truth, embellished and slanted to the glory of the family and aligned with the contemporary ideals of feudal honour and Christian virtue. William would have been well schooled in the principles of chivalry, which called for a noble magnanimity towards friend and foe alike. By precept and example he would have been introduced to the practice of what the French called *courtoisie*, the considerate behaviour essential for a harmonious life in the claustrophobic atmosphere of the courts: a modest civility and openness, a strict adherence to one's promises and obligations, generosity to one's fellows and especially to the weak and underprivileged. These 'courtly' manners were still in the process of refinement in the middle of the twelfth century. A particular concern was the increasing respect paid to women (it is no coincidence that the cult of the Virgin was growing in favour at this time), one aspect of which was to become enshrined in the 'courtly love' ideal. This raised the lady above her practical role as the provider of heirs to the point where she was at least the equal partner in a mutually uplifting relationship with her lover. All these ideals were, as we shall see, being promoted in the written literature of the day; and it too would have had some currency in the Scottish court.

By literature I mean in this context not the simple tales and songs of popular tradition, but consciously crafted works, for the most part in verse, such as were copied into manuscripts, even though they may also have been carried in the memories of the professional *jongleurs*. Their language would normally have been French, William's mother tongue. Works in English, a language in which he would also have been fluent, were negligible; and whether his Latin, assuming he had some, would have been adequate for the reading of a literary text is doubtful. So such literary culture as he acquired either in his youth or in later life would have been primarily in French. The authors of such works were often clerks. One who has left us his name, Denis Piramus, was perhaps typical. A monk, it seems, at Bury St Edmunds in Suffolk, he wrote his *Life of Saint Edmund* towards the end of the century, but only after some earlier indulgences. He regrets having hitherto spent his life in sin and folly. A frequenter of the court and its society, he says, he composed topical verse, rhymes, ditties and greetings passed between lovers. But that was at the Devil's prompting; and now, as old age approaches, he will turn to another subject.* The works Denis mentions represent only part of the range of literary entertainment that might have been enjoyed from time to time in courts, Scottish and English alike.

In the first half of the twelfth century the epic held pride of place among the narrative genres. The French *chansons de geste* were performed by the *jongleurs* to some sort of fiddle accompaniment and told of heroic deeds exuberantly multiplied round a grain or two of historical fact. The finest and most celebrated was the *Song of Roland* telling of the death of Charlemagne's nephew at the hands of the Saracens in the pass of Roncevaux. It was composed in about 1100; and the earliest surviving manuscript was copied in England. As he lay dying, Roland grieved lest his sword Durendal should fall into pagan hands, the mighty Durendal with which he had conquered so many lands for his uncle:

> With you I won Scotland and Ireland too,
> And England, which he held as his domain;
> With you so many lands and realms I've won
> That now white-bearded Charles holds in his sway.†

Roland's conquest of Scotland is, of course, an invention; but his name was honoured in the land, being borne by, among others, one of the lords of Galloway with whom William was to have a fluctuating relationship. The proud warrior of Roncevaux was surely one of his boyhood heroes.

Another popular genre was the saint's life; and some of these too would have passed young William's way. The Anglo-Norman *Voyage of Saint Brendan* by Benedeit, for instance, had been dedicated to his great-aunt Matilda (or in one manuscript to Henry's second queen Adeliza).‡ Brendan was a sixth-century Irish monk whom tradition presented as an intrepid traveller; and although his marvellous voyage in search of the Earthly Paradise contains more myth than reality, he does seem to have paid a visit to Iona towards the end of his life. The

---

* On Denis Piramus (or Pyramus), see M. Dominica Legge, *Anglo-Norman Literature and its Background*, pp. 81–85.
† *The Song of Roland*, tr. D.D.R. Owen, ll. 2331–4.
‡ *The Anglo-Norman Voyage of St Brendan*, ed. Ian Short & Brian Merrilees. See pp. 4–6 for the patronage question.

extent to which his fabulous journeys fired men's imaginations down the centuries is shown by the fact that even as late as the eighteenth century expeditions were mounted in search of the wonderful island that had been his goal. Such sparse records of these holy men as had been preserved in annals acted as magnets for all manner of ancient lore with which their stories were tricked out by their pious devotees. We shall return to the intriguing case of Saint Kentigern.

Pseudo-history had a wide appeal among the aristocracy; and when the Oxford clerk Geoffrey of Monmouth put together his *History of the Kings of Britain*, it rapidly became a 'best-seller'. Completed in 1136, it was translated into French in 1155 by the Jerseyman Wace who, if we can believe his English translator Layamon, presented a copy to Eleanor, Henry II's queen.* Geoffrey, who eventually became bishop of St Asaph, had it in mind to provide for the Britons a glorious past on which his fellow Welshmen could look back with pride; but at the same time his book would serve as an inspiration to the new Anglo-Norman rulers, successors to the illustrious line of British kings.

Geoffrey begins his story with the Trojan Brutus, who had left his homeland to found a second Troy beyond the seas; and he ends it with the death of King Cadwallader in the late seventh century. In this largely legendary version of history he gives pride of place to King Arthur, a figure who, whether or not he ever existed, had by now found a place in Welsh lore. But it was Geoffrey who made of him just such an exemplary ruler for the British as Charlemagne was for the French. And for him Albany, the modern Scotland, was to prove something of a thorn in the flesh.

Whereas now, says Geoffrey, Britain is inhabited by five races, namely Normans, Britons, Saxons, Picts and Scots, it was once occupied by Britons alone. The Scots were the product of intermarriage between the Picts and the Irish. Albany, whose first king was a son of Brutus, was the scene of much conflict when the Romans held the land. On their departure it came into the hands of the Picts, Scots, Danes and Norwegians. When, as a mere youth, Arthur came to the throne of Britain, he was faced by a threat from the Saxons in unholy alliance with the Picts and Scots. After a series of victories against the pagan Saxons,

---

* See Geoffrey of Monmouth, *The History of the Kings of Britain*, tr. Lewis Thorpe; and Wace and Layamon, *Arthurian Chronicles*, tr. Eugene Mason. Layamon was writing in the 1190s.

he marched with an army against the Scots and Picts in Moray, finally bringing them to bay at Loch Lomond, where they had taken refuge on its sixty islands. On each of these islands was a crag, and on each crag a nest of eagles which by their screeching foretold the occurrence of any dire event in the kingdom. After Arthur had wreaked great slaughter on his enemies, the survivors came to him with all their clergy and saints' relics, fell to their knees and begged his mercy. At this, the noble king wept with compassion and granted a pardon to the Scottish people. In York, which had been devastated by the Saxons, he found three brother princes to whom he restored their hereditary rights: the kingship of the Scots to Auguselus, the lordship of Moray to Urien, and the dukedom of Lothian to Loth, his own brother-in-law and father of his nephews Gawain and Mordred. All this Arthur accomplished before his marriage to the beautiful Guenevere, a girl of Roman birth.

His subsequent conquests included Ireland and the Orkneys as well as Iceland and Norway, which he made over to Loth of Lothian. Then, with a great army which included a Scottish contingent, he took the whole of Gaul. But when he was about to attack Rome, he learned that in Britain Mordred had usurped both his crown and his wife with Scottish, Pictish and Irish help. Returning home at once, he got to grips with the traitors. His own losses were grievous and included his nephew Gawain and Auguselus, king of Albany, who was succeeded by Urien's son Ywain. Though Mordred was slain, Arthur himself was mortally wounded; and yet, we are told, he was carried off to the Isle of Avalon so that his wounds might be tended. Geoffrey thus respects an ancient tradition that one day the great king will come again.

Avalon later came to be identified with Glastonbury; and Henry II, flattered no doubt by the legend, showed much interest in the abbey there where, two years after his death, the monks claimed to have discovered the remains of Arthur and Guenevere. It was not only for the Plantagenets that Arthur held a fascination. And there was another figure in the *History* who cast a spell over Geoffrey's public. This was Merlin the seer, whose arcane prophecies as reported by him gave rise in later writers to a host of topical interpretations. That the work or at least the lore on which it drew was known in Scotland at an early date is shown by the fashion of naming children after its characters. As early as 1154 we read of a certain Arthur who had committed treason against King Malcolm being killed in what appears to be a judicial combat. Five years later the record of Malcolm's great court at Roxburgh notes the presence of a certain Master Arthur; and we find a St Andrews charter of 1161 being witnessed by, among others, Master Arthur and Master Merlin. Presumably these men acquired their names in the first flush of the Arthurian vogue.)

By creating this hero-king out of a relatively obscure figure in Welsh legend, Geoffrey did a great service to literature in providing fresh inspiration for the new French genre of the romance, the ancestor of the modern novel. Originally treating Classical themes on the model of Virgil and other Latin writers, it now had a different fund of material to exploit, the so-called 'Matter of Britain', which incorporated a great deal of Celtic legend. The Frenchman Chrétien de Troyes is often styled the 'father' of Arthurian romance, his five main works being commonly dated between about 1170 and the early or mid-1180s.* It is, however, likely that he drew on earlier, simpler versions of his basic plots, and that these were being hawked around by the professional story-tellers on both sides of the Channel before they came to his notice. This was probably the case with the story of the celebrated lovers Tristan and Iseult, some form of which he claims to have treated in his youth; but his handling of it has not survived.

Tristan's historical prototype was Drustan son of Talorc, a Pictish king of the late eighth century, though his legend probably took shape in Wales with the use of mythical material from Ireland. Its currency in Scotland is once again proved by evidence from charters, where we find references to people named after both hero and heroine at least by the middle of William's reign. One of the witnesses to the foundation in 1200 of an abbey in Strathearn was a local landowner called Tristan, and a son of his bore the same name. Moreover, about a decade later Earl Gilbert of Strathearn took as his second wife an Iseult, sister to two Norman knights on his territory. The case for there being something of a Tristan cult in the area has been further strengthened by the excavation in Perth of a small thirteenth-century mirror-case showing a scene from the legend.†

* Complete translations of Chrétien's Arthurian romances are by D.D.R. Owen, Everyman, 1987, and William W. Kibler & Carleton W. Carroll, Penguin, 1991. See the bibliographies of these works for editions and other translations.
† For the Strathearn Tristans and Iseult, see R.L. Graeme Ritchie, *Chrétien de Troyes and Scotland*, p. 16, n.1; and A.A.M. Duncan, *Scotland: The Making of the Kingdom*, pp.448–9. For recent research on the Perth mirror-case see the Appendix below.

We can, then, be confident that stories from the 'Matter of Britain' were circulating in Scotland during William's youth; and where would they be more likely to be heard than in the royal court? As yet they were not necessarily in the form of full-blown verse romances. A vehicle for shorter tales were the *lais*, a term derived from the Celtic *làed*, 'song'. Especially intriguing is the case of one surviving *lai*, which shows some relationship with, on the one hand, the life of a Scottish saint and, on the other, one of Chrétien's romances. The life is that of Saint Kentigern, which was recounted in Latin, probably for the religious fraternity at Glasgow, some time between 1147 and 1160.* It is the circumstances of the saint's birth which interest us, for they are clearly based on Celtic folk traditions.

We are told that King Leudonus, from whom Lothian took its name, had a stepdaughter called Thaney. Although her father had pagan ways, she learned of the Christian religion and the Virgin Mary, to whom she showed great devotion, seeking to purge her mind of wanton thoughts. However, she had an ardent suitor, a most attractive youth named Ewen, descended from the noblest family of the Bretons, his father being named by the story-tellers as Ulien (= Urien). Although her stepfather favoured his approaches, neither by words nor by gifts could Ewen persuade her to marry him. In the face of her obstinacy the king gave her the choice of being wed to the prince or else going to live with a swineherd. She chose the latter alternative, only to find that the peasant was himself a secret Christian and encouraged her in her piety. Ewen sent a woman to her to persuade her of her error, but in vain. In his desperation, Ewen found her beside a spring and a stream where she used to wash, lured her away from it and took her by force, fathering on her the future Saint Kentigern. Discovering her to be pregnant, King Leudonus had her cast from a mountain-top, an ordeal which she miraculously survived unscathed. So he then set her adrift in a coracle on the open sea beyond the Isle of May. But again her faith was rewarded; for the boat drifted safely up the Firth of Forth, to be washed ashore at Culross, where in due course Kentigern was born.

This prose life was probably beyond William's reach in its original Latin; but there is no reason why he should not have become acquainted

---

* This anonymous *Vita Kentigerni*, which ends with the saint's birth, is printed in *Pinkerton's Lives of the Scottish Saints*, revised and enlarged by W.M. Metcalfe, pp. 99–109.

with the colourful legend its monkish author stirred in with apparent relish. He might have recognised a historical element or two: Urien, for example, was a sixth-century king of Rheged, a region round Carlisle and incorporating part of Galloway, and did indeed have a son called Owen. More likely is that he had come across these characters in Geoffrey of Monmouth's pseudo-history. He may too already have heard some version of the story of the rape of a noble maiden surprised beside a spring or stream; for this was one of the tales of the supernatural current among the Celts. Perhaps he knew it in the form, also with a Scottish setting, which found its way into the later French *lai* of *Desiré.*[*]

The father of the hero Desiré is the vassal of a Scottish king and hails from the district of Calatir (Calder, in Lothian). On his way to speak with a hermit in the nearby Blanchelande, the young man comes upon a beautiful maiden close to a spring; and she accepts him as her lover. Though herself a Christian, she nevertheless has a touch of the supernatural about her. She bears Desiré two children, a boy and a girl. The lovers suffer a long separation before being happily reunited at Calatir, where the King of Scotland is holding court. There, with the rulers of Moray and Lothian in attendance, their son is knighted by the king, who vows to take their daughter as his queen. Desiré is then at once married to his anonymous mistress, whom he follows to her own country, never to be seen again.

It is in the central plot of Chrétien's *Yvain*, dating from about 1177, that we find the third related motif, which is again a reworking of an earlier, probably Celtic, source. Yvain (= Owen or Ewen) is the son of King Urien, as in Geoffrey of Monmouth and the Kentigern legend. He takes as his bride, having slain her husband, the mistress of a magic fountain. She is named only once, and then as Laudine (or in some manuscripts as *la dame*) of Landuc, daughter of Duke Laudunet 'of whom a *lai* is sung'; and it is generally agreed that these names are derived from the district of Lothian. So once more we are led back to a source-tale localised in that region. With Chrétien, however, the story, which to all appearances once told of the union of a mortal with a water fay, has been fully integrated into Arthurian romance. Our conclusion must be that we have been looking at a cluster of legends which have made their various uses of some folk tale that was well known in southern Scotland by the middle of the twelfth century.

* In *Les Lais anonymes* ..., ed. Prudence Mary O'Hara Tobin, pp. 157–205.

It would be remarkable if all this passed William by. As an adolescent he would have been attracted by the chivalric adventures as much, perhaps, as by the love intrigues; and any qualms he may have felt about the basic immorality of it all would have been eased by a rather contrived deference to religion that seems to have become a feature of the tale and sets it apart from much of this type of courtly literature. There is in fact no reason why he should not have been introduced in his youth to the new courtly fashions in literature as well as living. It is not as if he spent all his days in draughty Scottish castles, whose amenities could hardly have matched those of the great royal residences in the south. We have glimpsed him, for instance, keeping high company in Henry II's favourite retreat at Woodstock near Oxford, where Geoffrey of Monmouth had once gathered his legendary material. And even before this he had tasted southern luxury when he followed Henry to the land of the troubadours, where his ears were surely not deaf to all but the clamours of the campaign. So we should beware of imagining him as a rough-hewn northern lad untouched by the culture of the Twelfh-Century Renaissance and the latest literary trends that were part of its secular manifestation.

They developed alongside and sometimes hand-in-hand with the new learning, as the more clerkish authors turned enthusiastically and often anachronistically to Classical authors for their subjects and style. It is no coincidence that in this age which fostered the ideal of 'courtly love' the erotic writings of Ovid were eagerly copied, studied and translated. Latin was, of course, the language of the schools, which grew in number and repute in the monasteries and especially the cathedrals. They provided basic instruction in grammar and rhetoric, theology and logic; and in the larger institutions the students could grapple with arithmetic, geometry, astrology (or astronomy) and music, whilst a few specialised in canon law and medicine. Although in William's day none of the Scottish schools had acquired a wide celebrity, this does not mean that there were no learned men in the kingdom. Most would have brought their knowledge up from the south, having been trained in England or on the Continent. One thinks of the connections between Dunfermline and Canterbury, where the erudite John of Salisbury spent some time as Becket's secretary, or between Glasgow and Tiron, or Jedburgh and Beauvais. The Scottish clergy must not be thought of as performing their duties in a state of cultural isolation.

It was in the library at Beauvais that Chrétien was to claim to have

found the source of one of his romances. The monastic libraries were
the chief repositories of books at this time, although the aristocracy were
increasingly making their own domestic collections. Much as we would
like to know the contents of those in Scotland or even where they were
located, the ravages of time have destroyed all but a few meagre records
and made a virtually clean sweep of the literary manuscripts copied in
William's own day. We do, for instance, have a select list of 174 Latin
manuscripts, mainly devotional, housed in the priory of St Andrews;
but though the record has survived, the books disappeared long ago. So
despite appearances, Scotland was far from being a cultural desert.

One small, intriguing piece of evidence for this is a short poem in
very accomplished Latin verse, which was composed by an eye-witness
to Somerled's downfall in 1164. The poet names himself as William and
dedicates his work to Saint Kentigern:

> Hoc quod vidit et audivit Willelmus composuit,
> Et honori et decori Kentegerni tribuit.*

After King David's death, he tells us, the barbarous Somerled and his
men from Galloway and Argyll came ravaging with fire and sword,
destroying townships and churches and putting the people of Glasgow
to flight. A certain Marcus remained alone in the cathedral, Bishop
Herbert being absent on a journey. In answer to his anguished prayers,
Saint Kentigern recalled the bishop, who returned post-haste, urged on
by Helias, his faithful attendant. Heartened by their bishop's arrival, the
Glaswegians became as bold as dragons and lions; and, though vastly
outnumbered, they miraculously put the invaders to flight and, as they
made for their ships, stained the land and waters with their blood. The
head of Somerled was hacked off by a cleric and presented to his bishop,
who ascribed the credit for the victory to Saint Kentigern.

We cannot pretend to any knowledge of William the Lion's
intellectual interests as a young man. He certainly had able scholars
at his beck and call whenever he needed them; and once he had become
king, he would have been accompanied by clerks of his household as
he moved from court to court. What we can be sure of is that he would
have been well versed in what passed for history in his day, including
that of his own family and kingdom. He would also have heard many

---

* *De Morte Sumerledi*, ll. 79–80; in *Symeonis Monachi Opera Omnia*, ed. Thomas
Arnold, Vol. II, p. 388.

a tale of stirring deeds and strange happenings, sometimes set in the familiar world of chivalry but often in the shadowy places of Celtic myth when the stories stemmed from the lore of his own land. As well as being nurtured on improving stories of moral rectitude and Christian devotion, he would have been initiated into the new, more adventurous ideal of profane love played out in a chivalric context. But Christmas of 1165 was no moment for him to dream of courtly dalliance with some peerless beauty: he had to turn urgently to affairs of state and the government of his kingdom.

THREE

The Young King 1165–74

Malcolm had bequeathed to his brother a kingdom in reasonably good shape. There were no pressing problems at home. The outlying regions were more preoccupied with their own affairs than with presenting any active threat to the royal authority. Since Malcolm's suppression of the earls' rebellion in 1160 and more recently the death of Somerled, wounds were being licked and internal rivalries developed. The lordship of Galloway had fallen to Fergus' two sons Uhtred and Gilbert, who showed little brotherly affection and in fact lapsed into a fatal rivalry. As for the northern lands beyond Moray, although the royal writ ran there in theory, in practice the Norse earl of Orkney and Caithness wielded the main power. In ecclesiastical matters, the question of the Scottish church's dependence on the metropolitan see of York was still unresolved, with Rome becoming increasingly concerned to assert its direct papal authority over Scotland in view of King Henry's challenge to it in England. In the main, though, William could focus his attention on the situation south of his border, alert to any development that might further his undoubted ambitions.

At the beginning of 1166 Henry II was not without his own worries. There was that continuing feud with Becket, who disputed the rights the king claimed over the church and had taken refuge in France, where he enjoyed the support of Henry's perpetual rival Louis VII. The previous year, Henry had hurried back from a visit to Normandy in order to deal with trouble in North Wales, though with little success. The news of the birth in August of a long-awaited heir to Louis would have given him little cheer: the infant was the future Philip Augustus, who would prove even more troublesome than his father. Then, early in 1166, Henry had to cross the Channel once more to confront a crisis in Maine where rebels, with Breton support, were challenging his wife Eleanor's feudal authority. So the dynamic Plantagenet had his preoccupations, to which the accession of a new Scottish king would have been a minor addition.

He had no reason to see in the spirited William a threat in the short term or for the foreseeable future. Certainly the Scottish king was likely to be more active than his dead brother had been at the end of his life; but in the event of his demise, his natural successor would be his younger brother David, still only in his early teens; and Ada, his worldly-wise mother would surely not have provoked William into any anti-English adventures. Nor would there seem to be any immediate reason for him to become embroiled in the Becket affair. It is true that the pope, Alexander III, had wasted little time in recommending the novice king to give the exiled archbishop his full support. But the missive to that effect should perhaps be read more in the context of the continuing rivalry for control of the Scottish church than as an active manoeuvre against Henry.

All these circumstances would have been considered by the far-sighted Henry. Unlike William, who still showed no sign of marrying and producing an heir, he looked beyond current problems and irritations deep into the future, even beyond his own lifetime. For he thought obsessively in dynastic terms, determined that the royal Plantagenet line should remain secure and flourishing after his death. No doubt Queen Eleanor's greatest merit as he saw it was to have provided him with the means to ensure the succession in the persons of five sons. The first, another William, had died in infancy; but already there were three more princes: Henry, Richard and Geoffrey, to be followed in 1166 by John. The king pinned his faith especially on the Young Henry, whom he had managed to marry off, as a mere five-year-old, to Margaret, the even younger daughter of King Louis of France. Any grand schemes he had of a merger with the Capetians were foiled by the arrival of Philip Augustus; but at least he could be confident that his own line was secure.

Although Henry had no reason to suspect any imminent menace developing from the substitution of one Scottish king for another, there were some purely formal steps that had to be taken. Malcolm had owed him allegiance for his English earldom of Huntingdon, whilst William had been granted the far from opulent fief of Tynedale. William had now inherited Huntingdon, for which he might be expected to pay the due homage. It is unfortunate that the chroniclers only provide sketchy details for the events in this first year of William's reign and omit to mention the performance of any act of allegiance. We must, however, assume that it did take place on one of the occasions when the two kings were together.

Whether on his own initiative or at the call of Henry, William had taken the road south early in 1166; and we can piece together the following account of his movements. If Fordun is to be believed, the two kings had a brief meeting, perhaps in early March, at Windsor, where William was warmly received. His objective was to negotiate a lasting peace, based on the return of the earldom of Northumbria to the Scottish crown. In this he was over-optimistic, and not for the last time. The conference was in fact interrupted by the arrival of the disturbing news from Maine which caused Henry to make a hurried departure for Normandy. William, it seems, went against the wishes of his own party and followed him to Southampton, where he took ship at Henry's expense.

His motives for this overseas adventure when he was scarcely settled on his throne were probably mixed. He is likely to have had that unfinished business regarding Northumbria still on his mind; and he had reason enough to remain for the time being in Henry's good books. There was also his interest in Breton affairs, which were at the root of Henry's present preoccupations. It will be remembered that William's sister Margaret was the wife of Duke Conan of Brittany, who had Henry's support in the troubled affairs of that unruly province. However, we must not overlook a more private ambition of the new monarch. This lay in his evident desire to win respect as a knight active in the pursuit of chivalry. That could be done in two ways: either on the field of combat, or in the practice of the relatively new 'sport' of tourneying. Owing to the church's disapproval of this bellicose and dangerous activity, Henry II maintained a ban on the holding of tournaments in England. As far as we know, none took place in Scotland at this period; so young nobles anxious to build a reputation on the jousting-field had to look for their opportunities on the Continent. Here was a chance William would not pass by.

From Normandy Henry headed for Maine. By Easter he had put down the rebellion there; and with Queen Eleanor he spent the festival in Angers. While elsewhere Becket was fulminating against his supporters in their increasingly bitter feud, he spent a couple of months on other business before, at the end of June, marching against the trouble-makers in Brittany. By mid-July he arrived with his army before the fortress of Fougères, which he captured after a protracted siege. From there he moved to Rennes, where he secured virtual control of the duchy by arranging the betrothal of his son Geoffrey, who was still barely eight years old, to its heiress Constance, Conan's only child and Geoffrey's junior by three years. After this satisfactory arrangement, Henry spent some further time in Brittany.

And what of William during these eventful months? We have no indication of his general movements, whether with or apart from King Henry. He is, though, reported to have engaged in some unspecified military activities, and indeed to have covered himself with glory. In the words of Andrew of Wyntoun, writing in about 1400, he

> prowÿd prowes
> Manhed and gret dowchtynes
> In tornementys and justyngys
> And mony othir knychtlyk thyngys.*

One imagines him showing off his prowess at the siege of Fougères, for example, as well as by breaking a lance or two in tourneys organised when no more serious business was afoot. One such occasion is described by the thirteenth-century biographer of William Marshal. It took place at Valennes near Le Mans; and despite some uncertainty about the date, King William's presence with a numerous following suggests that it was held some time during this summer. It was a grand affair, with many knights and horses captured and their ransoms duly paid.†

More reliable is the information supplied by Robert de Torigni, abbot of Mont-Saint-Michel, that in August or September William was received there by Henry as was the bishop of Man and the Isles. Perhaps he again raised the question of Northumbria; but if so, Henry was having none of it, and William returned to Scotland with only his enhanced chivalric reputation to show for his long absence. Nor had he endeared himself to the English king, who that October was provoked by a word on William's behalf to throw one of his notorious tantrums:

> Henry being at Caen and treating anxiously about a difference
> between him and the King of Scotland, fell into such a passion with
> Richard de Humez for speaking in favour of that prince, that he
> called him a traitor, and in the violence of his rage threw off his own
> clothes and the silk coverlet of a bed on which he sat, and chewing
> straws that he pulled out of the mattress underneath it.‡

* Quoted by Archibald Campbell Lawrie, *Annals* ..., pp. 113–4.
† *L'Histoire de Guillaume Le Maréchal* ..., ed. Paul Meyer, ll. 1319–41. See also Vol. III, p. 21.
‡ Quoted by Lawrie, *Annals* ..., p. 115.

Back on his own soil, William would have found no shortage of domestic affairs to occupy him; but apart from his presence as a dispenser of justice in Perth, we have no reliable records from his second full year as king. His surviving charters can seldom be precisely dated; so we must be content to assign most of them to a span of up to a decade. However, as the place of issue is normally given, it is possible to identify a fair number of the localities he visited at some time during the various phases of his reign. Thus, in the course of its first eight or nine years we find him travelling widely on his domestic business, both within his kingdom and beyond. In Scotland, we see him frequently in Perth and once at nearby Forteviot. His affairs also took him quite often to Edinburgh, which in one charter is given its popular name of Castle of Maidens (*Castellum Puellarum*). North of the Forth he appears at Dunfermline, Stirling, Forfar, Montrose, Brechin and as far afield as Elgin, as well as in his mother's favourite district of Fife, at Crail, St Andrews and Kinghorn. Other charters were issued at Lochmaben (Dumfriesshire), Clackmannan, Lanark, Linlithgow, Haddington, Peebles, Roxburgh, Jedburgh and Berwick upon Tweed, and also at places where he could combine business with the pleasures of the hunt: Alyth, Traquair, Selkirk and Yarrow Meres (St Mary's Loch). That his travels were not confined to Scotland appears from his recorded presence in his English domains at Huntingdon and Kempston near Bedford, whilst in Northumbria he paid visits to Durham, Mitford and the hunting-lodge at Donkley Haugh. He was by no means a stay-at-home.

One cannot, of course, suppose that he always took a deep personal interest in the matters dealt with in his charters. A large number record quite routine business such as the confirmation, largely no doubt soon after his return from the Continent, of provisions made by his predecessors. There were, for example, the details of the property and privileges of the great abbeys to be re-stated and approved by the new monarch; and this he duly did for Dunfermline, Holyrood, Cambuskenneth in Stirling, Newbattle, Jedburgh, Kelso, Dryburgh and Coupar Angus. These documents are of obvious interest to local historians; and they leave even the casual reader with an impression of the wealth of the foundations, whose possessions were not necessarily restricted to Scotland. Thus Jedburgh had property in Huntingdonshire and Northamptonshire as well as Cumberland. There were also religious houses in England that required a guarantee for some past arrangement;

the priories in Northampton, Huntingdon, St Neots and Harrol (Bedfordshire), and the abbeys of Elstow (Bedfordshire) and Sawtry (Huntingdonshire) are cases in point. William himself might even make new provisions, as when he granted to Westminster Abbey some land in Tottenham which had been held by Queen Maud's chamberlain and his son.

It was not only the religious establishments, large and small, that had to be confirmed in their rights: laymen too needed their titles to earlier grants of land assured. Take for instance William's powerful baron Robert Bruce (de Brus), whom David I had endowed with Annandale. William confirms his tenure of the fief, 'for the service of ten knights' and with certain rights reserved for the king, namely jurisdiction over treasure trove, murder, premeditated assault, the rape of women, arson and plunder. The provision of knights for service in the royal army was a common condition for the granting of land, their number being related to the importance of the tenure. For some modest property in Fife, to be held from Ada the queen mother, the requirement is one footsoldier. One Midlothian tenant's due is an archer with his horse; another's is one and a half knights, though he is conceded the right (otherwise the king's) to marry off his mother. A man in East Lothian has the unlikely commitment of 'the fifth part of one knight'. A certain William de Vieuxpont is more liberally endowed: for lands scattered over West Lothian, Berwickshire, Northumberland, Cumberland and Northamptonshire he must provide four knights. Lesser grants did not always involve knight-service, as when the Bishop of Caithness' nephew has to pay an annual due of one two-year-old hawk for property in Perthshire held from David the king's brother.

A charter addressed to the royal officers in Moray reminds them to pay to God through their churches and priests all the due tithes. These may take a variety of forms. Thus the people of Scone must render theirs to the local abbey in grain, cheese and fish. The same abbey is also entitled to the revenues imposed on one ship. The brethren at Dunfermline were granted a tithe of the annual supply of eels for the royal table. Other dues might be legislated for, like the offerings at Whitsun processions throughout his whole diocese granted by the bishop of St Andrews to the priory there. Another benefit afforded could be the freedom 'from all secular exactions' as enjoyed by the monks at Coupar Angus or from tolls on their merchandise in the case of the monks of Coldingham Priory.

Conditions of trading were spelt out in other charters. Those imposed on Kelso Abbey were rather complicated. Except on the day of the week when the king's market was held in Roxburgh, the abbey's men could buy and sell fuel, timber and grain, and might also sell in their shops bread, ale and meat in addition to fish brought by their own transport. Carts from elsewhere must unload only at the king's market; and on the day when that was held, the abbey's men must make their purchases there. Stipulations of that kind are absent from another document confirming the bishop and Culdees at Brechin in their right to hold a market every Sunday, as authorised by King David.

Special attention is paid in a number of charters to the Cluniac priory on the Isle of May, which is not to be exploited by anybody from outside. The community's tenure of property in various places of the mainland is confirmed, as is the monks' liberty to buy and sell throughout the kingdom free of toll. Provision is made for a berth in Dunbar for their supply vessel and for an annual payment from the royal dues levied on shipping coming to Perth. They are also entitled to a tithe of the fish caught in the waters round the island. The size of the community is fixed at thirteen monks and their prior, who is not to be removed except for obvious wrongdoing, and then only after the facts have been reported to the king and the bishop of St Andrews.

Royal and ecclesiastical justice is a frequent subject of comment in the documents. Scone Abbey, for instance, is empowered to hold its own court and may arrive at its verdicts through the procedures of judicial combat and ordeals by red-hot iron or water. The right of religious houses or even a layman to reclaim fugitives is sometimes confirmed; and in one case the authorities of a particular church are bound to return Kelso men and their cattle to the abbot there, provided he has offered them a proper hearing. There is even an instance of the king renouncing his right to a fugitive from Scone, having apparently discovered that his own claim on him was unfounded. We find him granting royal protection to favoured communities; and in the case of the brethren of the Hospital of St Andrews there is the added demand that debts to them are to be paid promptly. Hunting and the gathering of timber in the woods belonging to Coldingham are prohibited, with the proviso that any materials needed for the royal castle at Berwick may be taken from them. On two occasions the king's resolution of disputes is recorded: one charter announces the settlement of a quarrel over land between Dunfermline and St Andrews, and another confirms that an agreement has been reached in his presence between Durham and Crowland (Lincolnshire) as regards a property in Berwickshire.

King William's acts, then, did not deal solely with great matters of state. They were often the vehicles for even relatively trivial decisions. One called upon the royal foresters at Banchory to supply timber to the priory in St Andrews for the completion of their church and buildings. Another confirmed that the beasts of the Hospital there were to share pasturage with those of the local landowners. It was not always a question of rights of tenure or the transfer of substantial properties: even minor domestic arrangements had their claim on parchment and ink. For the lighting of the church at Scone Abbey specified sums were to be allotted from the revenues of a royal farm and mills at Perth; and for the same purpose at Cambuskenneth one silver merk was to be paid annually from Crail at the queen mother's behest.

We would like to have a full itinerary for William during these years while he was still in his twenties and to know how he passed his time both 'on and off duty'. His surviving acts are a precious record, but their formal Latin 'officialese' affords us no insight into his character or any glimpse of the private face behind the public gestures. On the other hand we can, as we leaf through them, learn something of the background against which he moved and obtain a partial picture of his generally peaceful kingdom going about its everyday business under his at least nominal supervision. Even the lists of witnesses are of some help in showing us part of the company he kept in his various residences.

A typical example is in the names appended to a charter confirming the property and constitution of the priory on the Isle of May. First there is David, the king's brother; then comes Nicholas of Roxburgh the chancellor, a capable man who had served under King Malcolm and represented him on a mission to Rome; the third name is that of Matthew, the worthy archdeacon of St Andrews, who later became bishop of Aberdeen; after him appear two native Scottish earls, Waltheof of Dunbar and Duncan of Fife; then we have the constable Richard de Moreville, whose family had possessions in England as well as Scotland and who had also held office under Malcolm; next comes the steward, Walter son of Alan, whose services began even further back, under David I; he is followed by David Olifard of Sawtry in Huntingdonshire, a godson of King David and justiciar in the early part of William's reign; then we find Ness son of William, who was perhaps of mixed Scottish and Norman parentage; and completing the parade are Hugh Ridel, who frequently appears in the witness lists, and another well-connected baron, Geoffrey de Melville. William did not lack men of experience to support and advise him, men of both native and French stock, though the latter were more numerous. We find several of them, the chancellor included, accompanying him to England; and their names appear in charters issued there along with those of a few men of a younger generation such as Philip de Valognes, lord of Benvie and Panmure (Angus), who became a frequent attender at William's courts. The king's brother David is found with him at Huntingdon and his mother Ada at Kempston, whilst the presence of a few members of the Anglo-Norman nobility is shown elsewhere by their appearance as witnesses.

From these dry documents, then, we can piece together a valuable if fragmentary picture of William's world both within and beyond his borders. We catch glimpses of the king's entourage and of his varied subject population ranging from the powerful French-speaking barons to their tenants and the native Celtic peasants working their land, and from the simple priests with their country churches to the religious communities comfortably settled within the walls of prosperous abbeys. We gain an insight into trade and tolls as we are introduced to merchants, some arriving in their ships from abroad, or to fishermen with their cargoes for sale. And we learn a little of justice, both civil and ecclesiastical, and of miscreants trying to evade it. Embracing all this is an overriding impression of a largely feudal mechanism of government ensuring the keeping of the king's peace. Much of that William could entrust to his own officers: he had less control over events in the wider world.

In 1167 King Henry might be thought at a safe distance, as he had not returned to England since William had followed him across the Channel: in fact he would not set foot on English soil until March 1170. Moreover, he would have had little time to worry about anything the Scottish king might be up to: he had too many more immediate problems. For one thing, his quarrel with Becket remained unresolved, leaving him concerned not only by the pope's evident displeasure, but also by the hostile meddling of King Louis as well as of several powerful barons, English as well as French.

If the Becket affair gave cause for alarm, there were more imminent dangers to be faced in a number of Henry's Continental territories. First there was unrest to be dealt with in Aquitaine; then the Count of Auvergne rebelled against his authority, and with Louis's support. Hostilities broke out with Louis in the north and were then replaced by a fragile truce. But no sooner had Henry secured peace on this front than he had to put down an uprising in Brittany with Aquitainian and French involvement or at least approval. Back in Normandy he spent an anxious Christmas before marching south again to quell a revolt in Poitou. His campaign there was interrupted by the need to hold fresh negotiations with Louis, since their earlier truce was to expire at Easter. Then before he could return to Poitou, he was once more diverted to Brittany, where a new rebellion was taking place. This he crushed by the summer, only to find the Capetian forces back on the offensive along the Norman-French border, no agreement having been reached with Louis.

William would have had wind of these events, but he is unlikely to have lost much sleep over Henry's problems. He admired Becket and had no quarrel with Louis, whilst his relations with the English king had been strained since their encounter at Mont-Saint-Michel. Was it even possible that he might turn the recurrent hostility between Henry and the Capetian to his own advantage? If we are to believe the usually reliable John of Salisbury, he did put out feelers during that turbulent year of 1168. For John divulged in a letter to Master Lombard, the papal nuncio, that at the time of Henry's abortive negotiations with Louis William had sent to the French king an offer of assistance along with hostages. Louis's response is not recorded; but no action seems to have been taken.

As it happens, Henry did reach a rather complex agreement with the Capetian in January 1169. It involved the payment of homage to Louis by Prince Henry for Anjou and for Brittany (to be held under him by his brother Geoffrey), and also by Prince Richard for Aquitaine, the fief of his mother Queen Eleanor. The eleven-year-old Richard was also betrothed to the princess Alice of France. The troubled waters in which William had tried to fish were thereby calmed for the time being. Henry, though, was left with problems enough; for apart from further unrest in the south, his feud with Becket came to the boil.

The exiled archbishop excommunicated some of his supporters; and when late in the year the two men met at a council with Louis, Henry refused to bestow on Becket the symbolic 'kiss of peace'. Having spent Christmas with Geoffrey in Brittany and delivered a further snub to the archbishop, he returned to England in March 1170 to play another of his cards. A role awaited the Scottish king and his brother David in the developing drama; and William would really come of age as a monarch.

At Windsor for Easter, Henry called a council on 5 April to enquire into the conduct of all persons in authority during his absence abroad. William was present, presumably as being answerable for his English fief; and he was accompanied by his brother. Henry lost no time in deposing those he felt to have failed in their duties; but the Scots were not directly involved in his purge. According to the unreliable Fordun, William took the opportunity to raise again the question of Northumberland. If so, he must have found Henry in an unreceptive mood. William, however, remained at court with his brother; and there, on 31 May, David was knighted by the Plantagenet. On the same day in far-off Poitiers, Richard was invested as Count of Poitou prior to his installation in Limoges as Duke of Aquitaine.

A fortnight later Henry made his most significant move, which he had been planning for some time. Early in June Prince Henry had been fetched from Normandy; and on the 14th he had him crowned as king presumptive in Westminster Abbey. The act was performed not by Thomas Becket, Archbishop of Canterbury, as was his right, but by the Archbishop of York. Henry's move was calculated to provoke the wrath not only of Becket and his supporters, including the pope, but also of King Louis, whose daughter Margaret had not been brought to England with her young husband to play her part in the ceremony. One assumes that King William and David were present. Certainly, on the following day, along with Henry's English lords, they pledged allegiance to the Young King, while reserving their loyalty to his father. Henry did not linger at the scene of his coup, but nine days later embarked for Normandy to face the hostility of the aggrieved Louis. William and David returned to Scotland.

We have no information on how the Scottish king passed the next couple of years, which were to prove for him the lull before the storm. For Henry they were filled with frantic action punctuated by tragedy; but we must think of William as reverting to the role of aloof and hardly sympathetic observer. For the rest of 1170 Henry sparred intermittently with Louis but also moved towards an accommodation with Becket, whom he permitted to return to Canterbury. But there, on 29 December, the archbishop was assassinated before his altar by four of the king's knights, the chief of them being Hugh de Moreville, whose father had founded Dryburgh Abbey and whose brother Richard we have met as William's constable. The murder, it appears, had not been sanctioned by Henry, who took it very much to heart. Doubtless William was equally shocked.

Henry now lay under the threat of excommunication, which was not lifted until just after Becket's canonisation in 1172. A passive repentance, though, was not for him; and he spent 1171 securing Brittany for Geoffrey, doing some cleaning up in Wales, then crossing to Ireland which, by the following spring, he had brought largely under his control. William may well have wondered if Scotland would be the next part of the 'Celtic fringe' on his list. In fact, after a spell in Normandy during which he received the pope's absolution, he arranged for a second coronation of the Young King, this time with Margaret at his side. He was not himself present at the ceremony in Winchester, having returned to the Continent. Young Henry proceeded with Margaret to the French court for a reunion with her father Louis.

Young Henry was now seventeen years old and already showing himself to be a spirited youth who was not content to idle away his time in his father's shadow waiting for his own call to the throne. He had been schooled by Becket, whom he admired; and the sorry feud which ended in Thomas' murder could not have been much to his liking. By all accounts he had spent something of a roistering boyhood and cultivated a taste for the chivalric life. Now he was impatient to have a substantial part of the Plantagenet domains to rule in his own right, though his father gave no sign of meeting his wishes. It would not be surprising if William, who was rather closer in age to the Young King than to his father, found him the more sympathetic character. They did, after all, have interests in common.

The older king, sensing potential trouble, was not happy to have his son lingering at the court of his rival Louis; so he called him back to Normandy for Christmas, while he himself went to Anjou to spend the festival at Chinon with Queen Eleanor and the princes Richard and Geoffrey. At the beginning of 1173 he found some business to transact in the south, and summoned the Young King to accompany the family on their journey. One purpose was to arrange the betrothal of the six-year-old Prince John; and this was effected at Limoges, but to the Young King's disadvantage, in that his infant brother was promised as part of the arrangement three strongholds which he himself coveted. With these matters settled, Young Henry was obliged by his father to set out with him for Normandy, while his mother made for Poitiers with Richard and Geoffrey. When the senior party was breaking its journey at Chinon, the Young King gave his father the slip and made hot-foot for Louis's court in Paris. There he was soon joined by Richard and Geoffrey; and some time later Queen Eleanor left Poitiers for the same destination. She, however, did not share their good fortune; for, travelling disguised as a man, she was caught and returned to her husband, who was to hold her captive in England for many years. By the middle of April the Young King and his brothers were in open revolt against their father, abetted by a number of disaffected English and Continental barons.

And what was King William's attitude to these dire events? It is time to turn to the graphic if somewhat biased account of them given by Jordan Fantosme.* Probably a clerk at Winchester and certainly an admirer of Henry II, Fantosme has bequeathed to us a verse chronicle written in Anglo-Norman French. In perhaps late 1174 or 1175 he devoted his real poetic talents to describing for us the Young King's rebellion and William's ill-fated embroilment in it. Fantosme claims to have been an eye-witness to some of the events; and for others he appears to have been given reliable information by participants. Usually considered trustworthy as regards the principal happenings, he does indulge in poetic licence for some of the details. Like so many of his contemporaries, he had been brought up on a diet of *chansons de geste*, as is evident from his style. But if we should treat with caution some of his embellishments, the fact remains that he has given us much of the flesh as well as the skeleton of history; and, writing as a contemporary, he succeeds in drawing us into the spirit of the time, at least as experienced by a supporter of King Henry's cause.

Fantosme opens his chronicle with a call to King Henry:

---

* *Jordan Fantosme's Chronicle*, ed. and tr. R.C. Johnston. My quotations are from this translation.

Noble king of England with the right bold countenance, do you not remember that when your son was crowned you made the king of Scotland do him homage, with his hand placed in your son's, without being false to his fealty to you? Then you said to them both: 'May God's curse fall on any who take their love and affection from you. [And you, William] stand by my son with your might and your aid against all the people in the world, save where my own overlordship is concerned!' Then between you and your son arose deadly ill will, which brought about the deaths of many a noble knight, unhorsed many a man, emptied many a saddle, shattered many a shield, and broke many a coat of mail. After this crowning and after this transfer of power you took away from your son some of his authority, you thwarted his wishes so that he could not exercise power.

Therein lay the seeds of a pitiless war, God's curse be on it!

(5—20)

We pass to the arrival of the Young King at the court of Louis who, on hearing his story, sends at once for Count Philip of Flanders and his brother Matthew of Boulogne. At the call of another of his fire-breathing lords for Henry to surrender England to his son while retaining Normandy for himself, the anxious Louis assembles a great army and, with the Young King and his brothers, invades Normandy, much of which is laid waste. A revolt by the Bretons is, however, crushed by Henry to the alarm of his opponents. King Louis then dictates a letter, which he has taken to Scotland by envoys on behalf of the Young King. It reads as follows:

To the king of Scotland, the most noble William, who has a common ancestor with us in former members of our line! King Henry the Younger with loving greeting thus addresses you: you must be mindful of me who am your liege lord. It seems very strange to me and amazement grips my heart that so powerful a king as you, and so valiant a man, with so many subjects and such personal vigour, does not aid me in war amongst the very first, helping me in person and with his nobles against my father. I shall give you the land your ancestors had – you never previously held in royal domain so great a landed fief – the land along the coast between Tyne and Tweed, I know of none better on earth. You will have the lordship in castle and keep. I shall give you Carlisle to increase your might, and the whole of Westmorland with none to gainsay you, on condition that

you come to my aid with all your fearless strength: send packing all
those who at present hold these lands.

(254–70)

King William is in a quandary because of his divided allegiance;
but he proposes to ask Henry for Northumberland. Should he refuse,
then William feels he may renounce his homage; and once Henry
accepts his renunciation, he will be legally entitled to avail himself
of the Young King's offer. In this he is backed by the wise Earl
Duncan; and envoys are sent to Henry the elder in Normandy. He
is told that William will send an army to his assistance provided he
surrender Northumberland; and it is proposed that William's claim
to the territory should be upheld by a knight in single combat. King
Henry will have none of it:

> Tell the king of Scotland that I am in no anxiety about any war
> my son is now waging against me, nor about the king of France and
> his men, nor about the count of Flanders, who is invading my lands
> not for the first time. I shall make their war bring wrath and sorrow
> on them, and, God permitting, I shall prove a deadly opponent to
> your king. But tell his brother David, my kinsman, from me to come
> to my aid with all the men he can command. I shall give him such
> lands and fiefs as will satisfy all his demands.

(342–51)

Henry's haughty rejection of the offer is brought to Scotland by the
envoys, who add that before granting William any land, he will see how
he acts towards him, whether like a fool or like a wise man. Some young
hot-heads demand instant war on Henry. However, Bishop Ingram of
Glasgow (who had been Malcolm's chancellor) and Earl Waltheof of
Dunbar caution against following the wild advice of these 'foreigners'.
But William's blood has been fired. He orders two of his lords, William
of Saint-Michel and Robert of Huseville to check on Henry's activities
and then to contact the Young King in Flanders. They must tell him
that if he sends a fleet with Flemish troops, King William will begin
hostilities. The envoys take ship at Berwick and, standing well off from
the English coast, make their way to where they find the Young King
in the company of King Louis and the Count of Flanders. Count Philip
fiercely urges acceptance of William's proposal and is backed by Louis;
and that is the message the envoys carry back to Scotland. Their news

is greeted by cries of 'Let's go and capture Wark Castle in England!'
But that was all empty bombast.

King William mustered his army at Caddonlee in Selkirkshire. It
included large forces from Ross and Moray, Buchan and Angus. With
them he marched on the border castle of Wark in Northumberland, which
was loyally guarded for Henry by one of his sheriffs, Roger Stuteville.
However, faced by the overwhelming strength of the Scots, he sensibly
approached William with a tactful request for a forty-day truce so that
he might report the situation to King Henry. Magnanimously William
agreed; but before the truce had expired, Roger returned from the south
with such reinforcements that he was able to defy the king to do his
worst with his Flemings, and he would await them with confidence.

William was forced to change his tactics. Having been assured by
the bishop of Durham of his neutrality, he announced to his knights
his determination to march on Alnwick and demand that the castellan
there, the bastard William de Vesci, either surrender the fortress or
agree to retain it without strengthening it in any way. From there he
would move down to the coastal fortress of Warkworth. Frustrated by a
stubborn defence at Alnwick, he managed to seize the weaker Warkworth
before continuing south to launch an assault on Newcastle upon Tyne
defended by Roger FitzRichard. Despite a siege in which the surrounding
land was devastated, William again had to give the garrison best.

His advisers propose another target:

> Go off and conquer Carlisle of which we have high hopes. Robert
> de Vaux will not have had such magnificent sables, nor eaten such
> delicious food, nor drunk such good wine, but that, when he sees so
> many fine shields and so many Poitevin helmets, he would wish he
> were a bishop on a chess board.

> (586—90)

But William's eyes are now on another castle, Prudhoe on the Tyne,
which he vows to seize from Odinel d'Umfranville, who had been brought
up by his father Earl Henry (and who, incidentally, had witnessed some
of William's own charters). So it is to Prudhoe that he leads his army; and
his tents are pitched below its walls. The Flemish mercenaries are all for
razing it to the ground; but his chief advisers, confident that it can be left
to be taken at leisure, call for the capture of Carlisle, a far greater prize. To
Carlisle, then, they go, wreaking havoc on the way, 'for they are terrible
in war and of the direst courage, as those well know whom they find in

their path. Those who are caught up with in the open country or in the forest will never live to tell the tale to any of their kinsfolk' (633–6).

Fantosme now gives a succinct and, it must be said, credible appraisal of William's character:

The king of Scotland was skilled in warfare and in inflicting damage on the enemies he fought; but he was too much in the habit of seeking new advice. He cherished, loved, and held dear people from abroad. He never had much affection for those of his own country, whose right it was to counsel him and his realm. In a very short time it became evident – you will hear me tell of it – how this war developed because of bad advice.

(636–44)

At Carlisle the Scottish army makes an immediate assault on the castle; but fierce as the attack is, the garrison puts up a heroic stand, and the defences remain unbreached. Fantosme says that William forbade any action against the church (and a surviving charter granting his peace to Furness Abbey may have been issued on this occasion). But this is a vain gesture, for 'that miserable race, on whom be God's curse, the Gallovidians, who covet wealth, and the Scots who dwell north of the Forth have no faith in God, the son of Mary: they destroy churches and indulge in wholesale robbery' (683–8). The rich land is ravaged; but God will bring aid to the defenders of the castle.

The bold and valiant king of Scotland was in his guarded pavilion surrounded by his chamberlains and intimates when an eloquent canon arrived bearing ominous news. He claimed to have seen a great relieving force led by Richard de Lucy, the chief justiciar of England. They would launch an irresistible attack that night, he said; and he advised William to retreat to the safety of Roxburgh, lest a mocking song be sung of him (that is, lest he become the subject of derision, a warning first found in the *Song of Roland*). William was enraged; and, invoking Saint Andrew, he declared:

We can stay here in perfect safety. If they want a fight they shall have one. Of course, an honourable man must win his heritage. My forebears of the kingdom of Scotland held this fief freely; by that Lord to whom pilgrimages are made on foot I too will hold it from my liege lord the king, the son of that father who granted me the right to it; in my lifetime I shall not yield an inch of it.

(738–46)

His counsellors, however, demurred: if he wished to preserve his reputation, they said, he should abandon the siege forthwith. Once again King William capitulated. Every one of his men made off like a coward without suffering any attack or damage. Losing no time, they entered Roxburgh by night. Robert de Vaux, though, collected much booty from the fugitives.

The picture of William that has been given by Fantosme thus far is by no means unsympathetic: he is a proud, energetic king, alive to his own honour and that of his family, as well as to his responsibilities to the church and its servants as he tries to curb the excesses of his motley army. Towards a submissive opponent he shows true chivalry, but on one whom he considers an ungrateful usurper he turns his full wrath. Yet, like Charlemagne in the *Song of Roland* and King Arthur in many of the romances, he places great reliance on his advisers and particularly the 'foreigners' among them, by whom he is too easily swayed in Fantosme's view. As portrayed here, he already has the makings of a figure of legend.

The chronicle now switches to the arrival of Richard de Lucy in the devastated territory of Northumberland. While his thoughts run on revenge, news reaches him that the Earl of Leicester has invaded England in the Young King's cause, bringing with him an army of French, Flemings and men from Friesland. Strategist as he is, the justiciar is wary of provoking King William further; but the constable of England, Humphrey de Bohun, has other ideas. To de Lucy's dismay, he has advanced on Berwick and put it to the torch, laying waste the surrounding land. De Lucy proposes that they seek a truce from William; and to this de Bohun agrees, provided he drop no hint of the danger in the south, which he will himself confront. He leaves at once for Norfolk, where the Earl of Leicester is confident of support in his enterprise from the king of Scotland and David his brother. In fact, his army is defeated in a fierce battle; and England is secured for King Henry.

Fantosme turns to the events of 1174. Earl David of Scotland, he assures us, was the noblest of warriors and a firm friend of Holy Church. William promised him the lordship of Lennox and the honour of Huntingdon in return for his aid against King Henry. So David marched south with an army and conducted a successful campaign in the Midlands. In the meantime William again succumbed to bad advice and flung his troops back into Northumberland. 'Ah! God!' cries Fantosme, 'what great harm

I saw come to them!' (1142) The King's first move was to lay siege to Wark; but by now that fortress had been strengthened. He therefore sent one troop to Bamburgh Castle led by an acquaintance of Fantosme's, whom the poet does not name because he lost his reputation on that expedition:

> It was early morning and the dawn scarcely breaking when the proud company of knights arm themselves. First they attacked the town of Belford. They spread themselves out over all the countryside.
>
> Some speed into the farms to wreak havoc, some take sheep from their folds, and some set fire to farmsteads. What more can I tell you? Never will a tale of greater loss be told.
>
> You could have seen Flemings tying up peasants and leading them off roped together like heathens. Women flee to the church only to be snatched away naked, leaving behind their garments and their valuables.
>
> (1159–70)

At least, says Fantosme, the people's mortal enemies the Scots were not there, for they would have beaten and killed them. The marauders returned with their loot to their quarters at Berwick.

At Wark, Roger Stuteville put up a gallant defence against William's Flemings and his archers and crossbowmen, his catapults, powerful siege-engines and slings. Failing to storm the castle, William ordered a heavy catapult to be deployed against the gate. But it scored what in today's parlance would be called an 'own goal'; for there was a malfunction, and the first stone it hurled felled one of his own knights. In his frustration he roared: 'This is indeed a priceless thing to happen! My heart is so full of terrifying rage and vexation that I would rather have been captured alive before Toulouse!' (1251–3) So heavy were William's losses, whereas the defenders suffered none, that he was compelled to abandon the siege. Next morning he assembled his leaders and instructed them to dismantle their camp and burn their huts before setting the army back on the road to Roxburgh. There was jubilation in the fortress at Wark; but Roger Stuteville showed his true chivalry in forbidding his men to mock the retreating enemy. Instead they celebrated with fanfares of trumpets and the singing of courtly songs.

William refused to admit the war lost; and in this he had the enthusiastic support of Roger de Mowbray. In council the unanimous but fatal decision was taken to return to Carlisle. William moved off with his army, some of the best knights ever known under their gallant leaders Mowbray and Adam de Port, and also the Scottish earls with their pitiless and hated followers. As they approach the sunlit walls of Carlisle they unfurl their banners and sound all their trumpets to the alarm of those within the stronghold. The castellan Robert de Vaux reassures them: he has no fear of the king of Scotland and his men.

William consults with his leaders and Walter de Berkeley (his chamberlain) and spells out the ultimatum to be taken to Robert. They find him on the battlements practising his sword-play; and there he courteously hears their terms. He must surrender the castle, William's rightful inheritance from which he has been illegally ousted by King Henry. Then, if he gives William his allegiance, he will be rewarded with a vast fortune; otherwise he will come to a cruel end. Robert refuses to betray his lord: but let William take his complaint to Henry, and if he authorises the surrender he will comply; otherwise he would rather die. The envoys return with Robert's reply. 'He is just joking', said King William.

The army, however, made no immediate move against Carlisle, but marched instead to Appleby. The castle there had no garrison or supplies, being in the charge of an elderly Englishman, Gospatrick Fitzhorm; and he handed it over at once. Leaving some of his own troops there to hold it against all comers, William continued on to Brough. That was a tougher proposition, being well guarded. The siege was immediately mounted; and on the first day the Flemings and Borderers took the outer defences and pinned the garrison in the keep, to which they set fire. All the men there surrendered except for one newly dubbed knight, who retreated to the battlements and from his vantage point hurled three javelins at the Scots, killing one of them with each cast and then doing more damage with sharp stakes he had there. But with the flames licking round him, even he had to give in.

From Carlisle Robert de Vaux sent to Richard de Lucy a messenger, who returned with the news that King Henry would be back in England within a fortnight, having been told of the serious situation in his realm and particularly in Northumberland. Henry's response had been to call upon Saint Thomas Becket, confessing his guilt and imploring him to keep his kingdom safe. In Carlisle Robert de Vaux temporised; and when William arrived to repeat his demand of surrender, he promised to submit should his king not arrive with help before a stipulated date.

Unaware of current developments, William turned his attention back to Prudhoe, still held by Odinel d'Umfranville and ripe, he believed, for the taking. Leaving his castle's defence to its garrison, Odinel rode off to scour the region for support, and had soon assembled a relieving force of four hundred knights. For three days at Prudhoe the king conducted a fierce and costly siege, while his men destroyed the surrounding fields and their crops, even stripping the apple trees there of their bark. Then, as before, William decided to leave the reduction of the stronghold for a more favourable occasion.

His new plan was to go to Alnwick himself to begin a siege, and to let the men from Galloway loose to ravage Odinel's territory, while the Scots would harry the coastal lands. For this he secured his advisers' approval. The Scots indeed rampaged through the countryside, desecrating a church, castrating three of its priests and killing some three hundred other folk. But Odinel was now on the move with the allies he had recruited, among them William Stuteville, Randolph de Glanville, and Bernard de Balliol, together with sixty horsemen sent by the archbishop of York. They came to Newcastle upon Tyne and there learned that William had arrived at Alnwick with a small company, including some French and Flemings. They therefore agreed to head that way and approach the castle with due caution, having sent their scouts ahead.

King William was riding early in the morning with five hundred of his men (other accounts say sixty), who assured him that Northumberland was at his mercy. In front of the castle he stopped to take a meal, the day being already hot. He removed his helmet and waited for his men-at-arms to bring him food, not realising that Odinel's men were lurking in a nearby copse (another source speaks of them emerging from a thick mist). But they, as soon as a scout had apprised them of the situation, armed in a trice, leapt onto their horses, and shouted their war-cries. All this Fantosme claims to have seen for himself. Undismayed, William was quickly armed and mounted on his charger, heading boldly for the fray. He unhorsed the first man he struck; but then a sergeant dashed up and plunged a lance into his steed. He fell to the ground with the horse on top of him and was unable to rise as the servants and squires swept past. It was the sins of the Scots, Fantosme assures us, that were his undoing.

The encounter was bloody and many of the Flemings were slain. At last the horse that pinned the king down was dragged off him, and he was taken by Randolph de Glanville, to whom he then offered to surrender. Again Fantosme insists that he saw this with his own two eyes. That was the most joyful day of Randolph's life. He accepted William's surrender, mounted him on a palfrey, then had him led away with all due consideration. His men had put up a gallant fight; but most of those who were not killed were captured and later ransomed. Roger de Mowbray and Adam de Port, however, managed to make good their escape. Fantosme is liberal with his praise for the valour of the leaders of both camps; but for the Flemings and more especially the brutal Scots he has no sympathy.

William was taken in the first instance to Newcastle upon Tyne, then on to Richmond to await King Henry's pleasure. Meanwhile Henry had landed in England and on the very day of William's capture had done penance in Canterbury at the shrine of Saint Thomas (other sources date that at July 13th: the coincidence was considered by some to be a miracle). Henry entered London amid general rejoicing, but with a heavy heart because of the war with Scotland. That night he was in his bed and dozing off when Randolph de Glanville's messenger arrived and begged the reluctant chamberlain to admit him to the royal apartment. Hearing them arguing, Henry called for the man to be brought in. On being told this was one of Randolph's men, he dreaded bad news:

> Has the king of Scotland entered Richmond? Has he seized the
> fortress of Newcastle upon Tyne? Is Odinel d'Umfranville captured
> or driven from his lands? And are all my barons ousted from their
> fiefs? Messenger, by the faith that you owe me, tell me the truth!
>
> (1984–8)

After some polite preliminaries, the man comes to the good tidings: the king of Scotland and all his barons have been captured. Henry had never been happier. He sent messengers to David in Leicester, calling him to yield up his castle and himself. David obeyed. Then the king ordered William to be brought before him. He himself must return to Normandy, having heard that his city of Rouen is under siege. David shall follow him to the coast, and Randolph is to bring the king of Scotland to Southampton with all speed. But when William and his escort arrived there, Henry had already departed to restore peace in Rouen, leaving the Scottish monarch to follow in his wake.

So ends Fantosme's stirring chronicle, which may have been written before he knew the final outcome of events. We are left to other, less vivid and sometimes conflicting, sources for the rest of the story. Henry appears to have spent some time in securing Huntingdon and pacifying further areas after he heard of William's capture. Roger of Howden (or Hoveden) says that he was in Northampton on 31st July, when William was brought to him with his feet shackled beneath his horse's belly. Other accounts suggest that Henry embarked at Portsmouth, taking the Scottish king and other captives with him. William was initially imprisoned at Caen before being transferred to the fortress at Falaise, where he was treated with proper respect, but was a captive none the less. As for David, it is likely that he had escaped Henry's clutches and returned to Scotland, although he too turns up later at Falaise.

What of the Young King, the instigator of this rebellion that had turned out so disastrously for William and his other allies? It was he and King Louis who had been besieging Rouen and thus precipitated Henry's return to Normandy. He had also been making preparations to cross the Channel and spread his rebellion in England. With his father relieving Rouen, he was forced to retreat with Louis into France. There he and his brothers Richard and Geoffrey were approached by Henry; and, realising the futility of pursuing their revolt, they accepted on 30 September his very reasonable terms for peace. Shortly afterwards, it seems, they joined their father at Falaise, where their agreement was formalised. It is interesting to find among its witnesses William Malveisin, a name with which we shall become more familiar, though a different person is involved.

King William was not kept in isolation in Falaise: a number of his lords and prelates crossed the sea to join him. There another document was drawn up on 1st December and ratified at Valognes a week later. This was the humiliating Treaty of Falaise, to which the captive William was forced to assent. By its terms he was bound to pay homage for Scotland and all his other lands to King Henry and to the Young King so far as this did not infringe his fealty to his father. The same requirement was to apply to his successors, to all his barons and their heirs, and also to his bishops, abbots and clergy as required. Further, the Scottish church was to be subject to that of England as 'in the time of his predecessors as kings of England'. This legal right of the English over the Scottish church was guaranteed by the bishops of St Andrews and Dunkeld and by the abbot of Dunfermline and the prior of Coldingham, and its strict observance by all prelates was demanded. It is significant that in this provision no mention is made of York or Canterbury; so the tricky question of which see should exercise the authority, so long disputed as we have seen, remained tactfully unresolved. Other minor clauses concern the mutual extradition of fugitives from the two countries and the continuing rights to lands held within them.

For Henry such largely theoretical requirements were not enough, so he added further demands that were to have immediate practical effect. The Scottish king was to place 'at his mercy' the castles of Roxburgh, Berwick, Jedburgh, Edinburgh (*Castellum Puellarum* in the document) and Stirling; and he was committed to paying for their garrisoning as necessary (in the event Jedburgh and Stirling would never be occupied by the English). Finally, to ensure compliance with his terms, Henry demanded hostages. Twenty-one are specified. The chief of them was William's brother David; then there were the earls of Fife, Dunbar, Strathearn and Angus; and among the rest, some of whom we have met before, were William's constable Richard de Moreville, his former chamberlain Philip de Valognes with his successor Walter de Berkeley, William de Hay his butler, the sheriffs of Roxburgh and Berwick, and Ness, son of William and lord of Leuchars. The king and his brother would be released once the specified castles had been made over; and in the case of the other hostages, their heirs might be surrendered in their place. All William's bishops and barons were to be bound by these terms; and should he break the agreement, they must remain loyal to Henry and the Young King, and the bishops were to place his land under an interdict until such time as he should conform.

On 11th December, the treaty having been ratified, the humbled but liberated king left Normandy for England and made his way back to Scotland. He might have done worse: at least he kept his throne, although he had been obliged to give Henry a firm foothold in his kingdom. But his cherished dream of lording it over Northumberland and the other coveted northern territories had been shattered, at least for the time being. And he would have to be careful not to give further offence to his English overlord. There were to be no more escapades with his erstwhile friend the Young King.

His was not a joyous homecoming. There would certainly have been no celebrations in Roxburgh or Edinburgh or his other southern strongholds. However, there was no occupying force in his lands north of the Forth; so William was from now on to make more use of his residences there such as Perth and Forfar. Not that he had much time to relax and mull over his past mistakes and present situation: there were pressing problems within his own borders that called for action.

But before he could attend to those, the last act in the settlement with Henry remained to be performed. On 10th August 1175 William, David and the great lords spiritual and temporal of his realm were present in the church of Saint Peter in York to proclaim in person their allegiance to King Henry and his son and confirm the transfer of his castles: in fact, of those specified in the Treaty of Falaise only Roxburgh, Berwick and Edinburgh were on the York list.

King William had certainly lost much, including the honour of Huntingdon and Tynedale; for whatever was implied by the 'other lands' for which he had done homage to Henry, they were not included. But from his bitter experience he had also learned a great deal. His youthful rashness may have been tamed, yet his pride remained and with it something of his ambition. Far from being eclipsed as a ruler of substance, he was now ready to start a new chapter in his reign.

FOUR

The Mature King 1175–89

In Geoffrey of Monmouth's *History of the Kings of Britain* King Arthur, once he had settled his Scottish affairs in York, was free to pursue his dreams of conquest elsewhere. Perhaps William remembered this when he came to ratify the unpalatable Treaty of Falaise in the same city. If so, he may have reflected ruefully that for him there was to be no more foreign adventuring in the foreseeable future: there were still problems to be grappled with at home; and the first of these concerned that perpetual trouble-spot Galloway, which tradition associated with King Arthur's nephew Gawain.

We last saw Galloway under the joint lordship of Fergus' sons Uhtred and Gilbert. They were probably half-brothers, with Uhtred, the elder, being a cousin of Henry II. During William's abortive campaigns, they had given him miltary support. But no sooner was he captured than the Gallovidians switched their allegiance. Returning to their own lands, they slaughtered any English or French they found settled there and could lay their hands on, and systematically destroyed all the castles belonging to the king. These bloody events are reported by the chronicler Roger of Howden, whom Henry had sent with Robert de Vaux to those parts for consultations.

Before their arrival, matters took a further vicious turn when Gilbert hatched a plot with his men to dispose of his brother. Uhtred was captured and, castrated and with his tongue hacked out, met a gruesome end. Then, as sole lord of Galloway, Gilbert offered his allegiance to King Henry with the promise of a rich tribute. Henry, however, whether because of the barbarous elimination of his kinsman or the fact that he had by then come to terms with the Scottish king, ignored the offer. Instead, he empowered William to send an army into Galloway to bring Gilbert to book. We have no information about the ensuing campaign; but it must have been successful, for in October 1176 we find William escorting Gilbert to Henry's court at Feckenham (Worcestershire) to make his peace for the fratricide. Gilbert obtained his pardon by pledging allegiance to Henry, disbursing a sum of one thousand silver Scottish merks, and leaving behind his son Duncan as hostage. He was, however, far from tamed. He continued to cause William trouble until his death in 1185; and he never, it seems, paid more than a small proportion of his fine.

At the beginning of 1176 William had been summoned with his leading clergy to a council in Northampton in the hope that a solution might be found to the dispute over the allegiance of the Scottish church. He duly arrived with the bishops of St Andrews, Glasgow, Dunkeld, Galloway, Caithness and Moray as well as various abbots and priors. When King Henry demanded that they be subject to the English church, they denied this liability, Bishop Jocelyn of Glasgow claiming papal authority for Rome's direct responsibility in the case of his own see. There followed an acrimonious dispute between the archbishops of York and Canterbury as to which should command the obedience of the Scottish church; and the council disbanded in a position of stalemate.

A letter was, however, sent to Pope Alexander III falsely purporting to come from King William and requesting that his church should be subject to York. The pope's reply deferred judgment until the question should be properly examined. To this end he despatched his legate Cardinal Vivian. He, however, was obstructed in his passage through England by prelates acting in the king's name; and it was not before diversions to Galloway, the Isle of Man and Ireland that he obtained Henry's permission to complete his journey to Scotland. A whole year had been wasted; and only on 1st August 1177 was he able to confront the prelates of the realm at Holyrood. An absentee was the bishop of Galloway, who refused to renounce his traditional allegiance to York and was consequently relieved of his office. Some routine business was conducted by Vivian; but after a month or two in Scotland, he was recalled on account of his own cupidity. The prelates were then summoned to the Lateran council arranged for March 1179. So there the matter rested, with the pope reluctant to grant York authority over the Scottish church, whose independence from England was thereby strengthened. William had no cause to be dissatisfied with this state of affairs.

Henry II's Continental possessions were by now considerably less secure than his lands on the English side of the Channel. At Christmas 1176 his sons were on their best behaviour, the Young King with his wife in Normandy, Richard in Bordeaux, and the two younger boys spending the festival with their father at Nottingham. During the following year there was sporadic unrest in different parts of the Plantagenets' territories across the Channel including Poitou; and this, as well as tourneying, kept Young Henry and Richard occupied for much of the time. A serious situation had also developed in the Middle East, where Saladin, the new sultan of Egypt and Syria, had turned his forces against the Christians. There was talk of the launching of a crusade; and some nobles, including the Count of Flanders, decided to leave for Palestine. Henry may have thought of joining them; but in the event he remained occupied with affairs in England until the summer. These included declaring Prince John King of Ireland and, of more immediate interest to the Scottish king, appointing his governors for the castles of Roxburgh, Edinburgh and Berwick.

Henry then summoned his vassals, including William, to a council at Winchester, preparatory to leaving for Normandy. It was held on 1st July; but what with unfavourable winds and the recurrence of an old thigh injury (he had been kicked by a horse a week before receiving the captive William at Northampton), it was mid-August before he was able to sail. Presumably William also made the crossing; but we have no record of the time he spent in Normandy on this occasion. As for King Henry, he had a meeting with Louis, who was urging him to expedite the marriage of Richard to his daughter Alice, as arranged eight years previously. No progress was made on that score; and the crusade, to which both kings pledged themselves, did not materialise. No doubt William lingered in Normandy no longer than he had to.

For him, so far as we can tell, 1177 had been a year more of observation than of action. Whether or not he met the papal envoy Vivian, he would have kept in touch with the debate over the position of the Scottish church; and while on the Continent he must have been brought up to date with the shifting relationships of the Plantagenets and Capetians and caught a whiff of the crusading zeal affecting some of the nobility. Back on home ground, it is possible that he held an assize in Aberdeen during Lent of the following year. More certainly 1178 saw the death of his mother the countess Ada de Warenne. He surely regretted the passing of not merely a mother, but also the chief lady of his court and an experienced counsellor throughout the early part of his reign.

We do not know the date of Ada's death; but it may not be a coincidence that William seems especially preoccupied during the latter part of the year with religious matters, by which I mean not the higher politics of the church, which had concerned him earlier, but with deeds that he hoped would promote 'the salvation of my soul and those of my ancestors and successors', as he states in the act announcing his foundation of the abbey church at Arbroath 'in honour of God and Saint Thomas archbishop and martyr'. Its initial handsome endowments are listed; and these are considerably increased in subsequent charters. Permission is granted to use material from the royal forests, certain fishing rights are stipulated, as also the ownership of a number of saltpans. The abbey may found a burgh, own a port, and hold a market every Saturday. Its own court may impose justice, including the use of judicial combat and execution by drowning or hanging. Another act, passed at William's Perthshire hunting lodge at Clunie in Stormont, grants one of his clerks land to be held from the abbey in return for a quantity of wax to be supplied annually on the feast of Saint Thomas (29th December). We notice that a benefaction of about the same period is made to Holyrood Abbey in compensation for the alms they have lost due to the garrisoning of Edinburgh Castle.

One other important document probably from 1178 announces William's conferment on his brother David of the earldom of Lennox, which was the northern part of the historical Strathclyde, and also various other properties including Garioch (an extensive territory in Aberdeenshire), Lindores and Dundee. His holding of Lennox proved only temporary, since he resigned it not later than the 1190s in favour of the line of native earls. Dundee was another matter. It was already an important trading centre and port, and David was to give it burgh status by 1195, when he may also have provided it with a castle. Thereafter he continued to take an interest in its development and growing prosperity. At Lindores he founded in the early 1190s an abbey as William had done at Arbroath; and as there it obeyed the Tironensian order and was established by monks brought from Kelso. It should be added that although the charter detailing William's grant seems to date from 1178, Jordan Fantosme states that already in 1174 he had pledged David the lordship of Lennox in return for help in his war against Henry. So the actual grant may have been made some years before its recording in the surviving document.

1179 brought William problems in the north of his kingdom. The earl of Ross until his death in 1168 was Malcolm MacHeth, possibly an illegitimate son of Alexander I and brother-in-law of the notorious Somerled. It was he who had suffered a long imprisonment at Roxburgh after he had crossed swords with King David; but he had then been given the lordship of the unruly northern province. Earl Harald of Orkney had married a daughter of his and may thus have harboured a tenuous claim to the Scottish throne. This might explain the state of affairs which now induced William to take a large army north in the company of his brother and construct two castles, one at Redcastle above Inverness and the other at Dunskeath opposite Cromarty. Another disaffected family in these parts, also with a claim to the throne, was the MacWilliams, Donald being a grandson, legitimate or otherwise, of Duncan II. It may be that he too was engaging in hostile activities in Ross and Moray. But whatever the threat, William and David returned south in the hope, vain as it turned out, that they had countered it with their defensive measures.

Henry II was back in England by the middle of 1178. For the rest of that and the following year he devoted himself to domestic affairs. The Christmas festival of 1179 he spent at Nottingham, where William and a number of his Scottish barons joined him. A few months earlier, King Louis, conscious of his own mortality, had arranged to have his son Philip crowned as his successor in his own lifetime, and had decided that the ceremony should be held in Rheims on 15 August. His plans were disrupted at short notice when young Philip fell gravely ill. On three successive nights, it is said, Saint Thomas appeared in a vision to the anxious Louis, urging him to visit his shrine at Canterbury. This Louis did in the company of King Henry. On his return he found his son restored to health; and the postponed coronation was held on 1st November, with the Young King Henry in attendance. Philip was to assume the throne on the death of his father in September 1180.

These happenings would surely have been the subject of much discussion and speculation at that Christmas court in Nottingham. It may be that a rumour was already circulating to the effect that Philip's illness had been brought on by his becoming lost in a forest when on his way to Rheims. The story was that after spending the night alone in its depths he had encountered a hideous, gigantic peasant, who was nevertheless good enough to guide him back to the royal party. I have shown elsewhere* that this tale as recounted by contemporary chroniclers contains, whatever its basis in fact, some lively embellishment inspired by a recent romance by Chrétien de Troyes. I mention it here partly as an example of the interaction

* *Journal of Medieval History* 18 (1992), pp. 141–4.

at this period of literature and history (of which we shall see much more later), and partly to suggest that William on his travels would presumably have become very familiar with such gossip and tall stories as well as with the literary culture enjoyed at the courts.

To return to ecclesiastical matters, the rivalry over the appointment of bishops to the Scottish church was coming gradually to a head since the death in May 1178 of Bishop Richard of St Andrews. He had not been replaced at the time of the foundation of Arbroath Abbey; but then the canons of the St Andrews priory elected as his successor 'Master John the Scot', a nephew of the earlier bishop Robert and also of the bishop of Aberdeen. This was not at all to the liking of King William, who had not been consulted in the matter. He therefore exercised what he considered his royal prerogative by making his own appointment in the person of Hugh, one of his chaplains; and he had him consecrated by certain unspecified bishops in the cathedral church at St Andrews. By then, however, John had left to obtain the support of Rome, and the pope's reply was awaited. It is ironical that in this Scottish variant of the Becket affair William was playing the role of Henry, not his revered hero Thomas, by placing his own authority above that of the church.

It was not until 1180 that Pope Alexander III sent another legate, Alexis, to Scotland with the bishop-elect John to enquire into this unhappy state of affairs. Despite the hostility of the king and his supporters, the legate found in favour of John, excommunicating Hugh and some of the royal clerks and in addition placing the bishopric of St Andrews under interdict. Alexis meanwhile arranged for the consecration of John in the abbey of Holyrood, his uncle the bishop of Aberdeen officiating. No doubt he chose Holyrood because, lying in the shadow of the castle with its English garrison, it was thought safe from royal interference. Hugh, however, continued to officiate in St Andrews, whilst John and his uncle were banished by William from his kingdom along with a number of their relations. King Henry having by now returned to the Continent, the exiles lost no time in taking refuge at his court in Normandy.

So matters stood until the spring of 1181, when William was summoned to consult with Henry, perhaps on promptings from Rome. He travelled to Normandy with his brother David. The deliberations of the two kings resulted in a compromise. Bishop Matthew was to be allowed to return to his see in Aberdeen; and John would relinquish his claim to St Andrews, receiving instead another bishopric of his choice (though only Dunkeld was vacant at the time) and also the royal chancellorship and handsome financial compensation. Unfortunately, when William sought papal approval for the arrangement, Alexander refused to condone it. Moreover, he appointed the archbishop of York as his legate to Scotland, empowering him and the bishop of Durham to take stern measures, should William prove obdurate.

The Scottish king was in no hurry to leave Normandy. Henry was in sporadic contact with Philip Augustus, the new Capetian monarch, doubtless assessing his present attitudes and future intentions. At one meeting they reviewed current developments in Palestine and reiterated their verbal support for the prospective crusade. All this would have been of interest to the watchful William. In July he was present, together with the Young King, at another conference between Henry and Philip. It was held at Gisors, the traditional meeting place on the border of Normandy and France; and it would be fascinating to know how far William and the Young King dwelt on times past in their conversations. That however, was of no relevance to the present business. Henry had been about to return to England after his deliberations with William when he heard that the Count of Flanders had invaded Philip's territory. At Gisors he was able to effect a reconciliation before travelling with William to Cherbourg, where they embarked on 26th July and made the crossing to Portsmouth. From there they showed their mutual devotion to Saint Thomas by making a pilgrimage to his shrine at Canterbury.

Henry then headed north, perhaps still in William's company. In any case, the Scottish king attended a council he held in Nottingham some time in August. Significantly, the archbishop of York and the bishop of Durham were also in attendance; but it is not certain that the pope's decision on the St Andrews affair was known at that point. By the time William reached Redden on the Scottish border, though, any hopes of papal approval that he may still have entertained vanished when he was confronted by the bishop of Durham, who had brought with him John, bishop-elect of St Andrews. Their one purpose was to have John reinstated and duly recognised as bishop. True to his mettlesome nature, William refused to bow to their demand and forbade John and his supporters to set foot in his kingdom. This was too much for the archbishop of York, who proceeded to excommunicate the king himself and lay his whole realm under interdict. Fortunately for William, however, and probably as yet unbeknown to the prelates, Pope Alexander had died on 30th August; and, by a further act of providence, his legate the archbishop himself died in November, leaving the legality of their measures in doubt. The outcome was that within the year William had sent the bishop of Glasgow and other of his loyal ecclesiastics to Rome, where they persuaded the new pope, Lucius III, to absolve him, quash the verdict in favour of John, and appoint another commission to solve the dispute. Lucius even went so far as to send to the king his Golden Rose, an ornament which the pope blessed each Lent and then awarded as a mark of his special favour. So by mid-March in 1182 William had recovered his advantage in the continuing struggle for control of the Scottish church. The contest, however, was far from over.

William's move to secure his northern territories had met with less success. While he was away negotiating with Henry in Normandy, Donald MacWilliam had seized his chance to further his sinister designs on the throne. According to Howden, after making a number of 'furtive incursions', Donald had answered the invitation of sundry powerful men of the kingdom and invaded Scotland, burning and laying waste to the land wherever he went. He put the inhabitants to flight, slaying all he could catch. The region is not specified, but was presumably part of Ross and Moray. The earl of Orkney may well have encouraged the aggression. It is said that William heard of it while still in Normandy. If so, he showed little urgency in his return to Scotland; and we know of no active measures taken to counter it during the next few years.

Perhaps he thought it better to let the storm in the north blow itself out, so long as it did not ravage his more settled lands south of the Moray Firth. An attempt to quell it risked drawing in not only Earl Harald of Orkney but even his nominal superiors in Norway. With the English occupying some of his chief strongholds and old wounds caused by the St Andrews affair not yet healed, prudence suggested he should cultivate his own garden for a while rather than go adventuring in regions where his writ did not run undisputed.

William's best option at present, then, was to concentrate on keeping order in the main part of his kingdom and nipping any internal disputes in the bud. One to which the Melrose chronicler naturally attached considerable importance was a quarrel between his abbey and Richard de Moreville, the king's constable. This concerned the rights to an area of forest and pasture in the vicinity of Melrose; and judging by the trouble taken by the king in resolving the matter, he did not treat it lightly either. A court was held at Haddington on 30th March 1180, which the rival parties attended in the presence of William and his brother David, the bishop of Glasgow, several other abbots, the earls of Fife, Dunbar and Strathearn, and ten more leading barons.

We have the charter confirming the settlement, which gives one of those fascinating insights into the life and preoccupations of the times. The area in question had been perambulated by the king himself, his brother, and the bishop of Glasgow; and its borders are specified in detail. Most of the forest area is to be freely held by the monks, who are also to have a site for a byre holding a hundred cows, a sheepfold and certain existing buildings. Richard and his heirs may retain one wood, but without erecting any building or fence or carrying out any manual work there; they are, however, entitled to its wild animals and birds (the record of a grant made to Melrose by another lord is more specific: deer, boars, hawks and falcons are reserved for him, the monks being allowed to trap nothing but wolves). Each party in the present case may have a forester to ensure that the conditions are observed. Provision is made for penalties should rights be infringed: in the case of any servant of the monks being charged, justice must be done to Richard at the abbey gate; and if the case is proved, the monks are to pay him the servant's wage for half a year, and the offender must be dismissed and not re-employed without Richard's consent. The monks, it is stated, have paid Richard in compensation one hundred silver merks.

For a proprietor who had to leave his estate for a long period, there was always the possibility of some unscrupulous person having designs on it. Travelling was a slow business at that period: sixty miles on horseback was a fair day's journey, and sea travel was always a hazard. So before leaving for distant parts, any man of substance whether layman or cleric should look to the security of his possessions. That was true as much for an abbot as for a king, as William was well aware. A king, though, had the further duty of reassuring a loyal subject against any infringement on his rights by himself or by another during his absence. So when the abbot of Kelso was about to journey on royal business, probably in this case as one of the envoys to Pope Lucius in 1182, we find William issuing a document guaranteeing the safety of his land, vassals and possessions until his return.

From that mission, as we saw, Bishop Jocelyn of Glasgow and his companions came back with welcome news. Jocelyn was evidently in William's good books. He was raised to the bishopric in 1174, the pope claiming direct jurisdiction over his well-endowed see, which William continued to favour with various grants. From one of the royal acts we get an impression of a prosperous region, as the population are urged to full payment of their tithes in corn, flax, wool, cheese, butter, lambs, calves, piglets, horses and foals and other unspecified commodities. Jocelyn also undertook extensive improvements to his cathedral church. Glasgow seems to have been equally well stocked with men of learning at this time; and on one of these we shall be keeping an interested eye.

This was a man called William Malveisin (or Malvoisin, a later form).* Unfortunately we can only conjecture about his early life. Plainly of French stock, he might have been the son of a person bearing the same name whose uncle was a count of Brittany; or more likely, perhaps, he was connected with another family of Malveisins who held lands between Paris and Normandy. In either case, he would have had relatives who appear in English records; and so he may have come to Glasgow from England rather than directly from the Continent. This seems to have been by the mid-1180s, when he first appears as a royal clerk witnessing a number of William's charters: he had taken his first step in a brilliant career under royal patronage within the church. But as well as serving as an example of how men of outstanding talent could make their mark under King William, he is of particular interest to us as a possible exponent of Arthurian romance, as will emerge in a later chapter.

When in 1182 Bishop Jocelyn had returned from Rome with the pope's Golden Rose, this signalled no more than another intermission in the St Andrews power struggle. Pope Lucius duly appointed two legates to undertake a further enquiry on his behalf. They travelled to Scotland and presented themselves to the king in council. Their discussions produced the proposal that both Hugh and John should renounce their claims to St Andrews and be given instead, with proper compensation, the sees of Glasgow and Dunkeld respectively. The assumption must be that Jocelyn would have moved to St Andrews. Then William had second thoughts, telling the legates that he would prefer Hugh to remain in St Andrews, and would welcome the opportunity of discussing this with John, who was awaiting developments in the security of Roxburgh with its English garrison. John, however, jealous of his rights and mistrustful of William, stubbornly refused to leave his sanctuary in answer to the royal summons.

---

* On Malveisin, see the article in D.E.R. Watt, *Biographical Dictionary of Scottish Graduates*, pp. 374–9. The French name means 'bad neighbour'.

All this the legates reported, with the recommendation that the two rivals should appear before the pope to argue their cases that October. It was early the following year that Lucius gave his ruling. Both men, he said, must renounce their claim to St Andrews. Yet a few days later, on the advice of all his cardinals and moved by pity, or so we are told, he changed his mind and awarded the disputed bishopric to Hugh and that of Dunkeld to John on the terms previously agreed between William and King Henry. To this judgment the two claimants had to submit: for John it was a bitter pill to swallow, especially as he never in fact received the chancellorship, which was part of the original deal. King William had, then, finally had his way, or so it appeared in the spring of 1183.

It was not only in matters of state, it seems, that William was wont to have his way — although in a less reputable sense. Aged forty and still unmarried, he had nevertheless not followed the chaste example of his elder brother Malcolm, but had sowed his wild oats in the past to produce a crop now ripe for harvesting. We know the names of six of his illegitimate children. Of these, four were girls, Isabel, Ada, Margaret and the shadowy Aufrica, the boys being Robert of London and Henry Galithly. His subjects must have wondered when, if ever, he would marry and be blessed with a legitimate heir. Even a daughter born out of wedlock, though, could be used to secure potentially useful family relationships. So in 1183 William bestowed Isabel on Robert Bruce, lord of Annandale. She too was of noble descent, having been fathered by William on a daughter of Robert Avenel, the lord of Eskdale. The marriage did not last long, for Isabel was widowed by 1191 and was then given a second husband, Robert de Ros, lord of Wark.

For another of his natural daughters (we do not know their respective ages) William secured an even more advantageous match. She had been named Ada after his own mother; and in the following year, 1184, he saw her married to Patrick, earl of Dunbar. Evidently of a pious disposition, she founded a nunnery at St Bothans (Berwickshire) before her death in 1200, thus following in her family's tradition. Her only daughter was also named Ada. At this time William would appear to have been particularly concerned with matrimonial affairs. Perhaps, with the passage of time and the absence of any major external preoccupations, he was turning his eyes to both his own future and that of his kingdom. So rather belatedly he considered the prospect of taking a wife himself.

We last saw Henry II at the council which William attended at Nottingham. The following year, at about the time the Scottish king

was making his peace with Pope Lucius, the English king returned
to Normandy, having first made a gesture to his own mortality by
drawing up his will. While he was there, Duke Henry 'the Lion'
of Saxony appeared with his wife Matilda, the daughter of Henry
and Eleanor; and with them they had presumably brought their own
daughter, another Matilda. Duke Henry had fallen foul of the German
emperor, been stripped of his lands and sent with his family into exile.
They were welcomed and given refuge at the Plantagenet court, where
they spent the Christmas of 1182. William kept an interested eye on
their movements.

At New Year, the Young King took an oath of allegiance to his father,
who required the princes Richard and Geoffrey to pay their homage to
their elder brother. Richard's refusal threw the Plantagenet household
into further turmoil, as he left the court at Le Mans for Poitou and
looked to his defences. The Young King, for his part, established himself
in Limoges. That spring saw a confusion of hostilities and manoeuvring
between the three princes, with their father vainly trying to damp the
flames. Then, in June, after a plundering campaign in the south, the
Young King succumbed to a sudden and fatal attack of dysentery.
His body was taken to Rouen for burial; and the family conflagration
smouldered to an end. A year later King Henry quit Normandy for
England, followed by his daughter the Duchess of Saxony and, soon
afterwards, her husband.

This was the moment chosen by King William to make his first
move in the matrimonial game. In the summer of 1184, taking with
him Bishop Hugh of St Andrews and a number of his lords both lay
and spiritual, he made the journey to Henry's court somewhere in the
south of England, where he was received with due honour. His purpose
was to petition the king for the hand in marriage of his granddaughter
the young Matilda.

We may notice in passing that her parents were leading figures on
the cultural scene and important patrons of literature and the arts. A few
years earlier Duke Henry had actually figured, in transparent disguise,
in Chrétien de Troyes's semi-Arthurian romance *Cligés.* Mixing fact with
fiction, Chrétien had told how the German emperor, having promised
the hand of his daughter to the Duke of Saxony, affronted the latter
by going back on his word. The disputed girl was ultimately won by
the hero Cligés, whose mother was the sister of King Arthur's nephew
Gauvain. The romance, which was in all likelihood known to William,

is often cited as an example of the deliberate intermingling of history and legend at this period. That William's own career was used by certain poets in a similar way is a possibility to be examined in a later chapter.

To return to William's own marital ambitions, we are assured by a contemporary chronicler that King Henry's response was not unfavourable. He may, though, have showed his reservations by insisting that the pope must first be consulted owing to a degree of consanguinity, since William and Matilda shared a common ancestor in the person of Malcolm Canmore. So messengers were despatched to the papal court; but they returned with the pope's refusal to make a dispensation. The disappointed king therefore had no choice but to return to Scotland.

Affairs there were not entirely as he would have wished, for in Galloway the murderous Gilbert was continuing to ravage the king's lands and put his men to the sword. William had made some attempt to intervene, but he had disbanded his army on hearing that Henry was back in England. Providentially, Gilbert died at the beginning of 1185, and so to that extent William might have rested more easily, but that was merely the signal for Uhtred's son Roland (who in some charters bears the Gaelic name of Lachlan) to go on the rampage through his late uncle's lands. This left the weight of the problem on the shoulders of King Henry, because Roland was thus dispossessing Gilbert's son Duncan, who was still a hostage in Henry's hands and consequently under his protection.

Meanwhile, in the autumn of 1184, William had been tidying up some matters of land tenure in Midlothian concerning the bounds of the properties belonging to the abbeys of Newbattle and, once more, Melrose. The latter adjudication involved the extent of the royal forest, within which the monks had pasture rights. King Henry, on the other hand, had wider concerns at this time. Apart from some relatively minor trouble in Wales, there was another family squabble to be defused, the princes Geoffrey and John in league with the Count of Flanders having ganged up in Normandy on their brother Richard. Then there was a dispute to be settled regarding a new archbishop of Canterbury as well as an attempt to reconcile the exiles from Saxony with the German emperor. For once Henry was playing, and with some success, the role of peacemaker. He had even relaxed the restrictions which had for so long deprived Queen Eleanor of her liberty; and that Christmas he held at Windsor a court attended by her, the princes

Richard and John, the Duke of Saxony and his family, and William's brother David. In the New Year he sent envoys to mediate between Philip Augustus and the count of Flanders; and then there arrived in England the Patriarch of Jerusalem seeking help against the infidels. In March Henry presided over a great council at Clerkenwell, where it was decided that the time was not opportune for him to go on crusade. But there was another and for us more significant item of business, for which Henry had summoned to his court King William and David his brother.

The previous summer the death had occurred of Earl Simon of Huntingdon, to whom Henry had made over that honour once he had wrested it from William on putting down the rebellion in 1174. Now Henry decided the time had come to extend his conciliatory gestures, at least in appearance, to the Scottish king and his brother. So, passing over claimants among Simon's kin (his son had predeceased him, but there were others with legitimate aspirations to his estates), he returned the honour to William. William lost little time in passing it on to David, who was to hold it under him while he retained it as Henry's vassal. It was probably at about this time that David resigned the earldom of Lennox, perhaps as part of the deal. Although his endowment with Huntingdon might be thought of as an honouring by William of the pledge he made in 1174, it may well be that it was a condition imposed by Henry. As earl of Huntingdon, David enjoyed a high position among the English barons and was thus firmly associated with Plantagenet interests. To have him as a buffer between the English and Scottish crowns might have seemed to Henry a good strategic move, especially in view of William's hankering after the recovery of Northumbria, an ambition he might for the moment have put on hold but had certainly not abandoned.

It was probably between the bestowal of Huntingdon on the Scottish king and its transfer to David that William was in Northamptonshire confirming the rights of an abbey within the earldom. If so, he would have been heading north on his return journey to Scotland. There is no evidence that he was present at the knighting of Prince John at Windsor, which Henry carried out at the end of March prior to sending the eighteen-year-old to Ireland as its king. News then arrived at the English court that Prince Richard was at loggerheads with his brother Geoffrey and causing trouble in Poitou. So this and other matters caused Henry to take ship to Normandy and remain there for a full year. The

Melrose chronicler reports further portentous events that occurred in 1185: a great earthquake throughout England, a solar eclipse and, of more direct concern to William, two bloody battles in Galloway, fought by Roland in his determination to seize all of the dead Gilbert's lands. As this went against King Henry's interests, William's disapproval may not have been absolute. On the other hand, when he learned of the death of Pope Lucius III in November, he perhaps felt that he had lost a sympathetic ear in Rome. As things would turn out, the St Andrews problem had not passed away with Lucius.

At the beginning of 1186 Henry II's mind was occupied with marriage affairs. Relations with his own wife Eleanor were back on a business footing after the ending of her captivity; and he had just had her temporarily retrieve the control of her inherited duchy of Aquitaine from their troublesome son Richard, to whom it had been transferred in 1170. By then, it may be recalled, the betrothal of the prince to Alice of France, King Louis's daughter by his second marriage, had already been negotiated with her father. Some seventeen years later the marriage was still eagerly awaited, not, be it said, by Richard but by Alice's brother Philip Augustus. It was never in fact to take place, but early in 1186 King Henry is found renewing the pledge to Philip. This, though, was mere prevarication: his real thoughts were revolving round a match which he supposed more to his advantage.

Towards the end of April he returned to England with Queen Eleanor, bringing with him his granddaughter Matilda of Saxony, whose marriage to King William had been vetoed by Pope Lucius. Henry had evidently been looking for an alternative bride, and one whose family connections would in the future pose no conceivable threat to his own interests. Once back in England, he summoned William to a council at Oxford, asking that he bring with him David his brother, Bishop Jocelyn of Glasgow, the abbot of Melrose and other Scottish lords. The council was held on 25th May; and at it Henry declared that he proposed to give William a wife of his own choice. This was Ermengarde, daughter of the viscount Richard of Beaumont in Maine. A great-granddaughter of Henry I, the Conqueror's son, by an illegitimate daughter of his, she was thus distantly related to William; but this time no questions of consanguinity were to be raised.

William had already acknowledged Henry's right as his feudal lord to the final word in his marriage arrangements when he consulted him regarding the suitability of Matilda. Nevertheless it was only after an apparently protracted discussion with his barons that he gave his consent to the proposal. This was made more palatable by the coupled offer to restore to William Edinburgh Castle, which was then to be made over to Ermengarde as her dowry together with land to the value of a hundred merks and forty knights' fees. There was no mention of the return to Scottish rule of the other occupied castles of Roxburgh and Berwick. Still, by accepting a French bride probably a good deal younger than himself and whom he may never have previously met, William had ensured the possibility of a legitimate heir to his kingdom and taken a significant step towards repairing the damage done to it by the Treaty of Falaise. With both parties, then, reasonably satisfied, the marriage was celebrated in the royal chapel at Woodstock near Oxford on 5th September. It was a sumptuous affair, with the festivities lasting for four days before the two monarchs adjourned to Marlborough. William entrusted his new bride to Bishop Jocelyn and his barons for the journey to her new home in the north. It is very possible that a certain ambitious young clerk called William Malveisin travelled in her company. So, for the first time in over half a century, Scotland now had its own reigning queen.

The atmosphere at the wedding celebrations could not have been entirely carefree in view of developments on the Continent, to which we shall return. Relations between the two monarchs must, though, have benefited from the fact that a potential source of conflict between them had recently been removed. This was their clash of interests brought about by Roland's seizure of the dead Gilbert's lands in western Galloway. Henry had lost patience with Roland's wild behaviour; so a few weeks after arranging the royal marriage in Oxford, he assembled a large army and proceeded to Carlisle, where he called William and Earl David to join him and secure Roland's appearance at court to answer for his actions. After some hesitation, Roland bowed to his superior force and presented himself before Henry in Carlisle. The Plantagenet's terms were less severe than they might have been, on condition that Roland would accept the judgment of his court in his dispute with Duncan over his father's lands, he might continue to hold from William his own inherited territory, while swearing fealty to the English king. William and David swore for their part to act against Roland should he break the agreement, in which case the bishop of Glasgow undertook to excommunicate both him and his land. For the Scottish king this settlement had the advantage of strengthening his hold on that turbulent region, in which Roland was later to serve as his justiciar.

In July of this event-packed year of 1186, the new pope, Urban III, decided to reopen the perennial St Andrews case. Having conferred with the rival claimants, who then seem to have returned to Scotland, he announced that they should report back to the curia on an appointed date, when the situation would be reviewed. In the event, whereas John dutifully obeyed his summons, Hugh ignored it and thereby incurred the penalty decreed by Urban: he was eventually suspended by the Scottish prelates from the bishopric of St Andrews, which he was still occupying, and was subsequently excommunicated.

We do not know when William returned to his kingdom. Although he had some cause for satisfaction in the return of Galloway to the fold, his northern territories were still out of his control, as was shown by a dramatic incident late in the year. Encouraged no doubt by the king's protracted absence and in defiance of the measures he had taken to guard against incursions by the MacWilliams and the MacHeths, a party of sixty outlaws had come raiding almost as far as the Tay. At Coupar Angus, however, they fell foul of the earl of Atholl. Showing no respect for the normal laws of sanctuary, he pursued them into the abbey there and slaughtered them to a man.

That was one dramatic incident in a situation which, while continuing to limit William's authority over the unstable highland region, was not an immediate threat to the foundations of his kingdom. King Henry found himself at this juncture facing a more radical problem. One lesson the newly-wed William might have learned from the Plantagenet was that the acquisition of sons and heirs could be a mixed blessing. He at least had no present worries on this score. In the event of his death, his natural successor would have been his brother; and as far as we can tell, he had always maintained good relations with David. Henry had been less fortunate. By prematurely crowning the Young King, he had given him ideas above his station and the hope of at least a share in his own power. Although Young Henry was no more, there still remained in the summer of 1186 his other three 'eaglets', to use Gerald of Wales's celebrated image; and they had already shown themselves equally sharp in beak and claw, just as capable of turning against him as against each other.

At the moment it was Geoffrey the Count of Brittany who was causing him some unease; for it was rumoured that the twenty-seven-year-old prince, instead of concerning himself with the affairs of his own province, had gone off to Paris, where he was scheming with Philip Augustus against the interests of his father and brother Richard. But the plot they were hatching, whatever it was, was fated to come to nothing because, on 19th August, Geoffrey was unhorsed in a tournament and trampled to death. Henry's grief as a father may have been outweighed by his relief as a statesman. In any case, far from attending his son's burial in Notre-Dame, he stayed to preside over the marriage of William and Ermengarde at Woodstock. The Scottish king would have shown more than a passing interest in Geoffrey's death, since his widow Constance was the daughter of William's own sister Margaret. Although their only child at that time was a girl, Eleanor, Constance gave birth in the following March to a male heir. He was named Arthur after the legendary king so beloved in Plantagenet circles.

After conducting some long-range negotiations with Philip, Henry spent Christmas with John and then in February went with him to Normandy, where they were joined by Richard. Together they prepared for the by now inevitable war with Philip. After a bout of hostilities, a two-year truce was agreed at midsummer, whereupon the untrustworthy Richard left for the Capetian court and a suspiciously warm reception by Philip. Then in October there occurred an event which sent a shudder throughout the whole of Christendom. After routing the Christian armies in the Holy Land, Saladin and his infidels had captured Jerusalem itself. This had the effect of persuading the two kings to sink their differences in the common cause. At a conference in January attended by Richard, they pledged a crusade, its cost to be met by a tithe levied in their respective realms. Richard immediately took the cross without his father's leave; and Henry and Philip followed suit before having the crusade preached throughout their lands.

After his return to Scotland, King William had not remained idle. In March 1187 he no doubt took some pleasure in the election of Richard, one of his clerks, to the bishopric of Moray and in his consecration at St Andrews by his protégé Bishop Hugh. Whether or not as a consequence, he then decided in a manner reminiscent of King Henry to bring that province to order. For this purpose and with the support of his earls and barons he gathered a large army and marched it to Inverness, determined to hunt down Donald MacWilliam. Some of the nobles showed less enthusiasm for the operation than others, being content to have the district scavenged for provisions. But a force of almost three thousand young warriors led by Roland, the erstwhile rebel of Galloway, set out to bring Donald to book. According to the Melrose chronicler, they came across him on an otherwise unknown moor called Mam Garvia. There they slew him with much of his army, putting the rest to flight. Among their spoils was Donald's severed head, which they presented to King William on their return. That was on 31 July; and it was a significant victory for William, heralding a long period of relative peace for this hitherto troublesome region.

By the end of January 1188 King Henry was back in England setting about raising the money for the crusade, the so-called Saladin Tithe. At Geddington (Northamptonshire) he held a council at which, after a fervent call to the crusade by the archbishop of Canterbury and the bishop of Rochester, it was decreed that a tenth of all 'rents and moveables' was to be levied throughout England. Moreover, the bishop of Durham was to require King William to raise the same tithe in Scotland. In the hope of making a deal with Henry, William had sent him an offer of four thousand merks in exchange for his lost castles; and in reply Henry now promised to give this favourable consideration once the tithe had been paid. The Scottish king with many of his leading prelates and noblemen met the English emissaries on the Tweed between Wark and Birgham and conferred together on their demands. According to one version, William's lords, evidently thinking more of their purses than of the recovery of distant Jerusalem, flatly rejected the terms, even if the king himself should agree. An alternative account is that William, having refused the embassy entry into Scotland, offered five thousand merks to cover castles and tithe. Whether or not William had been swayed by the parsimony of his magnates, the bishop of Durham went back to Henry with a proposal that he could not accept. So there the matter rested.

The English king was in no position to press his demands for the tithe, even had he wished; for yet again storm-clouds were gathering across the Channel. Philip had already threatened a move against Normandy if Henry continued to put off the marriage of his sister Alice to Prince Richard. Then, once Henry was in England, Richard became seemingly embroiled with Philip over his handling of a rebellious count of Toulouse, although there was some suspicion that the two had been acting hand in glove. Worse still was to follow; for in June Philip broke his truce with Henry by seizing some of his border fortresses. The Plantagenet had no option but to muster his forces and take ship for Normandy to counter Philip's aggression. The rest of the year produced a succession of hostilities, truces, and devious attempts by Richard to turn the situation to his own advantage. By Christmas the prince had defected to the French court; and for Henry the situation looked black indeed.

William was once again a remote spectator of the troubles of the English king with whom, as fate decreed, he was to have no further dealings. At home, the St Andrews dispute was entering its final phase, long though its echoes would take to die away. In December 1187 there was a new pope, Clement III, in Rome; and in the following month he solemnly ordered the removal of Hugh from the see and the holding of a new election. His recommendation was that his place should be taken by John. The papal decision was intimated to William and also to King Henry, with the request that he use his influence in the matter. The pope further urged recognition of John on Bishop Jocelyn of Glasgow and various other prelates of the Scottish church, which he then took under his immediate protection. But William had one final card to play: on John's return to Scotland, he was persuaded to renounce his right to St Andrews and accept Dunkeld, although the royal chancellorship, which had once been dangled as a bait, was no longer on offer. With John's destiny settled, Hugh travelled to Rome to seek the pope's pardon and absolution. This he was duly granted, but only to fall prey to a higher judgment. For in the August heat the Eternal City had been stricken by a plague, which carried off many of its cardinals and citizens, rich and poor alike; and among its victims was Hugh and almost his entire household.

In April of the following year, 1189, King William, no doubt with a sigh of relief, summoned his bishops and chief lords to a council in Perth. There he secured the election to the see of St Andrews of Roger, his chancellor at the time. William's triumph can be measured by the fact that Roger was his own cousin, son of the earl of Leicester. Bishop John of Dunkeld, we are told, was present but raised no objection. Roger's commitment to his religious calling seems to have been less than whole-hearted; for instead of plunging himself into his episcopal duties, he had his consecration postponed for nine years, remaining bishop-elect in the meantime; and even after being consecrated he is known to have spent a good deal of his time at the English court. On his election at Perth he surrendered his chancellorship, which was then conferred on Hugh of Roxburgh, one of the royal clerks.

Back on the Continent, King Henry's troubles were piling up. Not only was his health now giving cause for alarm, but the political situation, despite a papal attempt at mediation between Henry on the one hand and Philip and Richard on the other, went from bad to worse. In June the Capetian launched an attack with the errant prince in support. Driven from Le Mans, ailing and despondent, Henry was forced to negotiate with his enemy near Tours. The terms he accepted were humiliating: he had to do homage to Philip, surrender Alice for her marriage to Richard on his return from the crusade, have his vassals swear fealty to Richard as his successor and, among other provisions, make various reparations to the Capetian. The mortally sick king was taken the short distance from the scene of his capitulation to his great fortress of Chinon; and there, having learned that his favourite surviving son John figured high on the list of his foes, he died on 6th July. His body was borne for burial to the nearby abbey at Fontevrault. It is said that Richard came briefly to kneel before his bier.

Richard lost no time in being invested as Duke of Normandy and in reaching a firm accord with Philip, which included a renewed promise to marry the languishing princess Alice and the assurance that he would join the Capetian on the crusade. With that business completed, he crossed the Channel to his new kingdom, where he had spent little time in the past, but where his loving mother Eleanor was awaiting him. His glittering coronation took place at Westminster on 3rd September in the presence of the mighty of the realm. King William was not among them; but to his brother Earl David fell the honour of carrying one of the ceremonial swords. Thus began a fresh chapter in the history of England; and with it there opened a new phase in the reign of the king of Scotland.

FIVE

The Later Years 1189–1214

In September 1189 King William was confronted by an unfamiliar situation. For almost a quarter of a century he had grappled, successfully for the most part, with his duty to consolidate and protect his inherited kingdom. To the best of his ability he had defended it not against hostile external powers but against threats from within what we might think of as the interrelated members of the European family. These were principally the Plantagenet realm and Capetian France, with the German empire less directly involved, and Rome exercising its patriarchal authority and nominally spiritual but also temporal power. Tensions inside this 'family' strained its cohesion from time to time, accompanied as they were by rifts within the Plantagenets' own household. But although William had chosen to take sides in the gravest of these rifts, for him with his Anglo-Norman roots this was a domestic, not foreign, affair. The formidable Henry II seemed to accept the relationship, keeping an eye on the behaviour of the Scottish king, his junior, and putting him in his place when necessary, but without casting him out of his inheritance. Latterly, with William having learned discretion, the two monarchs had remained on reasonably good terms.

Now, with Henry's death and his branch of the 'family' in crisis, the relationship that had developed since William's coronation seemed to be in jeopardy. The irascible but far-sighted English king had been replaced on the throne by a more reckless, thirty-two-year-old troubadour prince, whose interests were centred on his southern provinces and who had shown little concern for affairs north of the Channel. William had spent a good deal of time with Henry over the years and must have gained a useful insight into his character. But his path had seldom crossed with Richard's: they might have met at Angers in 1166, when the prince was a mere lad, or at Falaise during William's captivity; but there is no record of any significant contact that might have produced a personal relationship.

There were, however, some reassuring factors for William in Richard's accession. From a neighbour with his back turned towards the British Isles there would seem to be no immediate threat to Scottish independence. Moreover, Richard's current plans were not directed to any part of Europe, but to the Holy Land, where he had vowed to go crusading. So he was likely to be long absent on an enterprise in which the Scottish king and his barons had decided to take no part, although some individuals among his vassals would eventually join the crusade. If William saw safety in his absence, there was one other circumstance that was greatly in his favour. Although he had as yet established no *modus vivendi* with King Richard, his brother David, Earl of Huntingdon, was well placed to act as a go-between. He too may have met the adolescent prince at Falaise; and certainly they both attended King Henry's Christmas court at Windsor in 1184. More significantly, since becoming earl, David had been in good standing at the English court and served as a natural intermediary in Anglo-Scottish affairs. This was a role he would continue to play.

After his coronation, Richard spent a busy few weeks dealing with affairs among his English subjects, assuring himself of their fidelity and especially trying to drum up funds for the crusade: he had now pledged Philip Augustus that he would set off for the Holy Land in his company the following spring. His hectic timetable included a meeting with King William in order to put the Anglo-Scottish relationship on a fresh footing. To this end he sent a delegation from York to join William on the Tweed and escort him with appropriate honour to his court at Canterbury. There William duly arrived; and on 5 December, having paid homage to Richard for his English possessions, he accepted from him the terms of what has become known as the Quitclaim of Canterbury. This in effect annulled the provisions of the Treaty of Falaise and restored to Scotland its rights as enjoyed in the reign of William's predecessor King Malcolm.

At last the castles of Berwick and Roxburgh were returned to Scottish control. William still had to pay homage to Richard for 'all the lands for which [William's] predecessors were liegemen of our predecessors', a formula which evaded the issue of Northumbria, since that earldom had once belonged to his father and himself, but never to his brother Malcolm. Not that its surrender was any part of the new king's plans, as was evident when, a few days before the Quitclaim, he had found it prudent and profitable to grant it to the bishop of Durham for the sum of two thousand merks. The customary rights to hospitality and other privileges traditionally enjoyed by the Scottish monarchs in England were, though, to be confirmed, once their details had been checked.

Needless to say, the arrangement was far from being a magnanimous gesture on Richard's part. On the eve of his departure to distant lands, it made sense in the interest of security that he should court the friendship of his northern neighbour. If at the same time he could swell his crusading fund, so much the better. William, therefore, was required to hand over as his part in the deal the considerable sum of ten thousand merks in gold and silver. That was twice as much as he had refused to Henry for the 'Saladin Tithe'. Perhaps William had been forewarned of this. In any case it seemed to him a price worth paying to make good his losses after Falaise and regain control over his entire, albeit impoverished, kingdom. Even his claim to Northumbria had not been explicitly denied; and he might find an occasion to reassert it later.

He would have had the benefit of his brother's advice in the matter; for David had been in England, frequently in Richard's company since his coronation and remaining with him until he embarked for Normandy a week after the Canterbury negotiation. His own title to the honour of Huntingdon was confirmed shortly afterwards. So back to Scotland went William with the satisfaction of having a weight lifted off his mind but the less welcome thought that his purse would be much lighter in consequence. At about the turn of the year he summoned his lords to a great council at Musselburgh and decreed what amounted to a national tax to pay, for his kingdom, a ransom which probably represented about a third of its annual revenues.

By now, with his necessary finances secured, Richard was back on the Continent, doing the rounds of his territories and preparing for his summer departure for Sicily on the first stage of his journey to the Holy Land. Fearing a possible attempt by his brother John to seize the throne during his absence, he had ordered him not to set foot in England for three years, a prohibition that turned out to be short-lived. Should Richard fail to return from the crusade, there was in any case the problem of his successor to be considered. No clear rule of succession to the English throne had as yet evolved; and a case could be made for John, as the king's younger brother, or for Arthur of Brittany, the posthumous son of Geoffrey, who, had he lived, would have been next in line.

King William had some interest in this, since Arthur was his great-nephew and would in all likelihood have received his support. Richard himself, once he had reached Sicily, had also declared himself in favour of Arthur, whose cause was espoused in England by William Longchamp, the ambitious bishop of Ely. One chronicler asserts that the bishop sent emissaries to King William setting out the position and enlisting his support; but the king's reply, if any, is not on record. The cleanest solution to the problem would, of course, have been for Richard to acquire a legitimate son of his own. This, however, was never to be, although his mother Queen Eleanor rushed him into a marriage with Berengaria of Navarre in the spring of 1191, when he was in Cyprus on the next stage of his journey to the east. King William was left to pursue the sensible policy of biding his time and awaiting developments.

We last saw David his brother in the south of England when Richard left for the Continent. His subsequent movements have been the subject of much romantic speculation. He had evidently not made the crossing with the royal party; for in the summer of 1190 he married into the powerful family of the earls of Chester, thus strengthening his ties and influence in Plantagenet circles. However, a number of late sources speak of his fighting the Saracens in the Holy Land with great valour. Sir Walter Scott, in his novel *The Talisman*, even made of him a dashing hero who, under the sobriquet 'the Knight of the Leopard', has a series of adventures that acquire for him both the friendship of Saladin and a Plantagenet bride. The fact is that, although he was at Henry's court on at least two occasions when the crusade was being urged, there is no evidence that he himself ever took the cross or participated in Richard's venture. It is true that we have no information about his activities before early 1194, when he reappears in Scotland; so it remains a possibility, if remote, that he answered the call to which King William had turned a deaf ear. Against this there is evidence to suggest that in the early 1190s he was preparing the way for his foundation of the abbey of Lindores in Fife, colonised by monks from Kelso; and it has been surmised that this pious act could have been performed by David as an alternative to active crusading.

While all that was going on, or was not as the case may be, Richard eventually reached Palestine, where he campaigned with mixed fortunes until the autumn of 1192 when, with Jerusalem still in Saladin's hands, he arranged a three-year truce and left the Holy Land. The Third Crusade was now over, but that did not spell the end of Richard's adventures. For, as every schoolboy used to know, on his way back he was first shipwrecked, then fell into the hands of Duke Leopold of Austria and ultimately of Henry, the new German emperor. From late 1192 he languished in captivity as a hostage while the terms for his release were painfully negotiated. As well as the handing over of two hundred noblemen as a surety, these included a ransom of a hundred thousand marks; and the dowager queen Eleanor was left to scrape the Plantagenet barrel in order to find this vast sum. Only after being held for some thirteen and a half months was King Richard able to return to England. His treacherous brother John, though, had been far from inactive. Back all too soon on English soil, he had sought support among the barons for his own cause, banishing King William's correspondent William Longchamp in the process. An attempt by him to hatch some plot with Philip Augustus was thwarted by Eleanor: the Capetian had abandoned the crusade early because of sickness, but was fit enough to put his hostility to the captive king into action. In the end it was left to Richard to defuse John's subversion once he was able to return to his kingdom and make it secure against his brother's supporters.

In Scotland, William must have had a few qualms on first hearing of Richard's captivity. He had continued to pursue his royal business, spending, so far as one can tell from his charters, a good deal of his time in Edinburgh and his newly recovered castle at Roxburgh as well as at Perth and other places both north and south of the Forth. He also arranged two strategic marriages for illegitimate daughters. In 1191, as we saw, the widowed Isabel was bestowed in Haddington on a Yorkshire baron, Robert de Ros. Then two years later Roxburgh was the scene of the marriage of Margaret, whose mother was the daughter of a certain Adam de Whitsome (Berwickshire), to Eustace de Vesci, the powerful lord of Alnwick and son of the man who had defended that fortress so courageously against William himself in 1174. By these alliances he was strengthening his position in the northern English territories where so much of his ambition still lay. In ecclesiastical affairs, he achieved in 1192 the effective freedom of the Scottish church from any threat posed by York, when he secured from the pope a bull declaring that with its bishoprics of St Andrews, Glasgow, Dunkeld, Dunblane, Brechin, Aberdeen, Moray, Ross and Caithness it was to be subject solely to the Holy See.

Clearly, with King Richard far away and possible trouble brewing in his English realm, William was intent on consolidating his own position in whatever ways he could. Having prudently declined to become involved with John's conspiratorial activities, he instead made a move calculated to retain the favour of the captive king. On hearing of the ransom demanded for Richard's release, he

Saint Margaret (c.1045-93). Wife of Malcolm III Canmore and
great-grandmother of William the Lion. She was canonised in 1250.
Copyright © The British Museum.

David I and his grandson Malcolm IV (right) portrayed in a charter of 1159 issued by Malcolm to Kelso Abbey. *Courtesy of the Duke of Roxburghe (per the National Library of Scotland).*

Seal of William the Lion. He is shown wearing a cap, probably as at his inauguration. *The Trustees of the National Museums of Scotland.*

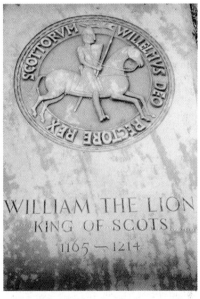

Detail of a modern slab at Arbroath Abbey, commemorating King William the Lion (1165 – 1214). *Crown copyright: Historic Scotland.*

Arbroath Abbey. The burial place of William the Lion,
who had founded it in 1178 in honour of Saint Thomas Becket.
From a watercolour by R.W.Billings (1813-1874).

Alnwick Castle. Besieged by King William and the scene of his capture in 1174. *Photograph by John Housby.*

Roxburgh Castle. The remains between the Teviot and the Tweed of the royal stronghold, which was occupied by the English from 1175 to 1189. It features prominently in *Fergus of Galloway*. *Crown copyright: The Royal Commission on the Ancient and Historical Monuments of Scotland (RCAHMS).*

The Mote of Urr. Site of the motte-and-bailey castle which once belonged to the royal chamberlain and may have inspired the fictional home of Fergus. *Crown copyright: RCAHMS.*

Dunnottar Castle. The ancient Mearns stronghold where, in *Fergus*, the hero acquires the marvellous sword. *Crown copyright: RCAHMS.*

Jedburgh Abbey was built for a community of Augustinian canons. Founded by David I c.1138. Jedburgh is the location of a tournament in *Fergus. Crown copyright: Historic Scotland.*

St Andrews Cathedral and St Rule's Tower. The cathedral was built between c.1150 and 1318. William Malveisin was the first bishop buried there. The earlier church of St Rule served the Augustinian canons from the second quarter of the twelfth century. *Crown copyright: Historic Scotland.*

The thirteenth-century mirror-case excavated in Perth. This small pewter case (54mm x 46mm) carries a scene from the Tristan legend and an assurance of joy to its bearer. *Perth Museum and Art Gallery, Perth and Kinross Council, Scotland.*

sent as his contribution two thousand merks taken from the royal treasury.

With the ransom paid, Richard returned to England on 13th March 1194. Early the previous month William was in Edinburgh, confirming an agreement between the church of St Andrews and that of Durham regarding certain of its properties and privileges within the St Andrews diocese. He then lost no time, presumably responding to a summons from Richard, in travelling to England, where Earl David had already had a hand in achieving the surrender of Nottingham Castle and its rebellious garrison. On 2nd April William joined Richard at nearby Clipstone. From there he followed him to Worksop, Southwell, and on to Melton Mowbray, where he judged the circumstances favourable to broach again that long-cherished ambition: would Richard restore to him the earldom of Northumbria along with Cumberland, Westmorland and the 'county' of Lancaster? To this Richard gave the diplomatic answer: he would have to consult his barons. Then they resumed their peregrination in daily stages by way of 'the house of Peter the forester of Rutland' and Geddington to Northampton. There, having conferred with his magnates, Richard gave William his disappointing answer: he could not grant his request for the strange reason that, if he did, it would appear that he had acted out of fear of the hostile lords of France.

If that had put William in a bad humour, the events of the following day added insult to the injury suffered by his pride. Heading south now, Richard made for Silverstone, while William relaxed with a day's hunting. He intended to spend the night at Brackley in lodgings to which Hugh, the long-serving bishop of Durham and now earl of Northumbria, claimed the right. When William's servants arrived with their provisions, they were refused entry by the bishop's men; and on Hugh's arrival he ordered the tables to be laid. The sudden appearance on the scene of the archbishop of Canterbury did not mend matters. So this was the situation that confronted William on his return from the hunt that evening. In a huff, he ordered his own provisions to be distributed among the poor, and went off to Silverstone to complain to King Richard, who took William's side in the sorry business and gave Hugh the sharp end of his tongue. Whether or not the events were related, a few days later the bishop surrendered his earldom to Richard, albeit with a recommendation as to his successor.

King Richard, meanwhile, had proceeded to Winchester, where he issued a charter noting in detail the Scottish king's rights whenever he was summoned to the English court. His daily expenses must be met by specified sums of money, and he must be supplied with given quantities of loaves, both wastel and simnel bread, of wine, of wax and candles, and of pepper and cumin. These spices, being imported luxuries, were highly prized and often figure in contemporary documents. Richard's decree was addressed to 'William, illustrious king of Scotland, our dearest friend and kinsman and our loyal liege'. It was issued in the presence of Queen Eleanor, the archbishop of Canterbury, the obstinate Bishop Hugh of Durham, and Bishop Jocelyn of Glasgow; and among the witnesses were, as well as the archbishop and Hugh, various leading prelates and barons, including Earl David and William's new son-in-law Eustace de Vesci.

These dignitaries had come to Winchester to attend Richard's second coronation. It was held on 17th April; and to William fell the privilege of bearing one of the three swords of state. After the ceremony Richard shed his robes and heavy crown for lighter ones; and William went in procession with the other great prelates and barons to enjoy a royal banquet in the monks' refectory. This may have sweetened his temper, but did not distract him from thoughts of how he might profit further from the occasion.

It was two days after the coronation that Bishop Hugh of Durham gave up the earldom of Northumbria. As soon as the news reached William, he made yet another bid for it. Reminding Richard that it had been held from Henry II by both his father and then his brother Malcolm, and no doubt reflecting on the Plantagenet's continuing financial worries, he offered him one hundred and fifty silver merks for the earldom. After taking the customary advice, Richard agreed to accept that sum for the whole of Northumbria except for its castles. This was not to William's liking; and he renewed his offer, only to be met with the assurance that it might be given more favourable consideration on Richard's return from Normandy. He in fact went there with his mother the following month in order to bring John to heel and confront the persistent threat from Philip Augustus. Fate, however, decreed that neither Richard nor the ageing Eleanor would ever tread English soil again. William had no choice but to return empty-handed to Scotland. Richard, though, had been able to pocket two thousand marks paid on the transfer of the earldom to Bishop Hugh's original candidate.

Still William refused to take no for an answer; and back in his kingdom, he dreamed up yet another scheme for getting control over the coveted northern English lands. Seven or eight years previously, Queen Ermengarde had presented him with his first legitimate child, a daughter Margaret. His present plan seems to have germinated when he lay sick in Clackmannan, probably in the summer of 1195, and turned his mind to the need to have an agreed successor. He therefore proposed to marry Margaret off, presumably with Richard's connivance, to Otto, son of the exiled Henry the Lion and so Richard's own nephew (he was eventually to become German emperor). Margaret would in due course succeed to the Scottish throne. Many of the Scottish barons led by Earl Patrick of Dunbar objected to this proposal, declaring that it would be wrong to have a woman as queen when William had a surviving brother and nephew, namely David and his son Henry. We can only guess David's views on the possibility of being excluded from the succession in this way.

Although William's recovery made the matter less urgent, he did not drop the idea, but in the following year pursued it at long range with King Richard. What emerged from their negotiations was an agreement that William would give Otto not merely his daughter but also the whole of Lothian, whilst Richard would endow the married couple with all Northumberland and Cumberland. The English monarch would have custody of Lothian and its castles, the Scottish of the lands and fortresses south of the Border. This settlement would seem the product more of William's obsessive desire for the English counties than of his statesmanship. Fortunately perhaps for all concerned, the protracted negotiations were not followed by action. Then, early in 1198, Queen Ermengarde was found to be pregnant again; and William, probably under pressure from his nobles, abandoned the project in the hope that she, with God's help, would provide him with a male heir.

Throughout the first half of the decade William had, of course, paid proper attention to the more mundane business of his kingdom, issuing charters in such places as Dunfermline, Clackmannan, Stirling, Jedburgh and Selkirk. Some of them made grants of land in exchange for knight-service as he continued to expand, especially north of the Forth, the class of landed gentry on whom he might rely in times of need. It is interesting to find some acts of about this period being witnessed by the chronicler Roger of Howden, who may have made more than one visit to Scotland in his capacity as servant of the English crown. Another name that appears with increasing frequency is that of

William Malveisin, who by 1193 had been favoured with the benefice of archdeacon of Lothian, which was in the gift of the king's cousin Roger as bishop-elect of St Andrews. So by now the young Malveisin was considerably extending his circle of acquaintances among the mighty of the land, and is very likely to have met the learned Englishman who was chronicling their part in the great events of the day.

In 1195, possibly as a result of the strain under which the kingdom's finances had recently come, William thought fit to 'renew his coinage', that is issue new coins with a modified design, belatedly following a move that Henry II had made fifteen years earlier. Considering the importance of trade by this time, the development of the Scottish currency had in fact been less than enterprising. There had been by the end of David I's reign royal mints at Berwick, Roxburgh and Edinburgh, the castles which William then had to surrender to English control. Although coins may have been struck elsewhere from time to time and William did open a further mint at Perth, it seems that the extension of the Scottish coinage had been low in the list of royal priorities.

In his Continental domains King Richard remained at odds with Philip Augustus, despite intermittent attempts to reach an accommodation. In 1196 he tried to obtain from the Bretons the wardship of his nephew and chosen successor, the ten-year-old Count Arthur. To his alarm, the boy was suddenly spirited away to the French court to be brought up with Philip's own son. Once again Richard was in danger of being outmanoeuvred by the Capetian. In the same year or the next, if not both (the chronicles conflict over the date), King William had to face a more immediate threat.

It seems that Harald Maddadson, earl of Orkney and Caithness, perhaps on the promptings of his second wife, the daughter of Malcolm MacHeth, continued in his hostile attitude to William. On one occasion Harald's son Thorfinn invaded Moray with a certain Roderic, but was put to flight by the king's troops near Inverness and Roderic was slain. 'Blessed be God over all who delivers up the ungodly!' exclaims the Melrose chronicler. Harald himself occupied Moray at one point; and William marched against him, continuing into Caithness and sending his army on to destroy Thurso castle. As gales prevented Harald from making his getaway to Orkney, he was obliged to submit to the king and promise to bring him hostages when he should next visit Moray. On these conditions and with the added stipulation that Harald Ungi ('the Younger'), who had pretensions to half of his lands as grandson of a previous earl, should share Caithness with him, William left the region.

The following autumn he travelled north again and waited in his new castle at Invernairn (now Nairn) for Harald to produce the hostages. Returning from the hunt one evening, he found that the earl had arrived by boat, bringing with him not the promised hostages, who included his son Thorfinn, but two young nephews of his in their place. Harald admitted that his son and heir was no longer in the land and that he had let the others leave. This was not good enough for William. He had Harald seized and hauled off to Edinburgh (or Roxburgh, according to some accounts), where he languished in chains until Torphinn was eventually brought from Orkney.

Harald was then freed and himself returned there. His troubles, however, were not over; for soon Harald Ungi appeared to claim his half of the earldom. Although Harald senior managed to kill his rival in a battle at Wick, he is said to have then been escorted to King William, to whom he offered a rich bribe to have his title to Caithness confirmed. To this William agreed, provided that he got rid of his present wife and took back his first, who was sister to the earl of Fife. But Harald was unwilling to reverse his marital arrangements; so William decided to settle matters by granting the earldom to the king of Man. This seems to have been the situation in about 1198 or 1199; and there we will leave it for the time being, with Harald, at least temporarily dispossessed, back in Orkney, and his unfortunate heir Thorfinn remaining in William's custody.

The charters of the period are of little help in sorting out the chronology of these events; but they do show William's presence in the north, and especially at Elgin, for extended periods in 1196 and/or 1197. In May of one of those years he was visited by his brother, perhaps in support of his campaigns against Harald. If David still entertained any hopes of succeeding him one day on the throne, they were much diminished when Queen Ermengarde gave birth at Haddington on 24th August 1198 to a son and heir, Alexander. Within a few months it was, in any case, the English not the Scottish succession that was to pose the graver problem.

By March 1199 King Richard had still failed to achieve any lasting agreement with Philip Augustus. It was, though, while he was dealing with a relatively minor affray with a rebel vassal at Châlus near Limoges that his rivalry with the Capetian was brought to a dramatic end. A chance shot from a crossbow inflicted a wound which turned gangrenous. His life could not be saved; and on 6th April he died with his mother at his side, and having named John as his heir and successor. His body was taken to be buried with his father Henry in the abbey of Fontevrault; his heart, it is said, was interred in Rouen cathedral. Years later, the archbishop of Canterbury was said to have seen his soul translated from Purgatory into Heaven.

Young Arthur, meanwhile, had been returned to his remarried mother in Brittany. It was no doubt because Richard mistrusted the baleful influence Philip would have had over the boy in Paris that he had, in his final hour, declared that John should follow him on the throne. Queen Eleanor evidently held the same view, which was soon justified when Arthur, his mother Constance, and King Philip joined forces to press his claim by invading Anjou, Maine and Touraine. Their thrust was countered by the doughty resistance of seventy-seven-year-old Eleanor; and Arthur was escorted to Paris again. John took advantage of the cessation of hostilities by returning briefly to England, where he was crowned at Westminster on 25th May.

In Scotland, King William, having completed the pacification of his own realm to his satisfaction, must have had some misgivings as news of these events reached him. Not only had he probably favoured Arthur as heir apparent, but word to that effect had once reached the ears of John, if one chronicler is to be believed. So whereas William lived in the hope encouraged by Richard that one day those coveted English territories might be his, the chances of his ambition being fulfilled by the dead king's suspicious younger brother would seem remote. Against this, he might have gained a little credit in John's eyes from the fact that his own brother David had been persuaded by an influential group of John's supporters to declare in his favour after Richard's death. Perhaps the situation might be turned to his advantage after all.

When John was still in Normandy, William had despatched messengers to him with the assurance that, provided he restored his lost patrimony of Northumberland and Cumberland, he would swear fealty to him and serve him against all men. However, the archbishop of Canterbury and others refused the messengers passage to the Continent. Instead, they sent Earl David to urge patience on his brother until such time as John should return to England. The prospective king himself informed William, through his son-in-law

Eustace de Vesci, that he would then give him satisfaction, if he kept peace with him in the meantime. William contained his impatience until John was safely crowned. Then he renewed his plea; and this time his messengers brought the reply that if William would come to him, he would see that justice was done.

Even as king, John was in no position to feel secure while there were still in high places supporters of Arthur's claim to the throne, in England as well as beyond the Channel. So as long as he was preoccupied with securing the allegiance of any waverers, William could afford to play hard to get. Consequently when, after his coronation, John sent by the bishop of Durham a summons to his Whitsuntide court at Northampton, William felt safe to respond with a message repeating his demand for Northumberland and Cumberland and saying that if it were not met, he would have to retrieve them as best he could. He was even bold enough to give John forty days in which to reply. The new king had not, however, lingered in Northampton; instead, having put the disputed counties in the charge of a new sheriff, he left on his way to the Channel ports. William's envoys followed him south, but may not have delivered their message before, on 20th June, John sailed from Shoreham for Dieppe to meet the threat to his Continental possessions. William, for his part, proceeded to muster a large army.

What, then, were his intentions? He was plainly smarting from John's delaying tactics. And his mood could not have been sweetened when, in late summer, his bridge over the Tweed had been swept away by a devastating flood. That was bad enough, but what further incensed him was the refusal of Philip, the bishop of Durham, to allow the end on his land to be rebuilt. We cannot know how near he came in this last year of the century to launching an attack on England. Perhaps it was with that danger in mind that the new sheriff of Northumberland and Cumberland intervened in the squabble over the bridge, which was finally rebuilt. Howden tells of another event which was crucial in persuading William to hold his hand. The king, he relates, went to Dunfermline and there spent a night of vigil before the tomb of the pious Queen Margaret. In the course of it, says Howden, he received in his sleep a divine warning against invading England. He thereupon disbanded his army.

A less romantic if more rational explanation of William's restraint might be that the advice he received was more human than divine. His barons had every reason to recall the disastrous events of 1174. And could his brother the earl of Huntingdon have played some part in staying his hand? After David had declared himself in favour of John's accession, he could be counted among his loyal subjects. Indeed by July of this year he had gone to join him in Normandy and is known to have spent several months in his service. For William to have attacked John's lands would surely have caused a rift with a brother with whom, as far as we can tell, he had always been on the best of terms: their relationship was certainly more stable than those between Henry II's fractious 'eaglets'. It may be, of course, that the mature William, now in his mid-fifties, simply changed his mind in the light of past experience and decided to play a waiting game.

In January 1200 John managed to reach an agreement with Philip which was ratified the following May. This involved the Capetian's recognition of John's right to the throne and the acceptance of his homage for his Continental lands, as a consequence of which Arthur was now John's vassal. While these moves were in train, John found time for a brief spring visit to England; and in the course of it, in late March, he held a council in York, to which he summoned the Scottish king. But once again William declined to present himself. The following month John returned to Normandy.

Was William, one wonders, still living in hope that John would fail to establish his authority and that Arthur could yet find his way to the English throne? The hurly-burly of European politics might still produce a situation more propitious for his own ambitions. If at this time he had recalled Geoffrey of Monmouth's account of that other Arthur, he could have ruefully reflected on how the legendary king had grappled successfully with the Saxons and then with his enemies in Moray to bring peace to Scotland. And how ironic that it was in York that King Arthur had restored to the princes of that land their hereditary rights! If Henry II had honoured in his fabled 'predecessor' the figure of a model king, why should not William too have once had his dreams of becoming a Scottish Arthur? Such dreams might now have faded, but something of his ambitions remained.

During the last year of the century William seems to have spent much of his time north of the Forth, especially in Forfar, where he celebrated Christmastide. An unfortunate gap in our knowledge is the role played by Queen Ermengarde at the royal court. She was evidently a lady of genuine piety, as her foundation of the Cistercian abbey of Balmerino (Fife) after her husband's death shows. But whether such worldly advice as she had to offer was of any account in the present situation cannot be judged. If it was, the fact that she is said to have applied her eloquence a decade later to mediating between William and John might imply that her voice would have been one of moderation. In this, as we have seen, she would have had the sympathy of her brother-in-law.

A mark of the favour in which John held Earl David was his issuing of a charter in favour of the burgesses of Dundee while he was at Château Gaillard, the great fortress built by King Richard on the Norman frontier. This was in October 1199, when David was still in his service on the Continent and may himself have been with him at the time. The inhabitants of Dundee, whose welfare was always close to David's heart, were to be free of tolls throughout John's realm except within the city of London. This is a further indication of the growing prosperity of Dundee as a trading centre at this period.

A few weeks before the death of King Richard, Glasgow lost its venerable and influential bishop Jocelyn, who had held the see for a quarter of a century. The chancellor Hugh of Roxburgh was elected to succeed him; but by July he too was in his grave. Hugh was another man who for years had served with distinction and whose death inspired an anonymous cleric to compose a fulsome eulogy in Latin verse, in which he is described as an adornment of the Scottish kingdom. To succeed to the offices of two such revered churchmen was in itself a great honour, and as such needed the full support of the king. The man chosen for both charges was our acquaintance William Malveisin, archdeacon of Lothian. In September he received the chancellorship; and in the following month he was elected to the episcopacy. For his consecration he travelled, at the instigation of Pope Innocent III, to Lyons. The ceremony was conducted on 23rd September 1200 by the archbishop of that see, with one of whose predecessors Malveisin corresponded, while still abroad, on the legal duties of a bishop; and he took the further opportunity of consulting with the experts in canon law in Paris. Having passed the best part of a year on the Continent, he returned to his new diocese early in 1201. There were weighty matters on which King William would need his advice.

During Malveisin's prolonged absence, relations between the English and Scottish kings had entered a new phase. In the summer of 1200, John had taken a second wife, his first marriage in 1189 having now virtually lapsed. It would be wrong to speak of a lightning romance, because the bride was a mere twelve-year-old, Isabella of Angoulême, whom he had snatched from under the nose of a prospective husband. Early in October he brought her to England; and in a ceremony at Westminster he had her crowned with him as his queen. After the coronation he sent a group of distinguished envoys, Earl David among them, to escort King William under safe-conduct to his forthcoming court at Lincoln. This was a summons he could scarcely refuse.

Accordingly, William had to swallow his pride; and on 22nd November he paid homage to John in a great assembly at Lincoln, pledging his loyal service, but reserving his own right, whatever that might imply. Among the gathering of lords and prelates were the archbishop of Canterbury, who administered the oath, William's brother David, and also Roland, that obstreperous lord of Galloway who had once been brought to heel by Henry II, but had latterly given William faithful service as justiciar and constable. Witnessing William's act of homage turned out to be one of Roland's last acts, for within a month he died while on business of his own at Northampton.

It must have come as no surprise to John that no sooner had William done his homage than he raised yet again his obsessive concern for his 'lost' English territories, petitioning him for the whole of Northumbria as well as Cumberland and Westmorland. Nor would John's reply have been entirely unexpected by William, requesting as it did a delay for consideration of the matter until Whitsun. There being nothing more William could do, he returned to Scotland for Christmas, which he spent in Lanark. The following May, John sent him a message asking that a decision on his plea should be further postponed until Michaelmas, a delaying tactic only too familiar to William. In the meantime, John was using occasional favours to secure the goodwill of a number of prominent Scottish barons and thus weaken any support among them for the Scottish king's cause.

Now that John's relations with Philip Augustus had been put on a better footing, and despite some unrest among his Poitevin barons, he chose to remain in England until June 1201. This gave him the opportunity, it seems, to do a little sabre-rattling, lest William's impatience should get the better of him. It may have been on his instigation that Earl Harald attempted to regain Caithness, from which William had ousted him a year or two earlier. In any case, Harald mounted an invasion, in the course of which he had the bishop of Caithness half-blinded and his tongue mutilated. William sent a punitive expedition to the region; and eventually Harald was brought to terms, his son Thorfinn having been blinded and castrated while in royal custody, or so the story runs. Harald was dealt with more leniently, for Caithness was returned to him on payment of two thousand pounds in silver. On the man who had mutilated the bishop the pope imposed a heavy penance.

Whether or not John had played any part in this affair, he did make it clear to William that it would be rash for him to come adventuring across his borders. For in February 1201 he made a personal inspection of his fortresses at Newcastle, Bamburgh and Carlisle. The likelihood of William trying to take the measures he had threatened two years previously was slim indeed. Quite apart from serious doubts he would have had about the support he might expect from his brother and those of his lords who were in John's good books, he was no longer a young man. The previous year had seen the deaths of Margaret, his sister and grandmother of Arthur of Brittany, and of Ada his daughter, whom he had married to the earl of Dunbar. Perhaps he was already feeling the weakness of his own flesh and thought it prudent to ensure an undisputed succession in the event of his death. Whatever his immediate reason, he called all the great and good of his realm to Musselburgh, near Edinburgh; and there on 12th October he had them swear allegiance to his son Alexander, now three years old.

This was not the only great assembly to take place in Scotland at that time. For Pope Innocent III had sent his legate Cardinal John of Salerno to tidy up some ecclesiastical business. To this end he held a three-day council in Perth, but spent far longer at Melrose grappling with a dispute (probably to do with boundaries) between the local abbey and that at Kelso. There seems a note of reproof in the voice of the Melrose chronicler when he tells us of the cardinal's sojourn there, in the course of which he made many promises to both parties but gave satisfaction to neither. For himself, though, the stay was extremely profitable; because before he moved on to Ireland, he had received many gifts (bribes might be the better word) of gold and silver from both sides, as well as a large number of horses. As for the dispute, he left it in much the same state as he had found it.

One of those present at the Perth council was the bishop of Glasgow, William Malveisin; and no doubt he followed proceedings with an ear attentive to all the points of canon law that were raised. He even enlisted the legate's help while he was in Scotland in resolving a dispute in which he was involved; and he may perhaps have had his support in furthering his own career. The occasion was the death in July 1202 of Bishop Roger of St Andrews, King William's cousin. The translation of Malveisin to what considered itself the senior Scottish see was quickly arranged; and by September, apparently having reliquished the chancellorship, he was already performing his episcopal duties there.

In that year of 1202 William remained nursing his grievances in his kingdom. He is unlikely to have been much cheered by a sop offered by King John when he ordered one of his constables to allow those wines imported for the King of Scotland from France to be free of any customs surcharge, provided his servants certified that they were for his own personal use. The toll usually levied was one cask from a cargo of up to twenty, and two casks from any larger shipments. But we must leave William quaffing his wine to follow his brother who that summer, after a visit to the Scottish court, returned to the Continent to continue his service to the English crown. There, events had taken an ominous turn for King John.

Philip Augustus had judged the time ripe for a final showdown with his Plantagenet rival. At the end of April he found an excuse for declaring his fiefs of Aquitaine, Poitou and Anjou forfeit. Then he proceeded to knight the fifteen-year-old Arthur, arrange his betrothal to his infant daughter, and accept his homage not only for his patrimony of Brittany but also for all John's Continental lands except Normandy, against which he now mounted an attack. Learning of these moves, John's aged mother Queen Eleanor left her retreat in the abbey of Fontevrault and with a small escort headed for her ancestral home of Poitiers. Having reached the castle of Mirebeau near the border of Anjou and Poitou, she was there cornered by her young grandson Arthur, whose French troops occupied the walled town, but failed to capture the citadel. One chronicler tells how from her refuge in the keep the intrepid octogenarian hurled rebukes at Arthur and told him to call his men off. He did not do so; but Eleanor managed to smuggle out a message to John, who was near Le Mans. After a forced march and a surprise attack, he retook the fortress and captured Arthur, who was carried off to be incarcerated in Falaise. His subsequent fate is a matter of speculation. According to one account, he was taken the following spring to Rouen, where John killed him with his own hands and had his body flung into the Seine. But all that is certain is that the young Count of Brittany was never heard of again.

Perhaps Earl David might have told us more; for he was at Le Mans in

August when John returned in triumph from Mirebeau. He is not known to have been back in Scotland before early 1204; but we may be sure that by then William would have been well apprised of the Mirebeau affair as well as John's subsequent misfortunes. David appears to have remained in Maine and Normandy until the early autumn of 1202, when Philip was securing his position and planning his final blow. In November 1203 his presence is attested in Rouen, by which time the Capetian's forces were already investing Château Gaillard, the great fortress that symbolised Plantagenet power. In December John virtually threw in the towel and returned to England. The following March Château Gaillard fell, and with it almost the whole of the Plantagenet dominion south of the Channel.

King William reaped no advantage from these calamities, for they served to confine John's activities to his English realm, making him jealous of his remaining power and suspicious of any internal threats that might arise. So he seems to have sat tight in his own kingdom, keeping a wary eye on the English scene and no doubt hoping for better days to come. Our knowledge of his affairs at this period is largely confined to the evidence of charters, the dating of which is often problematical. It was probably in March 1202 that we glimpse him in Roxburgh settling a lawsuit between Malveisin, when he was bishop of Glasgow, and a local landowner. In November 1203 he is in Forfar confirming a grant to Holyrood Abbey. But in 1204 the surviving charters are all from south of the Forth: Haddington, Jedburgh, and Selkirk where, in May, he gave his judgment on the dispute between Melrose and Kelso that John of Salerno had failed to resolve: William ruled in favour of Kelso, though with some compensation to Melrose.

During these years William lost a number of his leading counsellors. As well as Bishop Roger of St Andrews, they included Alan his steward for twenty-seven years, who latterly had caused him some irritation by marrying off his daughter without his customary consent. The royal justiciar, Duncan, earl of Fife for half a century, was another whose company must have been sorely missed when he died in 1204. No doubt it was reassuring for William that his brother was no longer abroad for extended spells and found time for an occasional visit to Scotland; and it was useful to have him in close contact with the English court, where he could act as a go-between if necessary and further William's interests as far as possible.

To the alarm of some of his barons, King John finally decided to do something about recovering his lost lands and planned an expedition to France. Earl David was not among those who opposed the idea; and he remained with the court while preparations were put in train. It seems that he was ready to leave with the king for Poitou, when John thought better of his project and cancelled his plans. Apparently he was nervous of unrest in the north of England, and rumours were circulating of a possible French invasion. So, thinking it more prudent to reopen with the Scottish king discussions about the territories after which the latter continued to hanker, he put out feelers, to which William was not slow to respond. Unfortunately there is no record of what transpired in the subsequent negotiations, since Howden, the faithful chronicler of such things, had himself died. That William had not been fully satisfied is clear from a letter addressed to him by John in July 1205. In it he speaks of his gratification at receiving a favourable reply from the Scottish king and mentions his retention of his Tynedale lands 'as an exception'. This seems to imply that the main territorial claim was shelved at that juncture.

Surviving charters, with the usual caveats about their dating, show a king active throughout 1205 in various parts of his realm. Early in the year we find him at Forfar confirming grants made to Arbroath Abbey, in one case by his illegitimate son Robert of London. Robert, who seems to have been in favour at the English court, held lands in Angus and Fife and was a frequent witness to William's acts from the latter years of the twelfth century onwards. The king probably spent the spring at Forfar and the nearby hunting grounds at Alyth before crossing the Forth for a visit to his lodge at Traquair. In May he is at Stow (Midlothian) confirming an arrangement between Bishop Malveisin and the prior of Durham regarding certain properties held by the latter in Coldingham and St Andrews and the rights, including that of hospitality, operating there.

At Lanark William announced the founding of a burgh at his new castle of Ayr, specifying the privileges of its burgesses. Summer saw him at Stirling and then returning to Alyth and Forfar; and then in October back he went to Stirling, where he was joined by his brother David and his bastard son Robert. There they witnessed a charter detailing the regulations and privileges of the burgh of Perth, including restrictions placed on foreign merchants, conditions for the manufacture and dyeing of cloth, and also on the siting and permitted number of taverns. Before the end of the month, William was at Clackmannan, granting holdings in and around Crail, a favourite residence of his late mother Ada, and where royal servants and officials appear to have been particularly thick on the ground. It was probably at about this time that Earl David paid homage, according to the Melrose chronicler, to his young nephew the heir-apparent Alexander. William's negotiations with John had not completely monopolised his time during what was clearly for him a busy year.

The upshot of those exchanges was the issuing by the English king in November of a comprehensive safe-conduct for William to go to York, where he would receive him early in February. At William's own request, John sent Earl David to Scotland, with instructions to stay there until his brother's safe return. The Scottish king's distinguished escort was to include the bishop of Durham and a number of John's senior barons. Frustratingly, the records are silent on the meeting itself. How long did the two monarchs spend together? Were their discussions friendly and frank, or coloured by mutual suspicions and conflicting interests? It is easier to imagine William sticking stubbornly to his territorial claims, so often repeated, and John offering sops of half-assurances than it is to think of them quaffing convivial cups in a spirit of mutual trust. But all we can say with assurance is that no significant agreement was reached.

The Scottish fourteenth-century historian Fordun says that William spent four days in York and mentions his auspicious return. But, totally ignoring the subject of the parleys, he tells how, in the presence of many English and Scottish nobles, William had there miraculously cured a gravely sick boy with a touch from his hand and a blessing.

Presumably inspired by William's posthumous reputation for piety and echoes from the life of his saintly grandmother Margaret, this anecdote redeems with a supposed spiritual triumph what in reality was yet another sorry failure to extend his worldly kingdom. As before, he returned empty-handed to Scotland; and any soothing reassurances he may have received from John would not have disposed him to let down his guard. He would have remembered how, once he had patched up a settlement with Earl Harald some four years earlier, John had been prompt to call the earl and his chaplain to consult with him in Northamptonshire. If William's suspicions on that occasion had been largely allayed, they may now have been revived by the news that John had sent from Salisbury a similar message, along with a safe-conduct, to Reginald (Ronald), king of Man and the Isles, whose father Guthred was one of the hostile MacWilliam tribe. Could it be that the Plantagenet was hoping to foment further trouble in the north in order to distract William from his tiresome obsession with his English claims?

If so, his plan may have worked. For, although Earl Harald died in this year of 1206, the charters suggest that William spent much of it ordering his affairs north of the Tay, residing chiefly at Kintore (near Aberdeen), Elgin and Aberdeen itself. One of his acts was to make Saturday a market-day at Inverness and grant his burgesses there much the same rights as those enjoyed by his other burghs. One difference from the document we noticed regarding Perth is the absence of any mention of foreign merchants; they may have done less business in what was still something of a 'frontier town'. King John himself made what might be thought a conciliatory gesture when he extended to Arbroath Abbey, William's own foundation, the privileges which, as we saw, he granted to Earl David's burgh of Dundee. We might also observe that, although now well into his sixties, William may still have taken some recreation in the hunting field, to judge by his presence on one occasion at his Perthshire retreat of Clunie in Stormont.

It is likely that by now John felt that William, with his advancing years and less than robust health, was losing something of his earlier resolution and could be played like a tiring fish. So rather than leave him to flounder in his disappointment, he decided to maintain at least the illusion of continuing negotiations. He therefore issued in March 1207 a further safe-conduct for William to return to York for another meeting, which in fact took place towards the end of May. John covered his expenses but otherwise, it seems, gave him no satisfaction. One more conference was planned for the same venue in November; but for some unknown reason it appears never to have been held. There is no evidence that Earl David played any active part in this bout of diplomacy; but that should not be read as marking any lack of interest on his part or implying that he was not available to advise both parties. The possibility of his engaging in some 'shuttle diplomacy' as the need arose is illustrated by his known presence, in July of the following year, at Selkirk with his brother the king, and his appearance a mere fortnight later at the English court.

William's visit to York is his only known activity in 1207; and the absence of any charter of his that can be firmly dated to that year might suggest some problem with his health. However, it was not only his physical wellbeing that could have given him some grounds for unease: his finances were by no means in good shape either. To pay for such things as their great building projects, their endowments, and their mercenaries when necessary, even the mighty of the land might be forced to take out loans from the 'bankers' of the day. This in practice often meant the Jews, who had followed the Conqueror to England in considerable numbers and set up their establishments in the large towns. Among the most important was Aaron, who had operated from Lincoln and from whom William, in his more profligate years, had borrowed on several occasions. Though Aaron had been dead for two decades, the debt remained; and the English treasury stood to gain handsomely from the crown's levy on its repayment. In William's case, it amounted to no less than £2776, for which Earl David stood surety, though he was himself saddled with other debts. So even in financial matters, both brothers were under some obligation to King John.

In his entry for 1207 the Melrose chronicler mentions a few things that we may note *en passant*. On Malveisin's translation to St Andrews, he had been succeeded as chancellor by Florence (Floris) of Holland, who was also elected to the Glasgow see. Florence was the son of the Count of Holland and Ada, William's sister; but although the king's nephew, he spent little time in Scotland and in 1207, as the chronicler tells us, resigned his see, to be replaced by Walter, the royal chaplain. We are also informed that Malveisin himself spent a period abroad: we in fact know that he was at the papal curia at least until the end of the year. Other items recorded by our Melrose reporter are that Ranulf de Soules, lord of Liddesdale and the king's butler, was murdered by his own servants, and that the greater part of Roxburgh was accidentally burnt to the ground. Lastly he tells us that a certain holy hermit was vouchsafed a vision in which an angel hinted darkly at civil commotion within the land, but that 'one is born who shall change the course of the world'. This last event is otherwise unknown to history; but we can imagine the stir the good hermit's story would have caused at the time.

One advantage held by King William over his Plantagenet rival was that he was evidently in good odour at Rome. An indication of this was Pope Innocent III's ready approval of the resignation of Florence, bishop-elect at Glasgow, and his replacement by the chaplain Walter. The largely political nature of such appointments is, incidentally, shown by a subsequent complaint from a Glasgow canon that Walter had obtained his promotion by bribing the royal chamberlain and even the queen and, as bishop, had continued in his corrupt ways. The pope would have been kept fully abreast of Scottish ecclesiastical affairs at this time by Bishop Malveisin, who was himself in good standing at the curia.

Malveisin had already given evidence of his combative nature in following up what he perceived as his own rights, not least in his relationship with the canons of St Andrews priory. The monks of Melrose were on one occasion to play on the meaning of his name by declaring him to be a thoroughly 'bad neighbour'. Dedicated to the strict governance of his see and putting his legal training to full use, he was by nature the complete opposite of the negligent Florence. It was on business of this nature that he travelled to Rome in 1207; and his purpose was served when at the end of the year he obtained a papal confirmation of the privileges and possessions of his diocese.

Meanwhile, King John's relations with Rome had gone from bad to worse. After the death in 1205 of Hubert Walter, the archbishop of Canterbury, a dispute had arisen as to his successor. Pope Innocent supported the election of his friend Stephen Langton, whom John obstinately refused to recognise. Although Innocent consecrated Stephen in June 1207, John would not allow him to set foot on English soil. The pope's patience finally ran out; and in the following year he laid an interdict on England and Wales suspending all celebration of Mass in those lands. In 1209 John was himself excommunicated; and it was not until four years later that he was obliged to make peace with the pope. Until then, far from being cowed by Rome, he took harsh measures against the clergy who opposed him, confiscating their property and banishing the bishops. Two of the latter, the bishops of Salisbury and Rochester, eventually found refuge in Scotland, in Roxburgh and Kelso respectively. It may have given William some small comfort to reflect that now right, if not might, was on his side.

In April 1208 Philip of Poitou, bishop of Durham, died, and his secular possessions came under King John's control. These included his newly-built castle at Tweedmouth which, according to one chronicle, he had named 'Mauvaysin' after William Malveisin, a doubtful tribute in view of the name's meaning and Philip's unneighbourly behaviour in obstructing the reconstruction of the nearby bridge some eight years previously. It was now John's turn to make a hostile gesture, which he did by putting in hand the construction of new and stronger fortifications at Tweedmouth. William's subjects took this as a provocation and a threat to Berwick on the opposite bank of the Tweed; and they are said to have crossed on at least one occasion to kill the builders and destroy their work. The records do not tell if this happened on their king's orders.

William appears to have spent most of 1208 south of the Forth; and we have noted his presence, together with his brother, at Selkirk in July. Perhaps he wished to be on hand for any emergency on his southern border, and would certainly have discussed the developing situation with David. Although the latter still spent most of his time in England, relations between him and John seem recently to have cooled to some extent; and his opportunity to plead William's cause would have correspondingly diminished. Bishop Malveisin, who may have attended the English court at Clarendon in November, now begins to share his role of intermediary in the exchanges between the two kings. John's increasing preoccupation at this time with affairs in his northern territories was shown when, in August, he appeared in Newcastle and from there paid a visit to Carlisle.

At the beginning of 1209 a serious illness kept William at his residence at Traquair. He then received from John a letter couched in the most solicitous terms rejoicing in his convalescence and requesting a meeting with him in April. William would not have been deluded by the smile on the face of the tiger; but he left Traquair and set out on what even he must have suspected was a futile quest, having take the precaution of mustering an army at Roxburgh. According to the *Melrose Chronicle* the rendezvous had been arranged for Newcastle. But William made for Alnwick, the scene of his humiliation thirty-five years earlier; and there he lodged at his own expense, although it was on English territory. John, meanwhile, had travelled up from the Midlands; and it seems that the two kings may have met at Bolton, near Alnwick, before moving to Norham, a few miles up the Tweed from Berwick. It could not have been an amiable confrontation, especially if John, as some say, was still smouldering after the affront to his authority at Tweedmouth Castle. On about 25th April, with no hint of an agreement, the talks were broken off and the kings went their separate ways to prepare for armed conflict.

Threading a path through the inadequate evidence of the chronicles, we can piece together an approximate account of the ensuing events. Both countries were now in the grip of war-fever; and William called together all his great lords, spiritual and temporal, to plan a course of action. Earl David was also present when the council met at Stirling on 24th May. As a result of its deliberations a deputation was sent to John, headed by the bishops Malveisin of St Andrews and Walter of

Glasgow, and the royal justiciar and chamberlain. They carried what was evidently William's reply rejecting out of hand John's latest, harsh demands. When the envoys came to the English court, they found the king in a furious mood, partly because of the Tweedmouth affair and also on account of William's harbouring of refugees from his land. The message they bore served only to unleash a storm of threats against Scotland and its king; and in a state of high alarm they returned to report to William, who was in Forfar at the time.

The king's first reaction was to go back into Lothian and look to his defences. Then, heeding the advice of his worried subjects and probably the moderating voice of his brother, his caution won the day to the extent that he despatched Malveisin, the abbot of Melrose and a few others with a message intended to placate John's wrath. This coincided with the Plantagenet's sending his own envoys into Scotland to reinforce his proposals. They were men very familiar to William: Saer de Quinci earl of Winchester and lord of Leuchars in Fife, and his own son-in-law Robert de Ros. They came up with the king in Edinburgh; and what they had to report induced him to send John an even more conciliatory message. At that juncture Malveisin returned and brought his alarming report to William, who had retired to Traquair: John was not merely in a fighting mood, but actually on his way north with a very powerful army. The bishop did, though, venture the opinion that the Scottish army was ready for them.

Again, William's first thoughts were of resistance. So for the third time he sent Malveisin to make contact with John, with the instruction to keep him talking until such time as he might make the final disposition of his own troops. This was to no avail; for John had soon advanced as far north as Bamburgh on the coast between Alnwick and Berwick, William being then at Melrose. They were, it seemed, on the threshold of a bitter war. Yet it may be that neither king relished the prospect. One contemporary chronicler speaks of some doubts among the English soldiery as to the justice of their cause when they were about to make war like pagans on the devoutly Christian Scottish king. But more telling was the opinion expressed at Melrose by William's counsellors that peace should be preferred to battle. This was the advice that prevailed. It was a fateful moment in Scottish history.

The outcome was in effect a humiliating surrender by William, whom one of the accounts describes as enfeebled by age and desirous of ending his days in peace and sanctity. He presented himself before

King John at Norham, and there agreed to his terms. It is likely that the Plantagenet had got wind of some plan by William to form a marriage alliance with the French royal house involving his still unwed eldest daughter Margaret. That would explain John's central demand, which was that the Scottish king should hand over both Margaret and her sister Isabel, who would then remain in his custody until he should arrange suitable matches for them. He had in mind that in nine years, when his elder son Henry came of age (he was born in 1207), he should marry Margaret, whilst Isabel would be destined for his other infant Richard, if not some appropriate lord of his choice. Provision was made for the earlier decease of any of the parties involved. (As matters turned out, Margaret was married in 1221 to the justiciar Hubert de Burgh, who had custody of the princesses, and Isabel three years later to Roger Bigod, the earl of Norfolk.)

Another of John's requirements was the payment of the vast sum of 15,000 merks in four annual instalments as well as £4000 in compensation for the destruction wrought at Tweedmouth. William was authorised, however, to destroy the castle there, which would never be restored. That was the only concession made in these severe terms, which further stipulated the delivery of hostages: the sons of at least thirteen of the Scottish nobility. When William accepted the treaty (the document itself no longer exists), he abandoned for ever his most cherished dream; because although there is no contemporary evidence that it contained a clause by which he renounced his claim to the northern English counties, that was the inevitable consequence. The pact having been concluded, says one chronicler, the two kings withdrew with the greatest joy. It is hard to believe that William felt any elation.

The agreement was reached at Norham on about 25th July and sealed there on 7th August. The only part of it which has survived, and that only in a late copy, carries the stipulation of the financial conditions. The leading witness is Bishop William Malveisin, the others being the king's chamberlain, his son-in-law Robert de Ros, and Robert de Vieuxpont, one of John's intimates. There is no evidence of the participation of Earl David, whose standing at the English court the settlement must further have undermined. The two brothers surely felt their age when they reflected on the implications for them of the Treaty of Norham.

In fact, despite the undeniable blow it dealt to William's political and territorial interests, not to mention the Scottish exchequer, his relations with its author seem to have undergone a surprising improvement. Far from brooding sullenly on his humiliation, William appears to have taken the initiative in rebuilding bridges between the two courts. A gift by him of falcons to John might appear trivial; but as a gesture it has its significance. Of far greater import was William's attitude to refugees from John's tyranny. In 1210 the Plantagenet was faced by a rebellion in Ireland; and his ruthless measures caused some fugitives to make for Scotland. Among them was a certain Matilda (Maud) de Briouze with her two sons and a dispossessed earl, Hugh de Lacy. Matilda and her family were arrested by Duncan, son of Gilbert of Galloway, whom William had made lord of Carrick. He handed them over to John's officers, who proceeded to return them to him in cages, ultimately to be starved to death in Windsor Castle. Hugh de Lacy did manage to find his way to St Andrews, but soon fled abroad to escape the knights who were still on his track. As for the refugee bishops mentioned earlier, one source says that John suffered their presence in Scotland. Also in 1210, Alan, the son of William's constable Roland of Galloway and holder of his title and office since Roland's death in 1200, was endowed by John with extensive properties in Ireland, for which he did homage to the English king with William's approval.

Was King William, then, trying to ingratiate himself with John out of Christian charity and a certain world-weariness, as that chronicler would have us believe? A cynic might suggest more devious reasons. Perhaps the ageing monarch was showing concern for the well-being of his family now that his two daughters were under John's dubious protection, whilst his brother David was still committed to his responsibilities as an English earl. Or did William even yet retain some glimmerings of hope for future concessions from the unpredictable Plantagenet (he may in fact have received a partial remission of the 'fine' levied by John)?

Such thoughts could have helped to take the edge off William's resentment; but it may well be that he had now set his sights on a new strategy. This would involve consolidating an alliance between the two kingdoms based on the prospect of a marriage between the young Prince Alexander and an English princess. If, as is likely, such a possibility had already been raised during the negotiations at Norham, it was given point by the birth in July 1210 of John's daughter Joanna. Such an alliance would have had real advantages for the English king too, plagued as he was by open rebellion in his Celtic fringe territories and by fears of insurrection in England itself.

William, for his part, had some cause to feel nervous about his own security, as the Norham terms were by no means welcomed by all his barons. One of them, Thomas de Colville lord of Carsphairn in Galloway, was actually charged with sedition and imprisoned at Edinburgh in 1210, though he was released in November after the payment of a ransom. On the other hand, William was happy to give his consent to the marriage of his brother's two daughters to prominent Scottish lords, whose loyalty was vital: Margaret, the elder, had married Alan of Galloway in 1209; and by the following year Isabel was the wife of Robert Bruce IV of Annandale. For Earl David this meant a perhaps prudent cementing of his Scottish ties.

According to one chronicler David was with William at Perth at Michaelmas in 1209 (or possibly 1210) when a natural disaster caused their sudden retreat. The river Tay and its tributary the Almond overflowed and flooded much of the town, washing away many buildings with great loss of life. The king and his brother managed to make their escape by boat, and soon afterwards were at a great council in Stirling, debating the means of paying the money due to John. William seems to have been at Stirling on other occasions in the early summer of 1210. One of his charters there confirmed the settlement of a long-standing dispute between Saer de Quinci and the St Andrews priory regarding the patronage of the church on Saer's land at Leuchars: Bishop Malveisin was the chief witness. In another document issued at Stirling the twelve-year-old Prince Alexander appears for the first time as a witness together with, among others, his half-brother Robert of London and Henry, Earl David's only legitimate son.

The year did not end well for William. He may have got wind of yet more potential trouble in the north which called for his attention, for that is where he proceeded. He is said to have spent Christmas in Moray, but was then laid low by illness at Kintore for the rest of the winter. In England meanwhile, if the Melrose chronicler is to be believed, King John returned from subduing the Irish rebellion to vent his spleen on the Cistercian monks, whom he plundered in various places, and especially the Jews. These he pillaged and drove from their homes, putting out the eyes of some and starving others to death, so that the survivors, despite their religion, had to go begging from door to door, asking for food in the name of Jesus Christ. Whatever the truth, the account surely reflects the reputation for savagery left by the Plantagenet among the Scots. He could never be a popular ally in their eyes.

William recovered from his illness to find that sedition was indeed brewing in his northern territories; for now Guthred, son of Donald MacWilliam, was on the loose. Although he had become established in Ireland, it is possible that he was one of those men recently expelled by John. What is certain is that he crossed from there to the Scottish mainland and, at the instigation it is said of the nobles in Ross, embarked on an aggressive campaign against the royal authority. William at once recognised this as a threat more serious than one of those private feuds for which the region was noted. If Guthred and his supporters thought they saw an opportunity to take advantage of the king's weakend state both physical and political, they reckoned without his resolution.

By the summer of 1211, with Guthred and his allies storming about the Highlands, William moved north with his own army. He first built or reconstructed two castles, probably those at Redcastle and Dunskeath on the further shores of the Beauly and Cromarty firths respectively. With his defences thus strengthened, the rebels were engaged. In the campaign which followed there was much savage skirmishing and pillaging; but when an attack was launched against Guthred's own headquarters, the engagement was not decisive; and in September William withdrew, leaving Malcolm earl of Fife as his commander in Moray. Almost immediately Guthred captured one of the new castles in Ross and, sparing the garrison who had capitulated, burnt it to the ground. The king was infuriated by the news; but, owing to the onset of winter, he was unable to take any punitive action. A position of stalemate had been reached.

In view of William's precarious health, it is unlikely that he played an energetic role in the field; but his presence in his northern lands does seem to be confirmed by the charter evidence. Those plausibly assigned to this year would show him in the early months at Forfar and Montrose before moving up to Aberdeen in June. A single document issued in August at Nairn refers to the help afforded by the vassals of Dunfermline Abbey in the recent construction of his castles in Ross and states that this service is not to be taken as a precedent. In October the king appears to have been at Forres, also south of the Moray Firth, before returning to Forfar by way of Fyvie.

The situation in Ross did not bode well for William. A full summer's campaign had not sufficed to quell the rebellion, so who knows what the next year might bring? The time had evidently come to test the solidity of his new working relationship with John; and the opportunity for this soon presented itself. In January a meeting was arranged between the two kings. We are not told on whose initiative it was called; but in view of their domestic difficulties, both parties stood to gain from an amicable arrangement. So John came north with some of his leading prelates and barons, whilst William made his way into England, bringing with him a similarly distinguished company, which even included his wife, Queen Ermengarde. They met first at Durham on 2 February, but soon adjourned as before to Norham to pursue their discussions.

The chroniclers frustratingly spare us the details and are not entirely consistent in their report of the conclusions reached. It was on this occasion that the queen is said to have acted as intermediary, putting her eloquence to effective use. The outcome appears to have been essentially a reaffirmation of the 1209 treaty, but with some additional provisions. Bower, the fifteenth-century continuator of Fordun's *Scotichronicon*, says that each king vowed to support the other in his just quarrels, and that when one died the survivor would give protection and aid to his heir with the aim of securing his succession. The agreement bore the seals of the kings and their magnates and was sworn by William de Harcourt and the constable Alan of Galloway. Prince Alexander, it is said, would add his seal once he was knighted. John further pledged that within six years he would provide the prince with a wife to his satisfaction, who would bring honour to the Scottish kingdom.

There survives a letter purportedly from King William which, though suspect in detail, seems authentic in its fundamentals. According to this, William grants to John the marriage of his son 'without disparagement'; and he further declares that, should anything happen to John, he and Alexander will support his son Henry and maintain him on the throne 'against all mortal men'. It is stated that the king has affixed his seal, as have the bishops William Malveisin of St Andrews, Walter of Glasgow, John bishop-elect of Dunkeld, Patrick earl of Dunbar, Alan of Galloway the constable, Philip de Mowbray and Walter Olifard.

Perhaps Ermengarde had a say in this sudden disposal of her son's marital fate which, it must be admitted, would seem a remarkable concession by William in the absence of any known preliminary consultation with all his lords, spiritual and temporal. Could her presence and participation in the discussions even reflect some nervousness over an ailing husband's total commitment to the affairs of state? Against this it could be argued that William's overriding concern was to ensure a clear path for his son to succeed to his throne when the moment came; and at the same time he was bidding for John's support in maintaining his kingdom intact in the face of the current rebellion. If this was his strategy, it was to prove successful.

William returned to Scotland and did not accompany Alexander when the prince, now in his fourteenth year, was packed off to the English court. At Westminster, on 8th March, he received from John the belt and sword of knighthood as, it is said, did a dozen other young Scottish nobles. One annal that reports the event includes the judicious comment that the prince, although of small stature, was attractive and distinguished in appearance. Some four years later, King John was to refer to him as a little red fox cub. A contemporary once called his father William 'the ruddy'; so it may be that red hair ran in the family and that 'the Lion' himself shared the feature. In an age when physical descriptions were largely conventional, one is reduced to noting such small touches as a guide to a person's appearance. If William was indeed a red-head, the fact is unlikely to have been advertised by well-disposed chroniclers; for that was traditionally the mark of a traitor, as typified by Ganelon and Judas.

When Alexander returned to Scotland, he was very possibly accompanied by a strong troop of knights and soldiers, including mercenaries from Brabant. For it seems that such a force, under the command of an English nobleman who may well have been Earl Saer de Quinci, was despatched by King John at about that time to help William suppress Guthred's rebellion. If this aid had been part of the bargain struck at Norham between the two kings, it would have made sense for the newly dubbed Alexander to have his first taste of chivalric action under the wing of the hardened Plantagenet troops. There was, however, to be no great campaign in which he might have shown his mettle. Instead, Guthred was betrayed by his own men and brought in shackles to Moray. There the governor Earl Malcolm had it in mind to bring him south to present him to William. But the king made it clear that he had no wish to see his enemy alive; so instead Guthred was taken before young Alexander, who was then at the Mearns castle of Kincardine; and there he was beheaded and hanged by the feet.

This must have been in the early summer of 1212. King William was at Stirling for at least part of that season and may have suffered another bout of illness, if one can judge by the fact that the queen appears to have been unusually active in the country at the time. On hearing of the end of the rebellion, he would have rested more easily. King John, though, had reason to feel less secure. He had again turned his thoughts to launching a campaign to recover his lost Continental possessions; and with this in mind he had once more called for a muster of an army. It was probably with an eye to persuading Alan of Galloway to supply a contingent of his fighting men that he went to Carlisle in the latter part of June. From there he proceeded to Durham by way of Hexham; and it has been suggested that King William was in his company. In the absence of any conclusive evidence and in view of William's frailty, this would seem unlikely, although one document does apparently anticipate a meeting of the two monarchs in Durham. Whatever the truth of the matter, John did not linger there and was soon on his way south again, having received word of a new revolt in Wales.

He handled that insurrection with his usual savagery, hanging twenty-eight of the ringleaders' sons whom he held as hostages. By then he had reminded Alan of Galloway by letter of his earlier request for troops. But now the ground was quaking under his feet; and according to the St Albans chronicler Roger of Wendover, he received from both King William and his daughter messengers warning him of impending treason in various parts of his kingdom. In a state of high alarm, John at once suspended his Welsh operations and set about collecting hostages from all his suspect barons. One of these was William's own son-in-law, Eustace de Vesci, who decided it would be best to leave his castle at Alnwick and take refuge at the Scottish court. All this put William's brother David in a difficult position; but although he too incurred John's suspicion, he weathered the storm of the royal wrath and is found still acting in the king's service not long afterwards. If the report of William's warning is correct, this must have earned him some credit with the Plantagenet, although at the cost of embarrassing his brother in the process. September saw John back in Durham, flexing his muscles in an attempt to intimidate his northern barons. But by the end of 1212 he must have supposed the danger past, for he then resumed his plans for an expedition to the Continent in the spring.

William probably occupied himself with domestic affairs, so far as he was able in this his seventieth year, while the younger Queen Ermengarde took her share of the royal duties as required. We find her, for instance, presiding with Bishop Malveisin over a court summoned to settle a dispute between Philip de Mowbray with his wife Galiena and Dunfermline Abbey. The case concerned the patronage of the church at Inverkeithing (Fife) and was held at Edinburgh on 31st May. Some time later, according to Bower, Malveisin received the king's permission to travel to France to visit his relatives there. He certainly does not reappear in Scottish records before the spring of 1213, when, with the bishop of Glasgow, he was empowered by the pope to whip up enthusiasm for the crusade. To this end he convoked a council of prelates and laymen in Perth; but although many were persuaded to take the cross, they included few of the kingdom's wealthy or powerful men.

1213 was another relatively inactive year for King William. Of the ten royal charters ascribed to it, the range is broad and not without interest. The first, issued in January at Traquair, confirms to his baker a parcel of land as well as the free use of his mill in Edinburgh. By contrast, the last, dated in December, is a confirmation made at Edinburgh of a settlement agreed between rival claimants to the earldom of Menteith. Apart from one concerning an annual payment due to him by Coldingham Priory, all the others are grants or confirmations made to religious houses. Pride of place goes to his own abbey at Arbroath (acts issued at Traquair, Selkirk and Haddington); but also favoured are North Berwick Priory, Holyrood Abbey, and the priory, later abbey, at Paisley (all made at Edinburgh). One senses that William, while still acting as the 'father' of his subjects high and low, is now preoccupied more with spiritual than with temporal concerns.

It has been suggested that King John, anxious to secure his position in the north and also hoping for military aid from William for his coming expedition, wished to have a meeting with him early in 1213. Moreover, he asked that Alexander should attend. The old king, however, feared that his son might be held hostage pending his expulsion of the refugee Eustace de Vesci; and in any case he had no stomach for the journey to England, so nothing came of any approach. All this seems very plausible, for John's habit of using hostages as pawns in his power game is notorious. He still held the ones surrendered to him by the Treaty of Norham; and these he ordered to be brought to him at Portsmouth where he was intending to embark in June. William had every reason to be wary of the Plantagenet.

In May 1213 King John, a prey to recurring fears of rebellion within his kingdom and by now even a Capetian invasion from without, thought it prudent to make his peace with the pope. But his projected expedition to Poitou only served to increase his barons' unrest; and again it was put off. When it did finally take place the following summer, it proved disastrous. Earl David, whose own stance remains ambiguous, stayed in touch with the English court, and no doubt kept his brother abreast of developments. William's only known contacts with John were in the form of minor requests, which the Plantagenet was pleased to humour. On one occasion he granted the release of a Scottish noble who had been captured in Ireland. On New Year's Day 1214 he gave permission for the sale to a servant of William's of fifty or sixty lampreys for the king's personal use. In July he met his request to restore to a burgess of Berwick goods to the value of £29 that had been seized from his ship at Bamburgh. He further ordered that ships from the lands of the German emperor and the king of Scotland should be allowed to proceed from English ports direct to their home countries, provided they carried no passengers but their goods alone.

King William's domestic activities were no more than routine, and must have been limited by the state of his health. At the end of April 1214 he was probably at Selkirk confirming the archdeacon of Moray in the possession of property in Sutherland, which was now back in the king's peace. A couple of weeks later at Jedburgh he confirmed a grant of land to a leper hospital in Berwickshire. Then in the summer he was strong enough to make the journey north to Moray for a brief stay, during which he concluded a pact with Earl John of Caithness, receiving his daughter as hostage. Since the death of Earl Harald the province had been divided between his sons David and John; and David having just died, John now had sole title to the earldom. Caithness had also recently acquired a new bishop, consecrated in May by Bishop Malveisin. While in the north William took the opportunity, at Elgin, of confirming the tenure of certain property and rights in the Mearns to Arbroath Abbey.

The long journey proved too much for the seriously ailing king. From Moray he was brought south by short stages to Stirling. There he issued what appear to be the last two of his known charters; and like those earlier ones we noticed, they stand in telling and almost touching contrast. In September he granted to a certain William the helmet-maker residing in Perth a plot of land between those of a die-cutter and a tinker, subject to an annual payment of two iron helmets. On 25th November he confirmed to the earl of Strathearn a considerably more extensive property for the service of one knight.

He would never himself have the benefit of that knight's service. For nine days later, on 4th December, he died, says the Melrose chronicler, a happy death, 'leaving his kingdom in a state of profound peace'. At his side in his castle at Stirling were, we can assume, Queen Ermengarde, his son Alexander and also Earl David his brother. This was the event he himself had anticipated when, in 1201 at Musselburgh, he presented Prince Alexander to his magnates as his rightful heir; and now, as he lay on his deathbed, he again had him recognised as such by his bishops and barons alike.

No time was lost. While King William's body still lay in Stirling Castle, the sixteen-year-old prince was escorted by six earls to Scone; and there, on 6th December, with Bishop Malveisin of St Andrews officiating, he was invested as King Alexander II. Leaving Scone after the required celebrations, the new king met the cortège of the old at Perth to proceed down the Tay to Arbroath. In his abbey there, before the high altar, William the Lion was laid to rest with great solemnity on 10th December. He had been Scotland's king for almost half a century.

It was fitting that, at his death, he had the chief members of his family with him; for unlike the rival Plantagenets, he had shown himself throughout his life to be a loyal 'family man'. He had revered his forebears and cherished his inherited rights; with his brother David he had maintained good relations when they could so easily have become strained; and he had jealously protected Alexander his son, insisting that he should be his successor in an age when the law of primogeniture had still to be firmly established. Brought up to respect the ideals of chivalry, he observed them to the best of his ability throughout his life. His loyalty extended beyond his family to all his subjects, rich and poor, native Scots and incomers alike. He was a 'lion of justice' according to Fordun, who is not alone in according him this virtue, just as there is general approval of his piety. Unlike King John of England, he can fairly be described as 'a good man'.

Among his achievements, the consolidation of Scotland as a cultured and peaceful kingdom within the European family must take pride of place. No doubt there were some who resented what they saw as his undue patronage of families of French extraction. It was in the context of Guthred's uprising that a contemporary chronicler observed that 'the recent kings of the Scots count themselves more as Frenchmen in race, manners, language and culture; and, having reduced the Scots to utter servitude, they admit only Frenchmen to their household and service'. This is perhaps a little unfair to William, since, although he was himself of almost pure French stock, we have no evidence of unfair discrimination on his part against any of his subjects because of their ethnic origins.

His judgment in matters of state is certainly not entirely above criticism, although to his credit he always seems to have been open to advice from his lords and counsellors. In this too he was following feudal principle if not universal practice. It was, we must remember, in pursuit of what he saw as his rights that he showed a stubborn streak, notably in his obsession with the recovery of the northern English provinces. If towards the end of his life he seems to have accepted that he would never himself realise this ambition, he had bequeathed it to his son as an aim to be pursued after his death.

Alexander inherited his father's disappointments with his throne. Resentful of the terms imposed by King John at Norham, he sided with the rebellious barons who forced John to accept the Magna Carta in 1215. Reviving the claim to the English counties, he was only to abandon it formally in 1237, when he concluded the Treaty of York with Henry III. Alexander, like his father, reigned for many years before, in an attempt to subdue the Isles, he succumbed to a fever and died on Kerrera, off Oban, in 1249. Earl David, who, according to Fordun, was 'neither alert in mind nor active in body' when he attended his brother's funeral at Arbroath, died in Northamptonshire in 1219. Though he had wished to be buried in Lindores Abbey, his foundation in Fife, his remains were in fact interred in his earldom at the Huntingdonshire abbey of Sawtry. Queen Ermengarde lived on until 1234, having latterly devoted herself to pious works including the establishment of an abbey at Balmerino in Fife; and that is where she herself was committed to the tomb. With the deaths of its leading characters, one of the richest chapters in Scotland's history had closed.

SIX

Legend: *Fergus of Galloway*

Now that we have tried to place William the Lion in his historical context and pieced together a record of his public life, it is time to see if a way can be found to get behind the façade of documented facts and catch something of the atmosphere of the society in which he moved. Having followed the professional historians through the main entrance to his world, we may find it revealing, and certainly adventurous, to try a little-used back door that will lead us to places hitherto unexplored. Turning away from the chronicles and charters, we shall enlist as our guide a man who frequented William's world perhaps as a leading participant in its affairs, but certainly as a keen observer bent on entertaining his courtiers.

This man, a poet as polished as his wit was sharp, has bequeathed to us what may claim, and with some justification, to be the earliest surviving work of Scottish vernacular literature.* By that I mean written not in Latin like the couple of remarkable texts we noticed earlier (both, as it happens, produced in Glasgow) but in one of the languages still widely spoken in Scotland outside the cloister. This was not northern English, the ancestor of modern Scots and in King William's day the common speech of many of the townsfolk, merchants and landowners too, especially south of the Forth but also as far as and to the east of the Highlands. Whatever literature in Scottish English may have existed at that time has been lost virtually without trace. Nor is our poem in Gaelic, which was certainly the vehicle for a great deal of story-telling throughout much of Scotland, although how much of it was ever committed to parchment within the kingdom is a matter of debate. It was in fact composed in French.

As we have seen, French was the everyday speech of a significant

---

* This claim has been staked for the Welsh poem *Y Gododdin*, which may have been composed about 600 A.D. It is a lament for a British war-band from the Edinburgh region, which was annihilated by the Northumbrian Angles at Catterick in Yorkshire. Its language, however, was no longer spoken in Scotland by William the Lion's day.

part of the population in William the Lion's Scotland, resented though the situation may have been by some among the older ethnic stock. It was the first language of the ruling aristocracy; and they were the main patrons of secular literature. But apart from them and their households, there was a leavening of less exalted French-speaking settlers, many of them from Picardy and Flanders. The latter were especially favoured by David I and Malcolm IV and included, as well as knights and landowners, many respected burgesses and tradesmen. They too, like their relatives on the Continent, may have had some taste for literature: not only was Philip, count of Flanders, one of the patrons of Chrétien de Troyes, but his town of Arras (ceded to the French king in 1191) was a thriving literary centre. It is interesting to find Philip himself exempting at about this time the monks of Melrose from toll on their goods, presumably exports of raw wool for his Flemish weavers. Perhaps they brought back from Flanders, along with other merchandise, a manuscript or two for the amusement of their more worldly brethren. For it would be wrong to suppose that the Scottish clergy, of whom many were French-speaking, spent all of their time with their noses in pious Latin texts. We noticed earlier that the Augustinians in particular had broader literary interests.

As an example of the ethnic and hence linguistic and cultural mix found in some of the Scottish towns, we may take the case of St Andrews. The burgh was founded by Bishop Robert with the authority of David I; and its first provost was a Fleming, Mainard, who had been brought from Berwick. Towards the end of the century we find charters specifying the dues to be paid to the local French canons by the burgesses, 'Scots, French, English and Flemings alike'. And it was, we remember, in cosmopolitan St Andrews that we encountered those two clerks 'Master Arthur' and 'Master Merlin' witnessing a charter a few years before William came to the throne. So we should not be too reluctant to accept the possibility that a man who spent many years there was inspired to compose a substantial poem in French – or that it was a romance in which both King Arthur and, albeit briefly, Merlin figure.

The poet names himself as Guillaume le Clerc (William the Clerk), but tells us nothing more about himself or any patron he may have had. His work is *The Romance of Fergus*,* a splendid tale which has been pitifully

---

* Guillaume le Clerc, *Fergus of Galloway*, tr. D.D.R. Owen, contains details of editions and sources. See also my study 'The *Fergus*-Poet', in *Medieval Codicology, Iconography, Literature and Translation*, pp. 233–9.

neglected in the past, partly no doubt because it has come down to us only in two thirteenth-century copies with a Picard colouring to the French and in a later Dutch version. Even when noticed and discussed by a handful of scholars, it has been generally underrated. For I believe it to be not only a milestone in the history of Scottish culture, but also a work of real significance in the development of European literature, marking as it does a reaction against the fashionable romance of the courts and, by cocking a snook at its latest and most enduring theme, distantly foreshadowing Cervantes and even twentieth-century film comedy.

Another disadvantage it suffers is that the poet has never been identified: such a common name as Guillaume was shared by numerous French clerks, even in Scotland. Although some scholars have supposed that he was working for a Scottish patron, others, myself included, have argued that he could equally well have been writing on the Continent and have come by his local knowledge at second-hand, or in the course of some brief personal visit. If that were so, although he tells a rattling good story placed in a Scottish setting, he could no more be thought of as a Scotsman than Sir Walter Scott, author of *The Talisman*, as a crusader based in Palestine.

There has been, too, a natural reluctance to give a French poem house-room within the Scottish cultural tradition, even if it was produced by a resident in the country. Despite the undoubted strength of the language in Scotland under William the Lion, it soon became more restricted and was little spoken by the end of the thirteenth century. So if anything that might be called a 'Franco-Scottish' culture ever existed, it could only have been an ephemeral precursor of the 'auld alliance'. In any case, where is the evidence? Most of it, sadly, has fallen prey to the ravages of time.

In the field of music one could cite the *St Andrews Music Book* which, like the *Fergus* texts, has found refuge in a foreign land, being now preserved at Wolfenbüttel in Germany. It is recognised as the most important source of our knowledge of early part-music and was compiled, it seems, at St Andrews some time after 1230, probably at the instigation of either our acquaintance Bishop Malveisin or his successor Bishop David de Bernham, who had earlier been briefly in charge of the choir at Glasgow. Most of its music derives from the school of Notre-Dame in Paris; but other pieces were composed specifically for St Andrews and do not suffer by comparison with the rest. Here at least is firm evidence of a thriving Franco-Scottish cultural partnership not long after King William's death.*

To return to the literature available during his reign, we have found a few small indications that there was a fund of legendary material circulating among his subjects; and this would in all probability have included Arthurian romance. We can add some intriguing evidence from an early German romance, *Lanzelet,* by the Swiss priest Ulrich von Zatzikhoven.† It is an ill-organised medley of adventures drawn from a number of sources including four of Chrétien's romances. The honest Ulrich admits that he found his material in a French book brought to the Continent by Hugh de Moreville when he stood as hostage for the release from captivity of King Richard in 1194. The Morevilles were a powerful Anglo-Norman family who held extensive lands in both England and Scotland, the English ones principally in the earldom of Huntingdon; and for these they were to owe homage to David, King William's brother, to whom they were eventually connected by marriage.

The first Hugh de Moreville whom we know was the constable of King David I, who endowed him with lands in Lauderdale and the Tweed valley; and in the early 1150s he founded the abbey at Dryburgh, where he died in 1162. His son, another Hugh, was one of the murderers of Thomas Becket. Forester of Cumberland, he had his seat near Carlisle, but also possessed until 1174 an estate in Galloway, ruled by Fergus up to his death in 1161. Although he has been proposed as the owner of the 'French book', this seems unlikely (he may have died while on pilgrimage to Jerusalem in the early 1170s). The elder Hugh was succeeded as royal constable by another son Richard, who served under both Malcolm and William and was one of the hostages provided by the latter at the time of the Treaty of Falaise. He was also, as we noticed earlier, involved in a dispute in 1180 with the monks of Melrose. His successor, in 1189 or 1190, as both lord of Lauder and constable was his son William de Moreville, who married the sister of Roland of Galloway; but in 1196 he died childless, and his fief passed to Roland. It is unfortunate that we cannot be sure which of this numerous family was the purveyor of Arthurian romance: another Hugh de Moreville

* On the *St Andrews Music Book,* see John Purser, *Scotland's Music,* Ch. IV.
† Ulrich von Zatzikhoven, *Lanzelet,* tr. Kenneth G.T. Webster. For the Morevilles (Morvilles), see Barrow, *The Anglo-Norman Era …*

was an archdeacon who became bishop of Coutances in 1207; and he
too has been offered as a candidate. So our only certainty is that the
Arthurian material on which Ulrich's source was based was circulating
in the family and hence probably in Scotland by the early 1190s. And
that material included the work of Chrétien de Troyes to which the
Romance of Fergus is a riposte.)

In the light of such evidence as we can draw together, tenuous
though it is, I think it reasonable to suggest that William the Lion
did indeed preside over the emergence of a distinct Franco-Scottish
culture which for a brief period made its own individual contribution to
that of Europe as a whole. I shall now propose that the most significant
surviving relic of that culture is in fact Guillaume le Clerc's neglected
romance. If this claim is to be substantiated, it must first be shown
that Guillaume had a knowledge of Scotland such as could only be
possessed by a resident in the country. I now believe the evidence for
this to be conclusive. Moreover, he will prove to be well acquainted
with contemporary courtly society. We may even be able to hazard
an identification of this Guillaume, or William; and it will come as
no surprise that, in our present state of knowledge, I put forward as
the most likely candidate for authorship our friend William Malveisin,
Bishop of St Andrews. Whether or not this is so, we shall find that,
in common with other romance writers of his age, this man was apt
to smuggle into his fictions oblique allusions to contemporary events
and figures. In other words, his poem contains some elements of the
roman à clef. To this end, and above all by deploying a subtle sense of
humour, he has contrived to make some personal comments on current
fashions and ideals. As a result, he has given us a precious glimpse into
the domestic preoccupations and general climate of the courtly society
of Scotland under King William. None of this, of course, can be taken
on trust; so his work must be examined in detail. First, though, let me
outline the story.

From near Carlisle King Arthur embarks with his knights on a
wide-ranging hunt for a white stag, which is finally caught in Galloway
by the grail-hero Perceval. As it returns, the hunting-party is spotted
by the naive Fergus as he ploughs the land of his father Soumillet.
That wealthy but low-born peasant has a handsome fortress by the sea,
built entirely of earth. On learning what this impressive cavalcade is,
Fergus is fired by the desire to become one of King Arthur's counsellors.
Reluctantly, Soumillet furnishes him with rusty armour; and he makes

for Carlisle, where he arrives bringing the heads of two robbers he had killed on the way.

Riding directly into the royal hall, he is received courteously by Arthur, but mocked by Kay the seneschal, who says he is just the man to go to the Nouquetran on the Black Mountain and there take the horn and the wimple from the neck of the gentle lion before bringing to heel the king's mortal enemy the Black Knight. Though Arthur tries to dissuade him, this Fergus determines to do; and he leaves the court to seek lodgings in the town. Soaked by the light rain that is falling, he is given shelter by the daughter of the royal chamberlain who, when he returns home, grants him hospitality, instructs him in knighthood and prepares him for his formal initiation in the morning. Fergus duly presents himself at court, to be armed and dubbed by Arthur with the warm approval of his nephew Gawain and Perceval, who presents him with his own sword.

The new knight rides forth to fulfil his vow and towards evening arrives at Liddel Castle. There he is graciously received by the castellan and his beautiful niece Galiene. Although the girl timidly visits his bed that night with a passionate declaration of love, she obtains from Fergus no more than a promise to return that way after he has dealt with the Black Knight. The rejected Galiene first contemplates suicide, but then decides to leave secretly in the morning for Lothian, where her father is king and is planning a royal marriage for her.

Early next day Fergus makes his way to the Black Mountain where, after an embarrassing encounter with a bronze statue, he retrieves the horn and wimple from the neck of a marble lion and vanquishes the Black Knight, whom he sends to give himself up to Arthur. Returning to Liddel, he finds the castellan distraught at the disappearance of his niece. Belatedly, he himself feels the pangs of love, whereupon, despite the castellan's disapproval and a moment of self-doubt, he sets off in quest of the missing Galiene.

He is not long detained by an affray with a hideous dwarf and a duel with his master, a lord who is bivouacking in the forest with his mistress; and, having defeated the knight, he sends all three packing to Arthur's court. A notorious robber who waylays him suffers the same fate. Then, on being denied a share of a barbecue being enjoyed by fifteen marauding knights, he helps himself to their food and slays thirteen, despatching the survivors to place themselves at the king's mercy along with the rest. Arthur meanwhile has been fearing the worst for the gallant young knight; but the arrival in succession of all those Fergus has conquered reassures him, yet does not diminish his grief at the hero's absence.

For more than a year the sorrowing Fergus roams the countryside, unkempt and half-starved, until he chances upon a marvellous spring, a draught of whose water restores him to physical and mental health. A nearby chapel is guarded by a dwarf with second sight; and he puts Fergus in good heart by assuring him that, should he manage to obtain a shining shield kept by a hairy hag in Dunnottar Tower, he may eventually win back his beloved. The dwarf will tell him no more.

His hope renewed, Fergus rides on, vainly seeking directions to Dunnottar. He passes through Lothian and lodges one night in Maiden Castle (Edinburgh); but even there he finds no one to give him guidance. Next morning he comes to Queensferry, where he embarks with some rascally boatmen to make the crossing into Scotland proper. A dispute over the toll ends with all ten ferrymen out of action and Fergus steering their craft to a landfall below the castle of Dunfermline. From there he goes where Fortune leads for over two months without discovering the way to his goal.

Then one day he sees in the distance a great radiance that he realises must come from the sought-after shield. Before long he arrives at the sea-girt tower, its bridge guarded, as predicted, by a shaggy old woman armed with a monstrous scythe. Fergus cleaves her with his sword and crosses the bridge to the gate. Passing through a hall beyond, he comes to a courtyard, where the brilliant shield hangs on a pillar protected by a somnolent dragon, which he accidentally wakes. Undeterred, he seizes the trophy, makes an end of the dragon, and jubilantly leaves Dunnottar.

Coming to the coast, he finds there a leather merchant with his ten boats waiting for a favourable wind; and the man is happy to transport him back to Queensferry. From there he continues his journey until he comes across three shepherds. They inform him that he is in Lothian, now ruled by a lady named Galiene, her father (as we learn later) having died. But she is being besieged in Roxburgh and her lands devastated by a powerful king, to whom she will soon have to capitulate. Fergus immediately sets out to her rescue.

Unfortunately, in a moment of inattention he takes the wrong road, only to find himself confronting the Dunnottar hag's giant husband in his fortress on Melrose Mountain. The monstrous fellow recognises his wife's shield; and a vicious combat ensues, from which Fergus emerges victorious though not unscathed. In the castle hall he finds the giant's son being massaged by two captive maidens; but of him too he makes short work. Although his horse had been killed in the fight, he discovers in a cellar a handsome replacement, which he has to break in before putting himself in the care of the grateful ladies. For three days they tend to his wounds. Then, from a high window, he catches sight of distant Roxburgh and its besieging army. At once he calls for his arms and sets out to aid his beloved.

Hurling himself against the men who are just beginning the assault on the castle, he wreaks great havoc among them, his victims including the king's seneschal and also his nephew, whom he unhorses. He has the steed taken anonymously to Galiene who, with her men, has been much encouraged on observing the prowess of the knight with the shining shield. The fighting breaks up, and Fergus makes his way back to his hostesses in the castle at Melrose; but every day for a week he repeats his performance, to the great discomfiture of the besiegers.

The hostile king decides to send his nephew Arthofilaus to demand Galiene's surrender or, failing that, to propose that his claim to Lothian be decided by single combat. Arthofilaus' message is received with scorn by the spirited Galiene, who declares that, given a week's respite, she will find a knight who will duel with any two of his own. Although she quickly repents her rashness, and none of her men are prepared to undertake the combat, one of her attendants named Arondele volunteers to go in search of the mysterious knight who has fought with such valour; and should she not find him, she will ask King Arthur for the service of one of the company of his Round Table. Galiene gives her permission.

Arriving in Carlisle, Arondele finds Arthur unable to help, since all of his knights are in distant parts seeking a gallant young man called Fergus, whom he had once knighted. The dejected maiden heads back for Roxburgh; and her road takes her through Melrose. There she is seen and offered hospitality by Fergus. She declines, but tells him her full story. Fergus sends her on her way with words of comfort but without disclosing his identity. Her news, when she arrives in Roxburgh, plunges Galiene into a suicidal mood, for the combat must take place on the following day.

In the morning, after Mass, she again appeals in vain to her company to provide a champion. Then, when the king and his nephew arrive and call for a man to fight them both, she climbs to her highest tower and prepares to leap to her death. But a mysterious voice bids her look to the woods; and there she sees the radiance from Fergus' shield. Before long the hero has triumphed in the duel, slain Arthofilaus and made the king renounce his claim to Lothian and then present himself to Arthur. From him Galiene learns that the victor was the knight who had once caused her such offence. The siege is over; but Fergus has once more disappeared from the scene.

The defeated king tells his tale in Carlisle and adds, like those sent there earlier, Fergus' warning that he has not forgotten Kay's mockery of him. The king is pardoned, as the others had been, by Arthur, who then declares that with Gawain's approval he will himself set out to search for Fergus. But Gawain has a better idea: let him arrange a tournament at Jedburgh, with the winner receiving a bride to his taste and the crown of some kingdom. Fergus will be certain to turn up when he hears of it. Arthur agrees with his nephew and proclaims the tournament far and wide. The news reaches Galiene; and she, with her lords' consent, decides to go to court and beg Arthur to give her in marriage to the knight with the shining shield.

The participants duly assemble in two camps, the knights of the Round Table beside Jedburgh and the cream of English chivalry, who wish to test their valour against them, in the nearby forest. The tournament opens with Kay demanding the first joust. Out of the forest charges Fergus, to upend the seneschal without ceremony in a swamp. He then unhorses Lancelot and for the rest of that day carries all before him until he withdraws from the scene in the evening. The next day Sagremor bites the dust; but the incognito Fergus merely halts Perceval in his tracks, out of deference for the man who had honoured him in the past. The Black Knight, however, he topples along with many another. For the whole week he remains invincible.

Then Galiene arrives at court and puts her plea to Arthur, who agrees to bestow on her the man with the bright shield, if only he can be brought to parley. To this end Gawain offers to be the first to encounter Fergus in the morning. Then, instead of the customary challenge, he requests that Fergus come to speak with Arthur. Mutual recognition follows; and together they go before the king. Galiene joins them and is bestowed by Arthur on Fergus amid general rejoicing. As well as the kingdom of Lothian, the hero will receive the district of Tweeddale. The next day, which is a Sunday and the feast of Saint John, the marriage takes place in Roxburgh and the couple are crowned.

After the celebrations, which last for three weeks, King Arthur and his company leave, with Gawain being assured by Fergus that he will not abandon knightly deeds for the sake of his wife. Nevertheless, the new king and his queen are united in their love.

Guillaume le Clerc has found nobody who can tell him anything more about the knight with the shining shield; so here he ends his romance. 'May great joy come to those who hear it!'

The first question we must ask is whether the evidence Guillaume provides in the course of his romance is sufficient to establish that he had a first-hand knowledge of the scene of its action. From my summary it will be seen that the route taken by Fergus on his quest is at least plausible: leaving Carlisle, he proceeds by way of Liddel Castle, Lothian, Edinburgh, Queensferry, Dunfermline, Dunnottar, Queensferry again, Melrose, Roxburgh and Jedburgh, then back to Roxburgh for his wedding and coronation. This reads like the route of a modern coach tour.

However, the work opens with an extended description of a hunt which describes a circuit so wide that we are put in mind of the fantastic geography more typical of the genre. King Arthur is first seen at his court in Cardigan, where he decides on an impulse to hunt a white stag in the Forest of Gorriende by Carlisle. Off he dashes with his company, and they pursue the beast there until mid-afternoon. The stag then heads for the Forest of Jedburgh before leading the chase through the district of Lammermuir, on to the Forest of Glasgow, then by way of Ayr into Galloway, where it is finally taken as evening falls. The hunt's sweeping itinerary is credible enough; and, although Gorriende has not been positively identified, the other two named forests did exist, that of Jedburgh belonging to the crown and that of Glasgow to the church. The time-scale, however (apparently a single day), is completely absurd, even though we are told that it all took place at midsummer.

This is an inauspicious start to my investigation, which relies on the belief that Guillaume le Clerc was essentially a realist. If that is so, what is his excuse for this initial flight of fancy, which takes us to the point where he first introduces us to his hero? Must we think of it simply as a case of naive inconsistency? To do so would be unfair to a man who elsewhere shows himself to be an extremely shrewd master of his material. Rather, I think, he was deliberately establishing from the outset his authorial attitude and giving us fair warning of his humorous intentions.

He begins by listing Arthur's companions at Cardigan: Gawain, Yvain, Lancelot, Perceval, Erec, Sagremor and Kay, as well as many others whose names he has not learned. All of these are prominent in or the heroes of Chrétien de Troyes's romances. Moreover, the opening court scene is a pastiche of that in Chrétien's *Yvain*, whilst the theme of the hunt for the white stag is a feature of his *Erec*. So Guillaume is at pains to draw attention immediately to the fact that he is using Chrétien's legendary world as a point of reference; and he proceeds to conjure up the vague and exotic topography typical of romance. At the same time he uses humorous touches to discourage our involvement in that world. There is the casual admission that many of the names escape him; and he pointedly excludes from the after-dinner conversation the ladies who were so prominent in *Yvain*. Arthur's queen makes her sole appearance as one of the hunting-party, but then almost as a figure of fun: she is wearing a fur mantle that reaches to the ground 'for the summer heat'! The stag, in full flight, plunges into a deep torrent, but needlessly, since its pursuers follow across a broad bridge. When Perceval finally wins the prize for its capture, the real merit belongs to his hound, who pulls it down into a swamp and drowns it, to the surprise of Perceval, who was far in the rear.

Perceval, then, who had been introduced as the knight 'who strove so arduously for the Grail', is the mock-hero of this preliminary adventure. It will emerge that Guillaume is preparing us for his supplanting by Fergus as the finest of all knights, with the sole exception of Gawain, the traditional 'flower of chivalry'. Fergus' succession will later be confirmed symbolically when, at his knighting, Arthur girds on him the sword presented to him by Perceval. Eventually we shall find Fergus in quest not of the Grail but of that other talisman, the shining shield. He is thus conceived by Guillaume as a 'neo-Perceval', but blessed by greater success than his predecessor. For whereas he won in the end both talisman and lady, by the point where Chrétien had broken off the story of Perceval, his hero had acquired neither the Grail nor the fair Blancheflor, whom he had abandoned as Fergus had left Galiene, with a vague promise to return.

Guillaume, then, has used his opening episode less as an integral part of his story than as a forewarning that what he is offering is not another Arthurian romance in the style of Chrétien, but something new: a travesty or burlesque of the genre. So it is no accident that he first subverts our expectations of a tale of romantic make-believe; and only when Fergus and his father appear on the scene does he begin to introduce elements of topical realism into the story. For now he turns to deal with characters who have historical prototypes, as his public would have known. These are the real Fergus of Galloway, who died in Holyrood in 1161, and Somerled (Soumillet in the romance), who met his end at Glasgow in 1164. From this point Guillaume abandons the legendary world of authentic romance for the one familiar to the subjects of William the Lion. However, by continuing to introduce fantastic elements, largely borrowed, into his story, he continues to maintain the illusion of romance. Yet he has given us the signal that there is, in modern jargon, a subtext to his work; and it is this that is of interest to us.

King Arthur's hunting party had entered Galloway from Ayr, 'the home of fair women', as Guillaume remarks. This comment would seem quite gratuitous at this pre-Burns period unless it was provoked by some tradition of the poet's own day. In that case it might have been of fairly recent origin, since the burgh of Ayr was only founded in about 1200, King William having just reinforced his authority in the area by building a new castle there. After the killing of the stag, the royal party bivouacs for the night, then takes the road back to Carlisle; and it is as they are leaving Galloway that they pass by Soumillet's castle, which prompts a long admiring glance from Arthur.

It was sited on a hill rising from a valley not far from the Irish Sea (that is, the Solway Firth) and was surrounded by walls of clay and wattle. The tower was not of stone, but had high earthen ramparts. I am not the first to suggest that the model for this is likely to have been one of the motte-and-bailey strongholds with which the nobility dotted the landscape before stone came into more general use in the thirteenth century. If Guillaume had been in these parts, he could well have had in mind the impressive Mote of Urr, set in a river valley between Castle Douglas and Dumfries. It had been the property in the latter part of the twelfth century of King William's chamberlain, Walter de Berkeley, and may even have received a royal visit when William was founding his castle-burgh of Dumfries in the mid-1180s. Had Guillaume been a clerk in the king's household at the time (as a certain William Malveisin appears to have been), one can imagine him seeing and admiring the chamberlain's residence.

The scene depicting Fergus at Carlisle has various touches of realism, not least the steady drizzle that seeps through his rusty armour as he wanders the streets in search of a lodging. The chamberlain's house is plainly a desirable residence by the standards of the day: it has not only two storeys, but a good stable and, for the guest, a separate bedroom decorated with a splendid painting of sun, moon and stars. The house is well furnished and staffed by an efficient group of domestics. We are given fewer details of the royal castle, but our overall impression of Carlisle is of a place worthy to have been the favourite residence of David I. Personal observation by the poet is certainly possible.

A day's ride takes Fergus from Carlisle to Liddel, a distance of just over twenty miles as the crow flies. The description of the riverside castle there is conventional enough. More interesting for us is the mysterious Black Mountain. It rears to the sky beyond a wide plain between two hills and hillocks separated by deep valleys. There is forest and heath in the vicinity (we can ignore a conventional olive tree!); and from its summit one can view the Irish Sea, England and Cornwall (the latter another example of poetic licence). Fergus' expedition there and back to Liddel seems to have been accomplished in a full day. If Guillaume had visited Liddel Castle, which was the seat of King William's one-time butler Ranulf de Soules until his death in 1207, he could have had one of the nearby mountains in mind. If so, it may be no coincidence that the map shows five or six hills containing the element 'black' (or Gaelic *dhu*) within half a dozen miles of Liddel. Moreover, another nearby peak used to serve as a landmark for ships at sea, whilst the English border is not far away. The whole district too is still rich in legends and prehistoric sites.

When he left Liddel for the second time, the love-sick Fergus rode aimlessly on, twice having to teach a lesson to petty brigands he met on the way. He is still plainly roving through the Border country; and this was a district notorious for its lawlessness in the Middle Ages. His fortunes change when he arrives at the marvellous, invigorating spring. That might seem pure fantasy except for one quite gratuitous detail given by Guillaume, namely that it discharged its waters to the east. Taken literally, this must mean that Fergus has crossed the watershed and reached the source of a river flowing to the North Sea. One thinks of the Tweed or its tributary the Teviot, which joins it at Roxburgh. And although it would be rash to give a precise identification to the splendid spring that restored our hero, he did proceed from it through the whole of Lothian until he arrived at Edinburgh. It may also be worth noting that King William had a hunting lodge at St Mary's Loch, a mere dozen miles from the Tweed's source. At the least we can say that Guillaume had a good grasp of the topography of this desolate region.

Fergus is now back in the heartland of the kingdom. Having taken lodging in the stronghold of Edinburgh, he rides west to Queensferry in order to cross from Lothian into 'Scotia' proper, that is the region north of the Forth. The revenue from the ferry established by Queen Margaret for the use of pilgrims to the shrine of Saint Andrew had been granted to Dunfermline Abbey, but with the proviso that no toll was to be exacted from pilgrims, messengers on the king's service, or members of his household. In the case of disputes, his judgment was to be final. The men of St Andrews Cathedral Priory were similarly exempt from the crossing fee. The boatmen who operated the ferry were also jealous of their rights, and are known to have later operated their business on a 'closed shop' basis. The trouble that arose when Fergus made the crossing stemmed not from his refusal to pay the toll, but from the fact that he had no ready cash and offered a silk tunic in lieu. The ferrymen objected that they were not in the bartering trade; and this Fergus took as a provocation.

The affray ended with the sailors disabled and the knight taking the tiller to guide the boat to land below the castle at Dunfermline, to which (unless the text is corrupt) Guillaume attaches the adjective *sarrasin*. The meaning here is unlikely to be 'Saracen': elsewhere it is found applied to Roman ruins in the sense rather of 'outlandish'. It is known that in the course of William's reign the royal burgh at Dunfermline fell into decay at the expense of a newer development by the abbey. So Guillaume may here be making an oblique reference to the dilapidated state of the royal castle, or even a sly joke at its expense.

The story requires that Fergus' next destination should be a remote and mysterious stronghold substituted by Guillaume for Chrétien's Grail Castle. His choice has fallen on Dunnottar; and although it is located in what, even in his day, was a populous and well-travelled district, his omission of any details of Fergus' wanderings north of the Forth seems designed to convey a sense of its isolation. Dunnottar lay, in fact, at the northern extremity of the diocese of St Andrews, on the coast between the royal residences at Arbroath and Montrose and the important centre of Aberdeen. The poet could have chosen no more dramatic scene for Fergus' conquest of the shining shield. The great rock had been the site of an ancient fort as well as an early ecclesiastical settlement; but the present ruins date from a much later period, and no trace remains of the motte-and-bailey castle which probably stood here in Guillaume's day.

The accuracy of his description suggests that it was based on personal observation. The dwarf had told Fergus of its impregnable situation, perched on a rock with the sea beating round it. Now the hero approaches by a causeway and, once he has circumvented the hag on the bridge, he climbs up to the gate, an ascent which still taxes the visitor. Beyond lie the hall and a courtyard, which may well once have existed. Because of the narrow entrance, Fergus had been obliged to leave his horse in front of the bridge; and that is where he remounted, to ride away flourishing his shining trophy.

Emerging from a forest, he came to the sea, where he found the merchant waiting with his ships. No sooner had he been welcomed aboard than a brisk northerly wind arose and sped them on their way to Queensferry, where they arrived by evening. The departure point is not named; but from the north shore of the Firth of Tay the voyage would have been straightforward and easily accomplished in a day, given the good speed Guillaume says they maintained.

He now has his hero making for Roxburgh but arriving instead at Melrose. The two places are not far apart; and it would have been easy for him to have Fergus stopping off at Melrose on his way. However, he seems well aware that the direct road to Roxburgh was the king's highway (following the line of the Roman Dere Street) that ran by way of Dalkeith, Soutra and Lauderdale and would have bypassed Melrose to the east. He therefore goes to the trouble of explaining that, occupied by thoughts of Galiene, Fergus took the wrong road in a fit of absent-mindedness; and that was how he found himself at the castle of the giant on Melrose Mountain. That mountain, also named the Dolorous Mount (*Mont Dolerous*) is generally agreed to correspond to the Eildon Hills overlooking Melrose, with their Roman fort of Trimontium. The giant's fortress has the descriptive name of the Castle of the Dark Rock (**Li Chastiaus de la Roce Bise**) and is probably a fanciful creation.

The Eildons command a panoramic view; and it is by no means implausible that from an upper window in the castle Fergus should have been able to see the eight miles or so to Roxburgh and the surrounding countryside with the tents of the besiegers. His future to-ings and fro-ings between Melrose, Roxburgh and Jedburgh do not strain one's credulity from the point of view of the distances travelled. So we are still in the real world and not being whisked through the imprecise landscape of romance.

Guillaume had been careful to mention that when the hostile king had been sent by Fergus to surrender to King Arthur, he had travelled to Carlisle by way of Cumberland, which is not the route the young knight had himself followed from Carlisle to Lothian. We notice finally that Arthur, as a marriage-gift, presented the new King of Lothian with a bonus: Tweeddale (until recently Peeblesshire), that is the upper reaches of the Tweed valley, where the royal lodge of Traquair was situated.

The *Romance of Fergus*, then, shows a topographical accuracy quite foreign to other Arthurian romances. Guillaume le Clerc, whoever he was, shows himself familiar with not only the lie of the land in the greater part of Scotland south of the Highlands but also with the general features of its landscape. Particularly significant are some of the small details he provides, unnecessary to the plot but demonstrably correct, whether it be the domestic scene in Carlisle, the eastward flow of the water from the marvellous spring, the Queensferry arrangements, the steep and narrow entry to Dunnottar Castle, the leather-merchants waiting for a northerly wind, Fergus taking the wrong road, or the views from the Black Mountain or the hilltop castle near Melrose. After the initial episode of the hunt everything, too, seems drawn to scale. Surely Guillaume le Clerc cannot have got all these things right by accident. The only reasonable conclusion must be that a great deal has come from the personal observation of a man who had lived in the country and travelled widely about it.

More than this, he had a particular interest in bringing into his story such realistic touches as would make his public feel at home. They provide more than general local colour and would lose their point for a Continental audience who thought of Scotland as some distant and probably barbarous land. This was not one of the typical run of romances where the setting was sufficiently vague to give them a universal quality. Guillaume was composing first and foremost for a discriminating Scottish public; and his poem is a romance only in name.

There is something of the impostor about Guillaume le Clerc in that he poses as a traditional purveyor of Arthurian fantasies, whereas his main interest, or so I maintain, is in probing the behaviour and manners of his own society. He is usually thought of as a second-rate romancer following in the footsteps of Chrétien de Troyes and plagiarising on the way the works of Chrétien himself and also of two of his successors who attempted to bring to an end the story of the Grail, left unfinished by the master. (This, incidentally, implies a date for *Fergus* of about 1200 or fairly soon after.) Yet, as we have seen, Guillaume himself drops early hints of an altogether more subversive purpose. It has, of course, always been fashionable to seek hidden meanings behind superficially straightforward texts; and in the Middle Ages this was encouraged by school training in exegesis and the hunt for allegorical interpretations. Chrétien hinted at a deeper sense he had put into his own romances. But such meanings, in so far as they existed, would operate on the general level: Guillaume's concern is with the particular.

Alerted by his tongue-in-cheek opening, his contemporaries would readily have tumbled to the fact that he was making fun of the Grail story, which others were already presenting as a quest for Christian revelation. Some of his techniques are obvious, as when he puts his talisman in the care of not a radiant maiden, but a hirsute old woman, or his frequent substitution of bathos for suspense. By deploying throughout a witty humour, he is calling above all for a thoughtful rather than an emotional approach to his tale. Thus his introduction of historical and topical reality will encourage his Scottish public to look behind the extravagant surface of his narrative for other references to their own familiar world. Might they not even recognise some of those characters who are more than the stereotyped figures of romance?

Many would no doubt be well aware of the poet's identity. If only we could share their knowledge! We can assume that he was a school-trained clerk (before the poem is thirty lines old he is showing off his knowledge of Achilles and Patroclus) and that his name was indeed Guillaume. Was he, then, merely some humble clerk in the service, perhaps, of a noble family? That is possible. However, medieval authors were sometimes coy about giving their full identity and even, on occasion, used jokey pseudonyms. So we are entitled to consider, as we search the romance for real personalities behind the fictions, the possibility of his being that more substantial Guillaume, namely Bishop William Malveisin: he was actually credited by late sources with literary compositions, both of them in Latin, on the miracles of Saint Ninian and the deeds of Saint Kentigern. That a bishop should have written courtly verse is perfectly possible, as witness Malveisin's younger contemporary, Robert

Grosseteste bishop of Lincoln, whose prolific output includes allegorical poems in French, though with a pious content. The grounds for the possible ascription of *Fergus* to Malveisin will emerge as we continue our investigation.

Let us, then, run once more through the romance, having assured ourselves of the reliability of Guillaume's geographical framework. We are now in a safer position to sift the nuggets of topical reference from the surrounding fictional matter, keeping an eye open for actual personalities disguised as characters of Arthurian legend and for apparent depictions of contemporary life, manners and attitudes.

It is from Chrétien's *Erec* that Guillaume borrows the departure of King Arthur and his company from Cardigan to hunt the white stag, although it was his idea to begin the chase in the vicinity of Carlisle. As in his source, the king cuts a vigorous and impressive figure; but there it is Arthur himself who takes the stag. We noticed, though, that Queen Guenevere, who plays a prominent role in *Erec*, is not even named by Guillaume, who reduces her almost to a figure of fun on her sole appearance. This could be an example of a rather anti-feminist streak that can be detected from time to time throughout his work. But if he is already drawing a tacit analogy with the entourage of William the Lion, it might reflect a relatively subordinate part played by the Scottish queen in court life.

Galloway is described in unflattering terms as a rich but uncivilised region, whose inhabitants are not only ignorant but irreligious. Chrétien had dropped a hint to that effect in his *Perceval*, describing them as perverse; and Jordan Fantosme had gone even further when he coupled them with the northern Scots as being quite godless, a 'despicable race, on whom be God's curse'. So Guillaume is echoing a widespread prejudice against the unruly Gallovidians, with whom the Scottish crown had had its problems in the past.

The wealthy Soumillet's fortress may have been modelled on the Mote of Urr, but if so he had nothing in common with its Anglo-Norman owner Walter de Berkeley. Nor does he owe anything but his name to the historical Somerled. He is depicted as a hereditary landowner of non-noble stock, whose uncouth manners betray his origins. He would come into the category of local lairds or thanes, though there is no hint of his owing service to the king, as the thanes usually did. So, despite an element of caricature, he would surely have been sketched from the life. No frequenter of courts himself, he had a wife with much better connections; and she, having married beneath her, was quick to point out that there had been many knights in her own family.

Fergus makes his appearance working for his father as a ploughboy. He watches as the royal party passes by: Arthur in close company with his knights of the Round Table, the counsellors in his sovereign chamber (the *camera regis*), a lame packhorse laden with silver vessels in the rear. The lad's accoutrements seem authentic; he wears a short lambskin jerkin and rawhide shoes and is armed with a club; for, we are told, in Galloway it was the custom for workers at the plough or harrow to go armed. Another realistic touch is that his team consisted of horses and oxen: such mixed teams are attested for England and were probably also used in Scotland. We shall see him later mount one of the sturdy horses of the region, which were especially suited to boggy land, says the poet. Galloway has in fact given its name to a small but powerful breed of horses. The short, broad sword with which Fergus then arms himself has been cited as another local feature; and we are assured by Guillaume that the knotted scourge he took with him was always carried by the men of his country.

Both Fergus and his mother swear by Saint Mungo or, as he says, 'Saint Mungo at Glasgow'. This was the familiar Celtic name for Saint Kentigern and is usually interpreted as 'dearest one'. We cannot be sure how widely it was employed outside the Glasgow diocese; but for Guillaume its use by Fergus before his knighting seems to be intended as a mark of his naivety; for thereafter the only saints he invokes are Denis and Nicholas. The poet has been at obvious pains to portray the lad as recognisably a native of Galloway just as Perceval, Guillaume's model, had been firmly placed in wild Wales, though with far less circumstantial detail.

We are reminded by the references to Saint Mungo and Glasgow that Malveisin had been bishop of that diocese before his translation to St Andrews. And we think of him again in the context of Fergus' reason for leaving his home for King Arthur's court. Perceval's aim had been to seek knighthood at the hands of the king; but, curiously enough, that was not the burning ambition of Fergus. His mother had persuaded Soumillet that he should be allowed to go away to make his reputation in some unspecified service. Fergus himself is more precise; no fewer than eight times Guillaume makes it clear that he is determined to serve King Arthur and, quite specifically, to become one of his counsellors. He says nothing about being made a knight. Here, we feel, speaks the clerk who is telling the tale and putting himself into his hero's shoes. If that clerk was Malveisin, he did in fact achieve the goal which Fergus so insistently declared; indeed, as chancellor, he had been for a time King William's foremost counsellor. The fact that the naive lad, as we later learn, thought that once armed he was already a knight does not make less remarkable his professed ambition not to win his spurs in feats of chivalry, but to join the king's company as a counsellor. One suspects the poet at this point of lapsing into autobiography.

We shall come across other passages in the romance where the hero speaks with what sounds much like the poet's own voice. But that is not to say that there is a consistent relationship between the two: it would be absurd, for instance, to suggest any correspondence between the extravagant adventures of the knight errant and anything that is likely to have enlivened the clerk's career. In this instance, however, Fergus' dreams of curial duties rather than chivalric exploits would seem more appropriate for the clerk than the knight; and that leads logically to the equation of Arthur with King William, in that Fergus is speaking for William's subject the poet. So a further line of investigation is opened: how far is it likely that Guillaume has the Scottish king in mind when he is portraying Arthur? Or perhaps more significantly for this study, to what extent is his public in Scotland liable to interpret his work in this way?

Arthur's knighting of Fergus in Carlisle would have evoked memories of earlier days. Between 1136 and 1157 Carlisle had been in Scottish hands; and it was there in 1149 that David I had conferred knighthood on the future King Henry II. Was this important ceremony in Guillaume's thoughts as he told of his young hero entering the order of chivalry in Carlisle's royal hall? And what of the more recent occasion when his own king William had as a youth received the accolade there, according to usually reliable chroniclers, at the hand of Henry II himself? If, as is quite probable, the ageing William read Guillaume's romance or heard it recited, he would have had memories of that ceremony some fifty years ago stirred by the account of the events in Carlisle.

To draw that analogy would be to equate William not with King Arthur but with Fergus. Yet taking the episode as a whole, the representation of the royal court in residence invites comparison with the Scottish court with William at its head. The portrait of the king is a flattering, albeit conventional one: he is courteous, fair-minded, attentive to justice and prompt to encourage a young man eager to make his way in his society. Here and elsewhere he is seen to value especially the advice of his dear nephew Gawain when he was at hand. In this respect, Gawain stands in the same relation to Arthur as did Earl David to his brother William. On the other hand Kay, the royal seneschal or steward, plays his traditional role as an insolent trouble-maker. It might be thought that Guillaume, if he did move in court circles, would have risked giving offence by perpetuating that image here. It so happens, though, that the royal stewards seem not to have been among William's more intimate associates. Indeed one of them, Alan, found himself in the king's bad books at the turn of the century by marrying off his daughter without royal approval.

Far more influential were the chamberlains. Just two men served William in this capacity throughout his entire reign, namely Philip de Valognes, from 1165 to about 1171 and again from about 1193 to 1214, and Walter de Berkeley in the intervening years. Malveisin would, of course, have known both intimately: he actually played a leading part with Philip de Valognes in the negotiations with King John at Norham in 1209. It may, then, be no accident that the role played in Guillaume's source by a hospitable nobleman remote from the royal court has been given by him to King Arthur's resident chamberlain. He is unnamed, so we are left to provide our own identity if we choose. Described as 'good-hearted, prudent and courtly and well versed in all customs', he prepares Fergus for knighthood and explains its legal basis before personally presenting him at court and taking part in the ceremony. He thus completes Guillaume's picture of the royal household; and it is one that would be entirely recognisable by his contemporaries.

One small but realistic detail is the sight of the king, back from morning church, engaged in a game of chess with one of his nobles. Also, the armour provided for Fergus, with its leggings of iron chain-mail, hauberk and conical helmet, has been shown to be typical of that worn by the Anglo-Norman knights of the period. It may of course be objected that there is little here that can be exclusively related to the Scottish scene and that to view Arthur's court at Carlisle as mirroring some gathering of King William and his household is to push the evidence to the limit. Perhaps so. But it cannot be denied that with Fergus' arrival at Liddel Castle we enter a genuinely Scottish milieu.

Under David I Anglo-Norman settlers from Northamptonshire were granted the lordship of Liddesdale; and one of them, Ranulf de Soules, was the first of a line of royal butlers. As such he served William during the early part of his reign and was then apparently succeeded by his nephew and namesake, who died in 1207, murdered it is said by his domestics. Although the butlers were not especially important members of the king's household, the second Ranulf appears frequently as a witness to royal charters. One of these, issued at Edinburgh in 1194, is of some interest to us, as we find him in the company of Malveisin, then archdeacon of Lothian, and Roland, the grandson of the historical Fergus and shortly to become royal constable. At Stirling in 1200 Ranulf appears with Malveisin, now chancellor, and the chamberlain Philip de Valognes. In the romance the hero finds the unnamed lord of Liddel Castle relaxing on the bridge in the company of a beautiful maiden and with a hawk on his wrist.

The girl is his niece, Galiene; and she is the daughter of the king of Lothian. The identification of Galiene, a name otherwise unknown to romance, is vital for us. There seems no doubt that she was the Galiena, daughter of Waltheof, who was given in marriage by King William to Philip de Mowbray. Philip's grandfather Roger had joined forces with William in the rebellion of 1173–4, and the family soon acquired land and favour in his kingdom. The earldom of Dunbar or Lothian was vested in a parallel branch of Galiena's family, whilst her father had inherited lands on the north shore of the Forth and shared with the abbot of Dunfermline the 'lordship of the ferries'. This interest in the Queensferry passage she inherited on her father's death without other heir; and it was in this context that there arose the dispute with Dunfermline, which as we saw was adjudicated by Queen Ermengarde and Bishop Malveisin in 1212. Her husband Philip de Mowbray was in frequent attendance at the royal court from the late twelfth century and on two occasions witnessed royal charters together with Malveisin, one of them in the company of Alan, the great-grandson of the historical Fergus.

Returning to the romance, one is tempted to see the fulsome praise of Galiene's beauty as a pretty compliment paid by the poet to the real Galiena. There is, though, more to his account of her burgeoning relationship with Fergus than meets the eye. The description of feminine beauty was a standard exercise in medieval poetics; and the portrait of Galiene was inspired by that of Blancheflor, Perceval's beloved, in Chrétien's romance. Guillaume even outdoes the master in his praise; but he does omit the conventional reference to lustrous golden hair, as though he were wishing to remain true to a real model. Faithful to the traditional representation of the onset of courtly love, he proceeds to describe the girl's eager contemplation of the handsome young knight. The god of Love sees his chance and, fitting a shaft to his bow, sends it winging through Galiene's eye into her heart. Again, this is totally conventional except for one playful twist: instead of using the familiar longbow, Guillaume declares, the god has recourse to the more powerful crossbow (and one operated by a windlass at that!) in order to drive home his gold-tipped bolt. So with one humorous aside, the courtly image has been undermined; and we have been put at an ironic distance from the evolving love situation.

That night, Galiene, racked by her love-sickness, tosses and turns so violently that she throws her bed upside down. Her father, she reflects, wants to marry her to a powerful king; but she will have none of it, although she realises that to make the first approach to Fergus would bring shame on her family. However, she finally overcomes her qualms and timidly goes to his bed, with the result that we know: Fergus will only contemplate an affair once he has vanquished the Black Knight. After a brief swoon, Galiene retreats to her bed and thinks of suicide. But then she tells herself that never had any woman of her family killed herself for love; and she would not want to be the first. She would rather go back to Lothian and submit to the wishes of her father, whom she had not seen for a whole year.

Fresh from his adventure with the Black Knight, Fergus returns to Liddel Castle; and there, confronted by Galiene's disappearance, he is so overwhelmed by the delayed effects of his own love that he becomes quite disorientated. His kindly host, though full of grief himself to find Galiene missing, tries to talk Fergus out of his misery: no knight should make such a fuss about any girl or woman, for people would consider him childish. The same thought had briefly crossed Fergus' mind: 'I'm stupid to dabble in love. My father Soumillet never in all his living days indulged in that sort of thing, yet his son wants to do so! God! How ridiculous I am to want to join the ranks of those who night and day serve as Love's mercenaries! – And why should I not join them? For then I'd increase my worth. Why not? Because it seems to me I ought indeed to have a beautiful mistress.' So that is what he decides; and he begins his quest for Galiene.

I have looked at the Liddel episode in some detail because it is so revealing of the poet's art and his relationship to his public. He begins by giving it a real location recognisable to a Scottish audience; and there Fergus is generously hosted by an anonymous castellan whom they would have equated with the lord of Liddesdale. His fictional niece, daughter of the king of Lothian, the poet has identified by name with a lady familiar in court circles and with strong Lothian connections. Within this setting Guillaume has played out a travesty of a conventional love affair as presented in the fashionable literature of his day.

The ideal courtly love situation as propounded and illustrated in countless texts usually begins with a well-matched couple falling instantly in love. For a while they may try to conceal their feelings, though the pangs of their love-sickness bring them sleepless and agitated nights. In the end it is normally the man who takes the initiative, assuring the lady of his total devotion, to which she responds, possibly after a show of coyness. Such a relationship engenders increased virtue and merit in both partners; but should the man be rebuffed, his unrequited passion will cause him mental and physical prostration and even derangement. In a serious romance like Chrétien's *Erec* any humour would be incidental and sympathetic to the lovers, producing a pathos aimed at touching the emotions. Guillaume's waggish embellishments are, on the contrary, designed only to bring a sense of absurdity to the whole affair and even, we might feel, a hint of disapproval.

The troubadours of southern France had developed the notion of courtly love (the term itself is modern); and they had evolved for its conduct various rules which were often debated in their verse. The fashion had spread to the north; and there, with the help of Ovid's writings, it was adapted to the needs of the romance. To discuss the finer points of amorous behaviour became an elegant pastime in some quarters. It has even been supposed, on fragile evidence, that 'courts of love' were sometimes held by noble ladies, Queen Eleanor of England among them, to refine the practice of courtly love and rule on particular cases. We catch echoes of that kind of amorous debate in the self-questioning of Galiene and Fergus, and strongly suspect that Guillaume's sympathies went with the castellan's down-to-earth attitude and Galiene's practical resolution of her problem.

All this would, of course, be lost on a public unfamiliar with courtly love and its literary expression. We can only conclude that the French-speaking majority of the Scottish aristocracy, so obviously targeted by Guillaume, would have been well versed in these matters. Although romances could be read privately by those with access to a copy, they would more often than not have been read aloud in instalments to audiences in the castle halls. This is what Guillaume implies when he wishes happiness on all who hear *Fergus*. And conversation being prized in his day as one of the social accomplishments, we can imagine episodes like that at Liddel giving rise to many a lively discussion on such matters as the priority to be given to love, or even its propriety in a society where the marriage of convenience was the norm. If Guillaume had been present, he would have been able to enliven the debate further with his witty, clerkish squibs on the folly of lovers.

It is not only the refined conceits of courtly love that he makes the butt of his humour. On other occasions he even reduces his hero's otherwise incredible prowess to human dimensions. When Fergus clambers up the Black Mountain, Guillaume forewarns us that the monstrous guardian of the Nouquetran will prove to be inanimate and the lion sculpted in ivory. Having attacked the bronze churl, Fergus is ashamed and hopes the court do not get to hear of it. Bathos is a keen weapon in Guillaume's armoury; and he is prepared to deploy it, so far as his plot allows, against the romantic extravagances in the field of chivalric and amorous prowess.

Another of his favourite tricks is to humanise the ferocious duels he describes by making the combatants indulge in outbursts of mocking repartee; and sometimes these seem to contain topical allusions. The Black Knight prefaces his attack on Fergus by pretending to take him for a mercenary sent by King Arthur, who is afraid to come himself: 'Instead he sends his menials who have come from other countries to serve at court as hirelings, when he's not prepared to take them permanently into his company'. The reference to Arthur's mercenaries might puzzle those familiar with conventional romance. On the other hand, at King William's court it could have touched a tender spot, especially with those who recalled the sorry events of 1174, William, it will be remembered, employed many mercenaries in his rebellion, mainly Flemings. It was they, says Fantosme, who launched the unsuccessful assaults on Wark Castle and then Prudhoe; and it was with a company of French and Fleming mercenaries that William marched to besiege Alnwick, where he was taken and led off into captivity. Perhaps it was tactless of Guillaume to arouse such painful memories; but at least the Black Knight was made by Fergus to pay for his taunts.

The hero's next trial of strength, as he begins his quest for Galiene, is with the knight bivouacking with his mistress in the forest. In the early hours the man had been roused by the cries of his guardian dwarf, whom

Fergus had wounded. Throwing on a tunic of Friesland cloth (a touch of realism), he accused the intruder of base conduct in his treatment of the dwarf. Fergus met his threats with a jeer: 'There's a magistrate in this district: you'd do well to lay a complaint with him, if I've done you any wrong. Alternatively, if I don't make you satisfactory amends, then don't hesitate to dispossess me of such lands as I hold from you until I've made you reparation for my offence in respect of your hunchback dwarf'. Part of my case for seeing Malveisin as our likely author rests on his particular interest in legal matters and his reputation as an expert in the field. On this and several other occasions we find the hero asserting his rights in a legalistic manner which would accord with Malveisin's known interests and confrontational behaviour.

Two more instances quickly follow. First there is the robber knight who illegally demands tribute from those who travel on his land and cross his bridge. Fergus deals him a crippling blow, then calls after him as he flees: 'Come back here, sir knight! I'm bringing you my charger because you want to be paid the toll you're demanding. I wouldn't on any account want you to think me a trickster or a base, very obstinate fellow by taking away your crossing fee'. We are told that by bringing the brigand to heel, Fergus had ensured that future travellers had free passage in the region.

There follows his purloining of the food being enjoyed by the knights round their fire. Their leader tells his companions to let Fergus eat his fill and then settle his account with them. The uninvited guest responds by invoking precedent: 'The custom of my country is this: when people have sat down to meal, share and share alike, they first of all eat as much as they feel like and then reckon up afterwards. I'm not asking to take away anything of yours, as God's my witness. I've a fine silk tunic I'll give you to cover the cost'. Fergus' behaviour here, with his plea for deferred payment, is much the same as in the incident at the Queensferry crossing, which we have already noticed.

As the victims of Fergus' prowess arrive to give themselves up at court, we are afforded an extended view of Arthur in council. He had assembled his barons to seek advice on the strategy to adopt in order to bring the Black Knight to book. When Kay, mocking as usual, is sharply rebuked by Gawain, Arthur refuses to have such squabbling in his council. Their enemy then entered the castle to throw himself on the king's mercy, whereupon Arthur turned first to Gawain for his opinion. His nephew spoke for clemency; and with the agreement of the barons, this was the policy recommended to and adopted by the king. The poet is not departing from tradition when he shows Arthur taking his lords' advice; and even in the *Song of Roland* we are told that Charlemagne relied entirely on his French barons. Nevertheless, Guillaume's insistence here on the consultative process and earlier on Fergus' ambition to be part of it, coupled with King William's known attentiveness to the advice of his leading lords, may well reflect his own experience of the Scottish *curia*. The association would have been flattering enough for King William, since Arthur shows the virtues of the model monarch. A dignified and magnanimous figure, he seeks to avoid offence to others and petty feuding in his court, while upholding the principle of rule by consensus.

Fergus comes to the wonderful spring, and the dwarf who guards the nearby chapel accosts him by name. Gifted with second sight and evidently a creature of legend, the dwarf predicts his coming trials and ultimate success in his quest. But even with this prophetic creature we are not entirely out of touch with the real world in which superstition had its place. We think of the monk of Melrose's hermit vaticinating from his remote cell to cause a stir among the credulous. At least there is nothing fanciful about the dwarf's description of sea-girt Dunnottar and its impregnability. 'I can tell you', he says, 'that if the whole of the English army were gathered and had sworn your death, but you had the sole advantage of being in that tower having raised the drawbridge, you would be in no fear of them all, provided you had a supply of food.' The prophecy was even more far-sighted than Guillaume realised; because, although the English were able to seize Dunnottar on a couple of occasions in the late twelfth and thirteenth centuries, as recently as 1651-2 it suffered an eight-month siege by Cromwell's forces before capitulating. It is significant that Guillaume, through his dwarf, is expressing a Scottish view when he thinks of the English as the hostile force.

Fergus, overjoyed at the prospect of recovering Galiene, longs for nothing more: 'If the Lord God were pleased to take me to Himself and pardon all the misdeeds I ever committed against Him, and if the bright-faced Galiene were in the darkness of Hell, then I should go there: for love of her I'd leave Paradise above to join her down below and suffer pain, hardship and torment until the great Judgment Day'. This seems an outrageous statement to come from the pen of a cleric who may even have been a bishop. In fact, it fits well into a tradition of clerical humour widespread in Guillaume's day, especially in anonymous Latin writings, prose and verse, by cloistered monks as well as wandering scholars. The most famous of these roving clerks is heard singing of his dedication to Venus and proclaiming himself more intent on the joys of the flesh than the salvation of his soul. Paradoxically, then, Fergus' irreverent outburst suggests rather than denies the poet's clerical background.

The hero makes his way through Lothian to Maiden Castle, the familiar name for Edinburgh, and thence to Queensferry, where he finds the boatmen more treacherous, the poet remarks pointedly, than any in the whole kingdom of England. If Guillaume's slighting reference to Dunfermline can be taken to imply some personal grudge, it may not be irrelevant that Malveisin was not always on the best of terms with the monks there. Some time during the abbacy of Patrick (1202–17) he exercised his episcopal authority by withdrawing the abbey's right to have its nominees given the charge of two local churches. The reason says more of his own fleshly appetites than his spirituality. For his complaint was that on one visit to the monks' establishment he had not been provided with enough wine to accompany his evening meal. In vain they protested that the wine had disappeared down the throats of his own attendants: they still had to pay for the lapse.

To set against the irreligious attitude struck by Fergus in his conversation with the dwarf, it may be remarked that Guillaume states explicitly that he survived his fights with the boatmen, the dragon and the giant only because God was on his side. Faint though the pious note is, it is not entirely typical of Arthurian romance to find the hero enjoying divine protection; and there are one or two later instances where we shall fancy we hear more clearly the voice of a cleric. The possibility that this could have been Malveisin is not lessened by the favourable impression left by the leather-merchant, whom Fergus greets in the name of the Creator. That would be consistent with the fact that Bishop Malveisin seems to have had good relations with merchants, at least towards the end of his life, when he used his influence with the English court to obtain licences for Frenchmen to trade in England. Small as they are, these grains of evidence may help to tilt the balance in favour of Malveisin's authorship.

An indication that Guillaume was familiar with heroic legends in Latin as well as French is found in his description of Fergus' fight with the hag's husband. Having killed the hero's steed, the giant seizes him bodily and, holding him under his arm, rushes off with the intention of drowning him. But Fergus manages to take his sword and, plunging it below his breast, deals him a mortal blow. Guillaume appears to have modelled this unorthodox victory on the widely-known *Pseudo-Turpin Chronicle*, a Latin prose spin-off from the Roland legend. Composed in the middle of the twelfth century, its highlight was the slaying of the pagan giant Ferracutus by Roland, who managed to loosen his opponent's grip and aim a deft thrust at his only vulnerable spot, his navel. Although French translations did appear from the beginning of the thirteenth century, Guillaume's source was more likely to have been the Latin text. He has already told us that Fergus, even before his knighting, had thought himself as good a man as Roland; and in a later scene he seems influenced by the original French *Song of Roland*. So there is no doubt that he was familiar with the legend and expected his Scottish public to be so too. After all, there were people in the kingdom named after Charlemagne's illustrious nephew, and not least the lord of Galloway.

To return from legend to harsh reality, the picture Guillaume gives us of Roxburgh under siege seems coloured by his knowledge of contemporary warfare, whether at first hand or by report. We see the tents and shelters of the besieging army encamped in the ravaged countryside. Then, when the trumpets sound the assault, there is the hubbub of the men manning the catapults, while the scaling ladders are set against the walls. Only the location at Roxburgh, though, is specifically Scottish. It was a scene that had been enacted time and again, for instance, during William's campaigns in England. But we are reminded of one specific siege, famous in its day, which may have been in the poet's mind; and that, as we shall see later, took place in neither Scotland nor England.

Within her castle at Roxburgh, Galiene is in dire straits when Fergus rides to her rescue. His valiant harrying of the besiegers gives their king pause for thought. In council, he takes up his nephew Arthofilaus' offer to go to the lady with a final demand that she should recognise what he considers his rightful claim to Lothian or find someone to defend her cause in single combat. When Arthofilaus arrives before Galiene, she is infuriated by his insolence, which she meets with a sarcastic sally of her own: 'Vassal, you've eaten or drunk on an empty stomach. I fancy you're one of Wasselin's three messengers. A curse on whoever gave you the wine that's made you so drunk! Aren't you used to wine being so cheap, then? Indeed, it was very wrong of that king who sent you here not to have let you sleep instead. Go and rest a little; and then you'll be good enough to come back to spin us some of your yarns!'

The reference to Wasselin's three messengers has puzzled commentators. The name appears nowhere else in romance or in any known proverb or saying that might explain the allusion. So where did Guillaume pick it up? I hit on the apparent answer with the discovery of a real-life Wasselin, or Wascelin to use the usual spelling; and it was no real surprise to find that he was a prominent member of Scottish society in King William's reign. William Wascelin was in fact a tenant of the king's brother Earl David and held lands at Newtyle, north-west of Dundee. He witnessed a number of David's charters, including that establishing the new abbey of Lindores in 1198 or 1199. Among his co-witnesses were King William, Patrick earl of Dunbar, and Philip de Valognes. Himself a benefactor of Lindores, he and his wife expressed the wish to be buried there, should they die in Scotland. Another of these charters, issued between 1202 and about 1208, is of particular interest: it records a grant of previously disputed land in Perthshire to St Andrews Cathedral Priory; and the list of witnesses, including Wascelin, is headed by Bishop Malveisin.

This associate of Malveisin and of the royal household is surely the Wasselin of the poem. There is nothing we know to account for his three messengers, of whom Galiene makes her disparaging remark; so the assumption must be that the reference is to some incident known to Guillaume and his public, who would have been amused to have it recalled. In that case, this would be another example of Guillaume's sly humour deployed not to give offence, but to draw his audience more closely into the story. Perhaps that is his reason for calling Galiene's attractive attendant Arondele; but if a young lady of that name did frequent the courts in his day, I have not traced her. However, with that exception and leaving aside for the moment the case of Arthofilaus and his uncle the king, we can say that the chief non-traditional characters of the romance either bear the names of or, if anonymous, can be associated with people prominent on the Scottish scene. They were also known personally to Malveisin.

A few more points may be adduced in favour of the bishop's authorship. His legal interests could be again reflected in the speech of his hero, this time when Fergus turns up to fight the judicial combat and discovers that he is to have two opponents, the king and his nephew, instead of the customary one. He calls to the king: 'Are these your conditions, now? Is this your way of fixing combats: two knights against one? This isn't at all a good arrangement. Are you and your companion twin children, then? In the old days they used to stipulate that a pair of twins would fight against one man, if they were summoned. This practice has lapsed; so it's a great shame and a pity when a combat of that kind is considered'. So here once more we have Fergus concerned, whether in jest or in earnest, about his legal rights. The lapsed custom he cites may be fanciful. But if anything of the sort did ever exist, Malveisin is as likely as anyone to have known of it, especially as rules governing the *duellum* were being regularised in his day. And if it is fantasy, who better to have invented it?

Noticeable too towards the end of the romance is the intrusion of rather more religious elements than we had found earlier. It was common enough in the earlier Arthurian romance to find characters swearing by God and the saints, and to see them performing their normal Christian duties, such as attending Mass or celebrating the main festivals. Less usual is to find them consciously putting themselves under divine protection when their prowess or love is put to the test. So it is noteworthy that the despairing Galiene is told by her maidens not to be dismayed, for the Lord God will help her, advice echoed by Arondele: 'Don't worry, but trust firmly in God'. Fergus, on hearing Arondele's story, assures her that her mistress will be defended 'if God Almighty pleases'.

When the time for the combat arrives and she has no champion, Galiene attends church to hear Mass and later goes up into her tower resolved on suicide. Having commended Fergus to God the Father, she 'makes the sign of the cross on her face with her right hand, then puts her head at the window to let herself slip down. But God is unwilling to suffer the loss of a soul there: she hears at that moment a voice saying to her: "Maiden, you are not at all wise: look over towards the woods!" That much it said, then fell silent'. She does as the voice tells her, and sees the light from Fergus' shield. When the heroine of Chrétien's *Erec* is about to kill herself, we are told that God in his mercy caused her to pause a little; and Guillaume probably had this scene in mind. He, however, has carefully prepared us for the divine intervention and then presented it in concrete terms. Such a clear manifestation of the Christian supernatural, rare as it is in these romances, speaks loudly for clerical authorship.

Fergus' participation in the Jedburgh tournament invites another

revealing comparison with a likely source. One of Chrétien's Con-
tinuators had told how Perceval came incognito to prove his mettle in
a tournament held between King Arthur and his knights on the one side
and the Irish and Scots on the other. Taking his stand with the latter,
he performed great feats against those of the Round Table, although
the kings of both Ireland and Scotland bit the dust in the course of the
action. Significantly, Guillaume, with an eye to his Scottish audience,
has the English as the 'outsiders'; and it is they whom Fergus joins.
Although on the Continent the Scots were renowned for their skill in
tournaments, none are in fact recorded as having been held at Jedburgh
or elsewhere in William's kingdom.

In his first joust, Fergus took full vengeance on Kay for his earlier
mockery by sending him flying head-first from his steed into a brook.
Now it was his turn to taunt the seneschal; and again he refers to his
legal rights: 'By my faith, good sir, you're very bad-mannered to fish in
my river without my permission: you really have behaved outrageously!'
The king, though, will have plenty of fish for his table in the evening
with such a steward in his service. Why, he has even made an eel-trap
with his coat of mail! Let him keep a reckoning of what he has caught;
but he must leave something for others to fish! The mention of eels
is not inappropriate, as they were a prized commodity in Scotland
at the time. We have seen Dunfermline Abbey confirmed by one of
William's charters in the annual receipt of a tithe of the royal eels
caught locally, Fife being especially rich in them. So once again we
think of Malveisin with his litigious reputation, not to mention his
banqueting in Dunfermline.

The ladies of Guillaume's public might not entirely have approved
of the way in which he brought his story to a conclusion. Spirited as
Galiene's rejection of her enemy's terms had been, it had not won the
support of her knights; and she herself realised that to propose a duel of
one against two was an act of pure folly. When, after Fergus had saved
the day and was carrying all before him at the tournament, she came
to Arthur's court, it was with a humble request that he should provide
her with a husband: 'Now I have come to put to you, as I should to
my lord, the request that you take care of me so that I don't become
disinherited. A land left to a woman is badly governed. It should not
displease you if from now on I should wish to improve my situation.
It is high time for me to marry; but you may be sure I would take
no man unless I had him from your court'. We know her aim was to

secure Fergus as a husband; and to this end, it seems, she exploits the no doubt common view that only a man can make a fit ruler. This is a point to which we shall return.

Having placed her fate in King Arthur's hands and been assured that she shall have a man of her choice, Galiene admits she has her eye on the knight with the blazing shield. Arthur, as usual, turns to his nephew for advice; and it is Gawain who is responsible for bringing about the lovers' reunion. We witness a long-drawn-out exchange of kisses and a great show of mutual affection, as we might have expected. But to our surprise it is Fergus and Gawain who thus indulge their emotions after recognising each other.

Guillaume's account of how the marriage was arranged is altogether more dispassionate. Arthur takes Fergus, Galiene and Gawain aside and offers the young man the lady, Lothian and Tweeddale if that is his wish. Fergus replies that he will do whatever the king desires: 'As far as I'm concerned, I wouldn't refuse her if I knew what she wanted'. Galiene thereupon places herself at the disposal of Arthur, who at once bestows her on Fergus. With dubious tact, Guillaume remarks: 'Now he has his beloved; now he is overjoyed. If he loves her, then she loves him three times as much'. So amid general approval the marriage takes place.

A fortnight later King Arthur left, with Fergus escorting him on the first part of his journey. Then, when they parted, Gawain bade Fergus farewell with many more kisses and embraces; and he made him promise never to abandon his chivalry for his wife. Back to Roxburgh went King Fergus and Queen Galiene. 'He loves her as his tender sweetheart and she him as her noble lover.' In his *Erec* and *Yvain* Chrétien de Troyes had illustrated a married knight's difficulty in accommodating the love of his wife with his duty to maintain his chivalric prowess. Here Guillaume gives his judgment on where the priority should lie.

Throughout the final scenes of the romance, then, Galiene has to take a back seat; and we must ask ourselves if this reflects a misogynistic streak in the poet's character such as we have had cause to suspect from his very first lines, when he avoided the mention of women at King Arthur's court. It would have been interesting to know if Malveisin, the ecclesiastic, possessed such a trait. One could argue, on the other hand, that this is is a tongue-in-cheek literary pose and helps to bring into gentle ridicule the whole idea of courtly love, the mainstay of the serious romance. How, then, would it have been received by Guillaume's public? The ladies might have been provoked by such a display of anti-feminism, leaving the men smiling discreetly behind their hands. It is unfortunate that we have so little evidence of the attitudes of the women at the Scottish court: the records speak of little more than their pious acts; but that must be far from the full story. It may well be that their role was less prominent in the male-dominated aristocratic society under King William than it was in the courts of France, or even England. But we are left to guess. As for the men, we shall find that at least some of them would not have been entirely out of sympathy with Guillaume's stance.

The wedding and coronation at Roxburgh take place amid celebrations that could have been sketched from the life, although such scenes are not uncommon in the romance. 'The town is full of noise and din: drums beat, horns and trumpets resound. Clouds of smoke rise from the kitchens. These were no mock marriage celebrations, for you could hardly move your feet in the town's streets ... The town was very full because everybody in the country was there: there were so many people that it was hard to find anywhere in the town to stay ... Upstairs in the paved hall they hold the great, lavish wedding feast. Never was any seen that was so costly or at which such rich dishes were served: the tables were so laden with them that before two people they placed as much as any six others would eat.'

It is possible that Malveisin attended such a wedding in Roxburgh; for it was there that King William, in 1193, bestowed his illegitimate daughter Margaret on Eustace de Vesci. At that time Malveisin was archdeacon of Lothian; and although as such he served the St Andrews diocese whereas Roxburgh came under Glasgow, so grand a royal occasion could well have called for his presence. We have come to suspect Malveisin of having a particular interest in gastronomic matters, so the emphasis on the bounty of the marriage feast would not have been out of character.

The poet's insistence on the date of the celebrations may be significant. That he placed them firmly on the feast of Saint John is not surprising, as major events in the romances were often assigned to one or other of the great Christian festivals. He is, though, more specific and, for no obvious reason, tells us that it was in fact a Sunday, and the weather was fine. Guillaume has not been in the habit of wasting his words, so one wonders if he could have deliberately given a final topical twist to the tale of his romance. The date of the marriage of King William's daughter is unknown; and in any case that lay in the fairly distant past.

Is it possible, then, that as our poet put together his last few lines he dropped a clue as to the year in which he was completing his task? Within the likely period of composition the feast of Saint John was celebrated on a Sunday in 1201, 1207 and 1218. Of these years, 1207 seems to fit most easily into the pattern of topical allusions, which include apparent echoes of incidents in William's reign, to which we now turn.

It has already been suggested that the rebellion of 1173–4 could have been in Guillaume's thoughts when he put into the Black Knight's mouth the sneer about the king who relied on mercenaries to invade his land. A more telling parallel is found in Galiene's rash decision to stake the future of herself and her kingdom on the outcome of a judicial combat. Although the siege of Roxburgh owes much to that of Blancheflor's castle in Chrétien's *Perceval*, where the hero does indeed fight man-to-man with Blancheflor's two oppressors in turn, there is in Chrétien's text no formal agreement to have the matter legally settled by a *duellum*. That, however, was the foolhardy proposal made by King William, according to Jordan Fantosme, to Henry II, then in Normandy: William would side with him against the Young King provided he first return Northumberland to him; and he suggests through his messenger that his claim should be upheld by a knight in single combat.

It seems safe to assume that Guillaume and his public would have known of this incident, if only by way of Fantosme's chronicle. More generally, the siege of Roxburgh by a hostile king would have stirred memories of the fifteen-year occupation of the castle by Henry II's English soldiery. When the king, defeated by Fergus and sent before Galiene, assured her that he would restore all her inheritances and not retain a single stronghold, William's Scottish courtiers would have allowed themselves a rueful smile.

There were also events in the more recent past that they would surely have recalled on hearing the story of Galiene. In this case too William's obsessive desire to recover the northern English counties had activated the rash streak in his character. In 1195–6, it will be remembered, he brought to a head his plan to marry his eldest legitimate daughter Margaret to Otto of Brunswick, son of Henry the Lion. Otto had pretensions, later fulfilled, to become Holy Roman Emperor. In anticipation of Margaret's succession to the Scottish throne, King Richard, Otto's uncle, would hold in trust for the couple Lothian and all its castles. Here, then, would have been another instance of a foreign king lording it over Roxburgh and the whole of Lothian, although in this case the lady involved would not have forfeited her inheritance. It is the chronicler Howden who tells us of the Scottish barons' opposition to William's scheme on the grounds that it would be flying in the face of tradition to have a woman on the throne. Our poet, very well aware of the plan and the misgivings it prompted at court, appears to have framed with reference to this historical fact his whole account of Galiene's situation and her doubts about her fitness, as a woman, to rule.

My proposition, then, is that Guillaume chose to base the climactic event in his romance on Chrétien's account of the siege of a lady's castle. In order to stimulate his public's interest, he filled out his ground-plan with features they would have recognised as relating to major events in the life of their own monarch, namely events in the 1173–4 rebellion against Henry II and William's abortive negotiations with Richard for the marriage of his daughter. This he managed with considerable ingenuity. To suggest now that he stirred into this rich mixture yet another ingredient from recollected history might seem to carry our detection exercise beyond the bounds of probability. Nevertheless I believe that he not only did so, but even left a cryptic clue to jog our memories.

This time he chose a dramatic happening which was of only indirect concern to King William. The year was 1202, and the event the confrontation at Mirebeau of the aged Queen Eleanor and her grandson the newly knighted Arthur of Brittany. It will be recalled that Arthur had been enrolled in the cause of King Philip Augustus, who had reclaimed three great Plantagenet fiefs. Hearing that his grandmother was at Mirebeau, Arthur and his French supporters had taken the town; and there they bivouacked as they laid siege to the castle, forcing Eleanor to retreat with a small company into the keep. An anonymous chronicler relates that Arthur managed to speak to her there, demanding that she evacuate the castle forthwith. The doughty queen replied that she certainly would not leave; on the contrary, if Arthur were a courtly gentleman he would himself be off and find some other castle to attack. She was amazed, she added, that he and his Poitevins, who should be her own liegemen, should besiege a stronghold knowing her to be in it. That was the end of their discussion. Somehow she managed to send an appeal for help to her son John, who was campaigning some eighty miles away.

After a forced march, he arrived at Mirebeau early one morning and caught the encamped besiegers off guard. John himself took part in the fighting, which ended with Eleanor rescued and Arthur carried off to his death. Philip Augustus, the prime instigator of the war, withdrew to his own lands.

This affair caught the imagination of contemporaries and was even used to colour the fictions of other romancers. It was certainly well known in Scottish circles. After all, Earl David had been at Le Mans when John returned there flushed with his success. Moreover, young Arthur was grand-nephew to both himself and King William and had probably been favoured by them to succeed to the English throne in preference to John. It would be interesting to know Bishop Malveisin's feelings on that score. But whatever they were at the time, we have seen him a few years later undertaking missions to King John and apparently in favour at his court.

Is it, then, by pure chance that the fictional events at Roxburgh remind us forcibly of aspects of the Mirebeau episode, and especially the disdainful rejection by the besieged queen of the young knight's demands, his elimination by her gallant rescuer, and the retreat of the king with designs on her lands? To think so would surely be to stretch coincidence to its limits. But fortunately Guillaume has tipped us the wink by the name he has given to Galiene's impudent young antagonist: Arthofilaus. It is a name unique to this romance and has all the signs of being invented as a mock-derivative of Arthur. Indeed, it is a near-synonym of Old French *Artu(s) li faus*, 'the false (perfidious) Arthur'. Guillaume, by one of his quirkish tricks, has made him the nephew of the hostile king, whereas the historical Arthur was the nephew of John, his slayer.

It is time to draw the threads of this investigation together. We first established the accuracy of the romance's geographical setting, including small details that could have been familiar only to someone who was, or had been, resident in Scotland. Encouraged by this, we went on to examine any elements that seemed to show knowledge of the social structure, manners and interests of the ruling class under William the Lion as well as various other realistic touches. Lastly we looked at certain historical events to which the poet seemed to make oblique reference. As we reviewed these features of the romance, we gathered some clues to the possible identity of Guillaume le Clerc. Let me now offer my conclusions, assuring the reader that there has been no conscious attempt either to force the evidence unduly or to pass over anything that might not have seemed to fit the general pattern.

It is undeniable that Guillaume introduced into his tale a good deal of topical material; and this he appears to have done systematically, thereby inviting his Scottish and largely aristocratic public to feel some involvement in Fergus' adventures. What, then, was his purpose in producing the romance? Medieval writers often give some indication that they are composing for a particular patron; but there is nothing to suggest that this was the case with *Fergus*. Naming himself in the final lines of the poem, Guillaume tells his audience that he finds no man in any land able to tell anything further of the knight with the shining shield; so this is the end of the romance: 'May great joy come to those who hear it!' His aim is therefore to give pleasure, to entertain. But with our experience of his impish sense of humour, we are wary of taking him at his word.

By fostering a sense of complicity in his audience, he is inviting them to give some thought to what he relates and look beneath the surface for some additional meaning, which they may ponder or discuss at their leisure. Very obvious is the way in which he pokes fun at the courtly romance and its conventions, taking the Grail legend as his prime target; and surely he does this not for his private amusement but because his public's knowledge of this fashionable literature would enable them to share the fun. Through gentle ridicule he has offered a new angle on the debate over the conflicting demands of love and prowess, exposing its artificiality in a society where political considerations were the order of the day. Clearly a realist himself, was he launching a tract against the secular idealism of the courtly world or simply accommodating his treatment to the tastes of a Scottish audience?

This is all too playful for us to think in terms of satire or the preaching of moral lessons. It is not impossible, though, that with most of the characters capable of being associated with living people, Guillaume was having a joke at the expense of an acquaintance or two: William Wascelin, for instance. Yet it would be hard to convict him of any malice. One sees him not as trouble-maker, but as a man of independent outlook thoroughly enjoying the intellectual game he is playing. Unlike some of his Continental fellows, and especially those who turned the Grail legend into Christian allegory, he has no great vision or moral truth to convey. With his feet firmly on the ground, his main purpose was indeed to entertain by putting his first-class poetic skills to the service of a sharp intelligence and impudent sense of humour.

This marks him out as an excellent practitioner rather than a genius. He is, though, fully worthy to represent almost single-handed the cultural revival under William the Lion and set Scottish vernacular literature on its way, albeit in the tongue of the French-speaking minority. It was his misfortune that what was in effect the secular Scottish component of the so-called Twelfth-Century Renaissance was based on a language with no future in his adopted country. It is Scotland's misfortune to have virtually forgotten his contribution to its cultural inheritance. Happily, however, his romance did find some favour on the Continent; and its influence can be traced on one or two later French works.

One of these is the sprawling hybrid, part-epic and part-romance, *Huon de Bordeaux*, composed between about 1216 and 1230.* Its poet has his hero, in the course of his many adventures, fight a cruel giant at Dunnottar Castle; and various details confirm *Fergus* as the source. The castle had been seized by the giant from the fairy king Auberon (Shakespeare's Oberon), son of Julius Caesar and Morgan the Fay. To our suprise we learn that it had been built over a period of forty years on the orders of Caesar himself. Influential though *Huon de Bordeaux* was, its literary merits cannot compare with those of the masterpiece *Aucassin et Nicolette*, a much shorter tale in prose and verse, which may date from about the middle of the thirteenth century.† Here the influence of *Fergus* runs much deeper, extending to the general shape and some of the details of the story as well as a great deal of the teasing, humorous technique. Among its author's more notable borrowings was the hero's irreverent preference for Hell over Heaven, provided his beloved was there. Guillaume would surely have been delighted that his romance contributed so vitally to the creation of one of the classics of European medieval literature. *Aucassin* in turn is likely to have provided Voltaire with much of the inspiration for his *Candide*; but that is another story.

So who was Guillaume le Clerc? We have assembled a good case

* *Huon de Bordeaux*, ed. Pierre Ruelle, who notes the influence of *Fergus*. It was composed in the Picard area.
† *Aucassin et Nicolette*, tr. Pauline Matarasso. See also the bibliography by Barbara Nelson Sargent-Baur and Robert Francis Cook; and D.D.R. Owen, 'Chrétien, *Fergus, Aucassin et Nicolette* and the Comedy of Reversal', in *Chrétien de Troyes and the Troubadours*, pp. 186–94. The dating of this work, which also seems of Picard provenance, has been much debated.

for seeing his name as the modest pseudonym of William Malveisin, former royal clerk and eventually bishop of St Andrews. An educated and sharp-witted man, he was widely travelled in Scotland, prominent in the counsels of King William and his leading magnates, and in touch with public affairs both in Scotland and abroad; a man reportedly with literary pretensions and certainly possessing a combative, legalistic temperament such as Fergus himself exhibits. Not renowned for his piety, he could nevertheless have been responsible for adding to his plot an element of the Christian supernatural, unusual in the genre. No other William I have found runs him close as candidate for authorship. So if it was Malveisin, when would he have composed the romance? I have suggested 1207 as a possible date. In view of its influence on *Huon de Bordeaux*, the end of the 1120s would seem the latest limit we could set. Malveisin actually remained in his see of St Andrews until his death in 1238, when he was the first bishop to be buried in its new cathedral. If he was not our poet, then it must have been some other William created in his image.

As well as for its literary qualities, *Fergus* is a precious document for the intimate glimpses it gives of the Scotland of William the Lion. Is it even possible to catch William himself lurking in its pages in one disguise or another? Some episodes do seem to carry distorted echoes of certain of his activities and behaviour, in particular as regards his participation in the rebellion against Henry II and his negotiations with Richard for the marriage of his daughter. It is too much to expect a close likeness; but William would probably have been happy to discover himself behind the dignified and benign features of King Arthur, a magnanimous monarch ruling with tolerance and justice, valuing his barons' advice but especially that of the most distinguished of his own kin. It is a flattering, if largely conventional, portrait. One cannot believe that the poet was oblivious to such an evident equation of king with king, or that it escaped the notice of his public.

Through this sophisticated and engaging romance we have been able to go beyond the cold chronicles and charters to enter briefly into the warm and living society from which it emerged and to whose delight it was dedicated. *Fergus* is a major document for the study of both Scottish culture and Scottish history during the eventful reign of King William the Lion.

SEVEN

Legend: The Legacy

As a vernacular legend of Scottish provenance *Fergus* stands alone at this period. It is quite possibly the sole surviving representative of a body of literature produced for the entertainment of the French subjects of King William and his son Alexander. There is no way of telling; but we can at least be confident that copies of secular works written in England and on the Continent would have circulated among the noble houses. It is of course not certain that Guillaume le Clerc, even if he was Bishop Malveisin of St Andrews, produced his poem on Scottish soil, although it is hardly likely to have been the fruit of some foreign visit: it must have taken many weeks to compose. But we are surely safe in assuming that it did the rounds in his adoptive land, whilst the evidence of the manuscripts shows that it quickly found an audience in north-eastern France. There it would have helped to familiarise the courtly circles with the contemporary Scottish scene or evoke memories of the country in the minds of all those who had travelled there in the past; for long-standing political, trading and social links had been maintained and strengthened under William the Lion. We may think that not the least of the achievements of Guillaume le Clerc was to promote the image of Scotland on the Continent.

By the early thirteenth century it was for many Frenchmen and other Europeans by no means a *terra incognita*; yet in the eyes of the majority it probably retained much of its earlier reputation as a remote and largely barbarous land where travellers journeyed at their peril and strange beings lurked among the mountains and forests. For those conversant with political matters, however, Scotland had been a power to be reckoned with at least since the Conqueror had marched north and sailed his fleet up the Tay in the 1070s. In the first half of the following century, largely through the efforts of King David I, it had become a modern state in the feudal mould with its frontiers open to ambitious *arrivistes* from both sides of the Channel as well as to foreign merchants or to the churchmen who occupied the new ecclesiastical foundations. David's knighting of the future Henry II was a mark of his own and his country's status in the wider world. Yet still in the popular imagination, fostered by the legend-mongers, Scotland retained something of its mystery and remoteness.

In his *History of the Kings of Britain* Geoffrey of Monmouth reached back into the largely legendary past to sketch a land inhabited by turbulent though nominally Christian races, prey to the marauding Saxons but eventually pacified and brought to heel by King Arthur. The northernmost part of his kingdom, it was left to be governed by three royal brothers, of whom the ruler of Lothian was his own brother-in-law and father of the gallant Gawain. But the Picts and the Scots remained a threat to Arthur and had a hand in the eventual downfall of his realm. Geoffrey's pseudo-history achieved wide popularity and coloured the general view of Scotland throughout the rest of the twelfth century. The new reality had somehow to reach an accommodation with the legendary background as Scotland emerged as a feudal power with its own cultural base and growing reputation for chivalric achievement. Under King William this transition was accomplished, and his kingdom was generally accepted as a full member of the European family. Something of the process is reflected in the French literature of the period. *[margin note: Kingdom respected]*

We saw elsewhere how some early material from Celtic folklore had found its way into the Latin life of Saint Kentigern and how elements from the same ancient source were worked into the French *lai* of *Desiré*, which probably dates in its present form from King William's time. Although the tales are localised in the Forth-Lothian region, this is clearly the stuff of myth; and the French poem gives no real impression of the country or the society in which the events take place. By now the legend of the originally Pictish hero Tristan was also being turned into French verse, but in a form in which the central action takes place in Cornwall; and if, as has been conjectured, the forest of Morois in which the lovers take refuge, ultimately derives its name from Moray, it too has migrated south to the Cornish domain of King Mark and would have been unrecognisable to those who came across it in the accounts of the star-crossed lovers.

For the weavers of Arthurian romance, including its acknowledged 'father', Chrétien de Troyes, Scotland was still part of the landscape of legend and little more than the source of an evocative name or two. Chrétien himself, whose activity coincided with the first half of William's reign, was by no means averse to bringing into his works echoes of real events or places familiar to his public. For instance, in *Erec*, his first romance, a coronation at Nantes recalls Geoffrey Plantagenet's investiture there; and in *Cligés* we find a realistic description of Windsor Castle and also thinly veiled allusions to contemporary marriage negotiations in Germany, not to mention accounts of various journeys including a Channel crossing to Britanny, a ride from Southampton to Winchester, and a visit to a tournament on the plain between Oxford and Wallingford. Yet when he permits himself the occasional Scottish reference, all becomes vague.

Erec is himself presented as a Scot, son of King Lac of 'Estregales', which is probably Strathclyde, and nephew of a king of Galloway. Among the knights listed as members of Arthur's court are Yvain son of Urien, whom we have already met in a Scottish context, and a certain Yder 'of the Dolorous Mount', usually identified with the Eildon Hills. The dignitaries at Erec's wedding include Aguisel the king of Scotland accompanied by his two doughty sons, a sure sign of Chrétien's reliance on Geoffrey of Monmouth for a little name-dropping. After the marriage a grand tournament was staged on Scottish soil, in the plain below Edinburgh; but the reason for the choice of venue is unstated, and we must suspect that for Chrétien it was just one more exotic touch that betrays his ignorance rather than a real knowledge of the Scottish scene.

As we have seen, the early legend from which he derived his *Yvain*, doubtless by way of some lost intermediary, was firmly localised in Lothian and its environs. But after an opening scene at Carlisle, we are unaccountably transported to the magic spring at Brocéliande in Britanny, and all Scottish associations are lost; except, that is, for the name of the heroine. This is given only once in the romance, and even then not in all of the manuscripts, the commonly accepted form being Laudine, which is supposed to be the last lingering evidence that in an earlier incarnation she was not the lady Laudine, but the lady of Lothian.

Chrétien did not complete his last romance, which goes under the title *Perceval* or *Le Conte du Graal*. There are in fact grounds for considering the text which has come down to consist of two unfinished works, one telling the story of Perceval and the other presenting a series of Gawain's adventures. Although Perceval himself was brought up by his widowed mother in the remote Welsh forest, he learns that his parents hailed from 'the Isles of the Sea', which have been plausibly identified as the Western Isles. Like Fergus, he was inspired by a meeting with a party of knights to seek knighthood at Carlisle, where King Arthur was holding court. Later he witnesses the mysterious Grail procession at the castle of the Fisher King, having been given by his host a sword of rare workmanship. He is subsequently informed that the weapon is destined to break at one moment of peril and might then be repaired only by its maker, the smith Trebuchet, at 'the lake below Cotoatre'. Here again Chrétien appears to be choosing a name more or less at random, because 'Cotoatre', far from being a hill or some such feature as his words imply, seems derived from 'Scottewatre', as the Firth of Forth was known in the Middle Ages.

At the beginning of Gawain's adventures there is a further passing reference to the 'Dolorous Mount'. More mystifying is the hero's crossing, after a tournament at Tintagel, of the 'bounds of Galloway', a region from which no knight may ever return. He then makes his way to a splendid castle, the home of a host of ladies and maidens, which he enters, only to be detained there against his will. For his description of this stronghold, which has a touch of the otherworld about it, Chrétien may well have been inspired by the Castle of Maidens, the contemporary name for Edinburgh also found in the pages of Geoffrey of Monmouth's history. At the point where the romance breaks off, Gawain has managed to send a message to King Arthur, then resident in 'the city of Orkney'. One can only conclude that to Chrétien Scotland was known merely through his reading of Geoffrey and similarly vague accounts; so for him it was a land of legend, a useful source of Celtic colouring to enliven his tales of mystery and adventure. As a frequenter of the courts of northern France and enjoying the patronage of Marie of Champagne and Philip of Flanders, he may be thought to reflect a fairly widespread ignorance of Scottish geography and society in the latter part of the twelfth century.

Among the composers of romance who followed in his footsteps was Renaut de Beaujeu, a poet from the north-east of France who produced *Le Bel Inconnu* ('The Fair Unknown'), probably in the 1190s.* It is the story of a novice and initially unknown knight who turns out to be Guinglain, the son of Gawain, and eventually takes the Queen of Wales as his bride. Among his early exploits is the rescue from a knight's clutches of a maiden

---

* *Le Bel Inconnu* is the earliest surviving treatment of the 'Fair Unknown' theme, which is also exploited in Ulrich von Zatzikhoven's *Lanzelet* (see D.D.R. Owen, *The Evolution of the Grail Legend*).

of surpassing beauty. Her name is Margerie; and she tells him that she will return to Scotland, her father's country, where her brother Agolant is now king. It has been suggested that her name could have been derived from that of King William's sister Margaret, countess of Britanny. While Guinglain, like Fergus, is adventuring far from the royal court and sadly missed by Arthur, the king plans to lure him back with a tournament. It is to be held in the plains near the Castle of Maidens which, for us if not the poet, has associations with Edinburgh. Among the illustrious participants are Erec of Estregales (identified with Strathclyde) and the King of Scotland himself, named in this episode Aguissans. He is evidently Geoffrey of Monmouth's Anguselus and the double of King Aguillars, who appeared as one of Arthur's courtiers at the beginning of the romance and was said to be the brother of Lot and Urien. So here we have a poet fully in the Chrétien mould who has used his master's technique of stirring into the narrative a few Scottish ingredients to heighten the Celtic flavour characteristic of these Arthurian stories. To find the real Scotland of William the Lion behind such fictions we have recourse only to Guillaume le Clerc's *Fergus*, which is a further measure of his remarkable innovative talent.

If we now turn to non-Arthurian verse tales, the first to claim our attention are two more *lais* which, like *Desiré*, make use of Scottish localisations. The first, *Doon*,* opens with the claim that virtually all good harpists can play the tune of this well-known *lai*, to which the Bretons have given its name. From this and similar statements in other examples of the genre it has been supposed that the poems were composed to be sung and hawked round the courts on both sides of the Channel by bilingual Breton minstrels. Most, though not all, contain elements that seem to derive from Celtic tales of the supernatural, as we saw with *Desiré*. The case of *Doon* is less clear-cut, and we would certainly be rash to assume that its French or possibly Anglo-Norman author found his matter on Scottish soil.

In the north near Edinburgh there lived a beautiful and courtly maiden. She was heiress to the whole region and lived in a castle known, after her and her company, as the Castle of Maidens. So proud was she on account of her wealth that she looked down on all the men of her land and had no wish to enter the servitude of marriage. So she made it known that she would take no husband unless he could travel

---

* In *Les Lais anonymes*, ed. Tobin, pp. 319–33.

to her from Southampton in a single day. Some attempted this feat, and a few succeeded but arrived exhausted. These were then shown to a splendid but perilous bed where, during the night, they were put to death. Word of this reached a knight in Brittany named Doon, who owned a marvellous horse. Having travelled to Southampton and warned the haughty maiden of his coming, he achieved the journey to Edinburgh one Saturday. Like his predecessors, he was received there with much honour; but once in the room with the perilous bed, he remained awake and was found alive and well in the morning. However, when he called on the maiden to make good her pledge, she refused unless he could, on his horse, outstrip a flying swan for a whole day. In this too he was successful and duly received the lady's hand and the lordship of her domain. The wedding celebrations lasted for three days, at the end of which Doon abandoned his grieving wife to return to Brittany, having predicted the birth of a son, whom she should send to be raised by the king of France. So it was; and, when of age, the boy was knighted by the king. By chance, at a tournament at the Mont-Saint-Michel he fought an incognito combat with Doon, whom he unhorsed. Mutual recognition followed; and the *lai* ends with Doon being taken by his son back through England to his still loving wife and all three spending the rest of their lives in great honour.

It is possible that some folktale featuring a supernatural horse lies at the root of this tale, in which the poet takes the opportunity of explaining the name 'Castle of Maidens' (Edinburgh is also given its alternative name of 'Daneborc'). It is more doubtful, though, than in the case of *Desiré* that it was taken from local lore. Edinburgh may have been selected simply for its remoteness from Southampton, given the choice of a location in Britain. Perhaps the Scots' reputation for chivalry played some part; but in general it would appear to be another example of Scotland providing an exotic scenario for a tale of the supernatural.

King Haakon IV of Norway, from whom William the Lion's grandson Alexander III was to wrest the Western Isles and who died in Orkney, was a man of literary interests; and about the middle of the thirteenth century he had a collection of French *lais*, including *Desiré* and *Doon*, translated into Old Norse. One of them, *Gurun*, has survived only in the Norse version;* but its French original probably circulated in William the Lion's day. It is, however, of particular interest for us in that a

* Translated in *Les Lais anonymes*, ed. Tobin, pp.365–70.

substantial part of it appears to relate to historical events in the north of Scotland in which William may well have taken part.

Gurun was of high parentage, his father being king of Brittany and his mother sister to the Scottish king, into whose service he was sent when he came of age. He was much favoured by that monarch, who knighted him and then made him a count. At the Scottish court, Gurun fell secretly in love with the queen's niece. Much later he was able through intermediaries to arrange a rendezvous with the girl, with the result that she agreed to take him as her lover. At that time a great army of rebels assembled in the north of Moray and swept through the king's lands, killing many of his men and carrying off their womenfolk. Summoning all his troops and allies, the king launched a series of raids against them in the forested countryside. On one occasion his nephew Gurun, bearing a silken sleeve given him as a favour by his mistress, opened the assault by jousting with the king of Ireland's son. Although he toppled his opponent from his horse, another of the rebel knights thrust at him with his lance just at the moment when one of their archers let fly an arrow that struck home below his shoulder. Wounded as he was, Gurun cut off the knight's head before retreating to his own company. On being told of his nephew's plight, the king was much distressed and threw his whole army against his enemies, slaying over three hundred and capturing even more. But when the rebels turned to flight, he did not pursue them for fear of having his troops ambushed in the forests. He then put Gurun in the hands of an expert doctor, who soon healed his wound. When the news of her lover's misfortune reached the king's niece, she was beside herself with grief. All, however, ended happily with first an elopement and then full royal approval.

Gurun is one of the few *lais* without any supernatural dimension: instead, it is strongly marked by historical reality. If we redesignate the rulers of Brittany count and countess instead of king and queen, we immediately recognise the latter, the king of Scotland's sister, as being the double of Margaret, sister of King William, who married Duke Conan of Brittany in 1160. Pursuing the equation, we see the Scottish monarch as William himself. Conan and Margaret were blessed with no male heir; but their daughter Constance became the wife of Geoffrey Plantagenet, who thereby inherited Brittany. Their son, the ill-fated Arthur, was thus King William's great-nephew, whereas Gurun in the *lai* has no direct counterpart in history.

We already suspect that the original poet had some knowledge of

Scottish affairs; and this would appear to be confirmed by the central episode treating the rebellion in Moray. That region, as we know, caused William a good deal of trouble; and it was not until two years before his death that it was finally pacified. That was on the occasion of the rebellion led by Guthred who, we note, had crossed from Ireland to launch his campaign. This could have been what prompted the poet to have Gurun joust with the king of Ireland's son; but although the latter was unhorsed, it was his companion who literally lost his head, whereas the real revolt ended with the decapitation of Guthred. Remembering that this took place in the presence of the newly knighted Alexander, we may be tempted to see that prince lurking behind the features of the fictional Prince Gurun, with the Scottish king's fictional nephew playing the part, much dramatised, of his actual son. If so, the *lai* could not have been composed long before William's death. But there is another possibility.

In 1187 the king had gathered his barons and marched with a great army to Inverness, intending to put an end to the depredations in Moray of Donald MacWilliam. While he himself hung back and little effective action was taken by his leading vassals, Roland of Galloway ran Donald to earth and returned bearing his head in triumph to the king. That year of 1187 also saw, as it happens, the birth of Arthur of Brittany. The *Gurun*-poet could have had in mind either of these expeditions by William to deal with insurrections in Moray. If in portraying his hero he gave any thought to the chivalric activities of young Arthur of Brittany, then the earlier events would have been a more likely source of inspiration, since Arthur was dead by 1203. Is it even possible that in his *lai* he was wishing to promote the image of William's great-nephew in the context of his claim to the English throne, favoured in Scottish circles? That, no doubt, would be carrying conjecture too far.

Whatever the precise circumstances of the composition of *Gurun* and the inspiration behind it, it does mark a significant development in the representation of Scotland in courtly literature. In the other pre-*Fergus* works we have looked at, the Scottish setting, while providing a backdrop to the action, serves also to transport us from the everyday world into a remote land where supernatural events are a matter of course. *Gurun*, on the other hand, antici-pates the new realism of a Guillaume le Clerc. Placing a typical courtly love affair within a historical context, the unknown poet contrives to hint at more mundane problems with which the real

King of the Scots had to grapple. And that king was William the Lion.

Let us now consider a romance of a different type. This is *Guillaume d'Angleterre* by a certain Chrétien,* who is in all probability not to be identified with his namesake from Troyes, although they do appear to have been contemporaries. In the poem the supernatural again plays a crucial role, but not in association with those magic springs or fairy mistresses that found their way into Arthurian romance from ancient Celtic lore. Here it takes the form of destiny as decreed by the Christian God. Medieval man was fascinated by the marvellous, being surrounded by so much that could not be explained by such limited science as he possessed. Though thought of by us as superstitious, he placed great reliance on what he considered to be firm authority as handed down by the writers of past ages or even in time-honoured oral tradition. Free, if he chose, to remain sceptical about some of the wonders of the Celtic or ancient worlds, he was committed to an acceptance of the miracles vouched for by the Scriptures and by the Fathers of the Church and was predisposed to credit the marvels related in many a saint's life or other pious legend. The twelfth century abounded in such legends; and for the poets of the time it was an act of piety to propagate them in their verse.

One such tale was Benedeit's *Voyage of Saint Brendan*, mentioned in an earlier chapter. There Celtic myth and Christian legend are closely intertwined, and the story may even carry traces of seafarers' accounts of real islands seen in the north and west. It is said on doubtful authority that as well as his likely visit to Iona, Saint Brendan's own travels ranged from Brittany to Orkney and the Shetlands. The story of Saint Kentigern, no stay-at-home himself although principally associated with Scotland and Glasgow, similarly contained a blend of pious and profane that set the popular imagination running. Another moral tale, this time with its origins in the East, passed through Latin to an eager public in western Christendom. Known as the Placidus-Eustachius legend, it relates the miraculous conversion from paganism of the future Saint Eustace, the separation of his family and their chance reunion. The basic theme of family dispersal and reunion is also found in the early legend of

---

* *Guillaume d'Angleterre*, ed. A.J. Holden, who discusses the question of authorship. Although still sometimes ascribed to Chrétien de Troyes, its subject matter, style and probable circumstances of composition make his authorship most unlikely.

Apollonius of Tyre; and from one or other of its forms Chrétien derived his pious story of the unhistorical King William of England. He tells us, in fact, that the true account can be found in the abbey of Bury St Edmunds and that he heard it from a friend, Roger.

King William lived in Bristol with his queen Graciene. They remained childless for six years; but in the seventh, to their joy, they found that Graciene was pregnant. On three successive nights, at the hour of matins, the king heard a great thunderclap, and his room was filled with a dazzling radiance, whilst a voice commanded him in God's name to flee into exile. After the third bidding, and having distributed all his wealth to the needy, he left the castle at dead of night, accompanied by his faithful queen and without the knowledge of his subjects. With his sword girt and Graciene at his side he made for the depths of the forest. There they fended for themselves as best they could until one day they arrived at the coast and took refuge in the fissure of a rock, where Graciene gave birth to twin boys. Tormented by hunger, she was tempted to eat one of them; but the horrified William was about to cut for her a slice from his own thigh when she repented and asked him instead to see if he could find food in the neighbourhood.

In a nearby port he comes across merchants loading their goods into a ship. Disbelieving his story of a starving wife and infants, they follow him to see for themselves. Graciene's beauty convinces them that this rough beggar must have abducted her; and despite her protestations and William's resistance, they carry her off to their ship and set sail. A purse containing five gold besants which they had flung as a sop to her husband is left hanging on a tree. The distraught William thinks he must find a ship to take him and his sons away from England, where his subjects will be searching for him.

He takes one of the babes to a vessel he finds by the shore, then returns to the rock for the other, just in time to see a wolf retreating with the infant in its mouth. There is nothing he can do; so he slumps by the rock and falls asleep. The wolf, meanwhile, is forced by a party of merchants to drop its prey. One of them decides to adopt this handsome child; and they return to their ship where, to their amazement, they find his twin. Another of the merchants vows that he will bring up this second boy as his own son. Without more ado they put to sea.

On waking and finding both his sons gone, William puts his trust in God, then goes to recover the purse; but an eagle snatches even that from his grasp. This must, he thinks, be a punishment for his past covetousness. Wandering aimlessly, he encounters another party of merchants; and they, after a hostile reception, agree to give him passage in their ship. He sails with them to Galloway, where he is taken into service under the name of Gui by an honest bourgeois, whose trust he soon wins.

In the meantime the queen has been transported to 'Sollin', which the latest editor takes to be Sutherland, although it is later represented as a stronghold (other scholars have opted for the less appropriate Stirling). There Guiolaïs, the elderly lord of the region, takes her into his home and, on the death of his wife, begs her to marry him. Graciene demurs and appeals for a year's respite, which is granted. Her pretext is that she has led a dissolute life, for which she wishes to atone. The betrothal is nevertheless announced and celebrated, with all Guiolaïs' subjects pledging their fidelity to the much loved Graciene.

The poet turns to the fate of the infants. They were now in the hands of the merchants who, sailing, as we later learn, from the port of Yarmouth, headed north and finally made harbour in Caithness. There the twins were christened according to the circumstances of their discovery: the first was named Lovel ('young wolf') and his brother Marin. They grew to be fine and well-mannered boys and close companions, though unaware that they were brothers. When their adoptive fathers wanted to apprentice them to the furrier trade, however, the prospect did not appeal to them, and they decided to seek their own fortune. They were roughly equipped and mounted on horses by the merchants who had fostered them and who now also gave them the swaddling clothes in which they had been found; and so they entered the forest, accompanied by a lad to act as their servant. As they prepared to dine off a deer they had killed, they were discovered by a forester, who hauled them off before the king of Caithness to answer for their poaching of the royal game. But he was impressed by their noble appearance and kept them instead at his court, where he instructed them in the art of hunting.

King William, meanwhile, had earned the trust of the bourgeois in Galloway to the point where the good man launched him on a new career as a trader in furs and fine cloths. On one occasion he lent him his ship to carry a cargo to the fair at Bristol. There William finds that his young nephew is now king. In the town he sees a youth carrying a hunting horn which he recognises as once having belonged to him, and which he is happy to buy back. People begin to recognise him. He even meets the new king, who would gladly surrender the throne if this should prove to be his uncle. But William insists that he is only the merchant Gui of Galloway; and he hurriedly leaves Bristol.

Back at sea, he is driven northward by gales and eventually makes a landfall by the castle in Sutherland, of which Graciene is now mistress, the old lord having died. The custom there is that a heavy toll has to be paid: first the lord, then the lady, and after her the seneschal may select from the cargo the object, however precious, that most appeals to them. In the absence of the lord, Graciene is the first to choose. Her face is hidden by her wimple, so William does not recognise her. She, however, suspects the truth when she sees not only his face, but also the horn he has hung at the mast, and the ring on his finger, which had once belonged to her. It is the ring that she chooses as her toll. In return, she offers him and his companions hospitality at her castle.

By now their recognition is mutual; but nothing is said. Suddenly, some hounds come into the hall; and William, carried away by thoughts of his once favourite pastime, gives a loud hunting call. Amid the general amusement, Graciene puts her arms round his neck and asks the reason for his outburst; and when he says that he has not indulged for more than twenty-four years in the sport he loved the best, she declares that she will turn his daydream into reality. They take to the hunting-field; and there they abandon all pretence and tell each other of their adventures since their separation.

Then Graciene speaks of her present situation. For some time, she says, a neighbouring king has pressed her to marry him; but her refusal has led him to wage a bitter war against her. His lands lie on the other side of a river running through the woods where they are hunting; and she begs William not to cross it in pursuit of a fine stag that has been started. Having given his promise, William resumes the chase; but, carried away by the excitement of the hunt, he forgets her request. Beyond the river, he encounters two armed knights intent on his death or submission. Faced by their threats, he names himself as King William of England and recounts his whole story. When he tells how the eagle had flown off with his purse, a miracle occurs: the very purse falls among them from the sky, still with its gold besants. At this the knights, who are none other than Lovel and Marin, recognise him as their father and the fact that they are brothers. As evidence they produce their swaddling clothes, made of cloth William had torn from his own tunic. They and their lord the king of Caithness learn with consternation that the lady whose lands they have been harrying is none other than their own mother.

Next day Graciene, riding with her men to launch an attack on her neighbour, is met by her husband returning with his sons. She is overjoyed at their news; and together with the king of Caithness they go to her castle in Sutherland. With her husband's agreement, she makes over to her erstwhile enemy the title to her own land. Her sons' foster-fathers are sent for and richly recompensed for having cared for them. Then William returns with his whole family to his kingdom of England and resumes the crown restored to him by his nephew. To his court in London he summons the honest bourgeois of Galloway, who becomes his chief counsellor. His bounty extends even to the youth who had sold him the horn and is now made his chamberlain. As for Lovel and Marin, he makes them knights and arranges their marriage to the daughters of two powerful counts.

The lesson underlying this exemplary romance with its strong religious colouring is clear if unoriginal: divine Providence will ensure that essential virtue has its ultimate reward. We are shown as proof an extreme case: the humbling and dispersal of a royal family followed by its reunion after many years. For a courtly public the story would have the attraction of conveying a moral appropriate to their class through a series of lively adventures with a good dose of the supernatural and travels to outlandish parts. The source legend had a Mediterranean setting; but Chrétien chose to play out his drama in Britain. This, together with his claim, genuine or fictitious, that the original text of his version was to be found at Bury St Edmunds suggests that, though a Frenchman himself, he had an insular public in mind. So he provided for his characters itineraries which, allowing for the exaggerations inherent in the genre, were not totally impossible.

From Bristol the royal fugitives made their way across England to Yarmouth, where they were separated. Their journeys continued by sea, William's ending in Galloway, Graciene's in Sutherland and their sons' in Caithness. Subsequently William sailed to Bristol, after which his vessel, driven by gales, also made port in Sutherland. Reunited, the family travelled south to the royal court in London. Implausible as all this is, the voyages involved would have been recognised by an English public as at least feasible, given the vague timescale provided. The poet evidently had some notion of the geography of England and Scotland; so we are justified in looking further for the kind of realistic detail that could have come from first-hand observation.

Of the places he introduces Bristol must have pride of place. He shows it as a favoured royal residence with the castle near a port and a prosperous township noted for its important fair. This corresponds with reality. Henry II had himself been brought up there by his uncle Robert of Gloucester, and he granted the town its first charter in 1171. Yarmouth was also well known at this period as a thriving port which handled a good deal of commerce from Scotland (especially Berwick) as well as from other parts of Europe. However, such further realism as we find in the romance appears in its descriptions of the trade and life of merchants and seafarers, good-hearted men for the most part, but tight-fisted as they sought to make their livings in a hard world. There are scenes too of life in the courts and on the hunting-field; but it is these more humble folk who make the strongest impact and are duly rewarded for their efforts by the poet. Yet authentic as much of his detail appears, there is little other than the geography that demands a localisation north of the Channel. So we are left with an impression, but no more, that Chrétien had at least visited England and had some acquaintance with the country south of a line from the Bristol Channel to the Wash.

This has encouraged scholars to think of him as working under English patronage, despite the fact that there is no trace of Anglo-Norman in his language and the only surviving manuscripts of his romance were both copied in France. On the basis of the name Lovel given to one of the king's twin sons some have been bold enough to label *Guillaume d'Angleterre* as an early example of the 'ancestral romance', composed in honour of one or other branch of the Lovel family, who had come to England hard on the heels of the Conqueror. Despite the most recent editor's opinion that the identity of the names is mere coincidence, that of the prince being adequately explained in the story by his seizure by a wolf, the patronage theory cannot be dismissed out of hand: such name-play was not uncommon among medieval writers.

There was one Lovel family, whose name was to be perpetuated in Minster Lovell in Oxfordshire, who had once had some connection with Bury St Edmunds, where Chrétien tells us the source story was to be found. More promising, however, as regards likely patronage is the branch which had become established in Somerset, at Castle Cary some thirty miles south of Bristol. By the time William the Lion was on the Scottish throne they had acquired by inheritance the Roxburghshire barony of Hawick; and they maintained both estates into the fourteenth century. Patronage of Chrétien by these Lovels would provide a neat explanation (some might say too neat) of his coupling of Bristol, in Somerset, with Scotland when he decided to reorientate the original legend.

Let us then suppose that Chrétien was composing at the behest of the Somerset Lovels, or at least had them in mind as a likely audience (he, like Guillaume le Clerc, drops no hint that he is writing under patronage). This could account for the generally favourable impression he gives of Scotland, or rather of the outlying regions where his action unfolds. Both Caithness and Sutherland are shown as ruled by courtly and well-meaning figures; and even Galloway, despite its unsavoury reputation, is the home of a god-fearing and magnanimous merchant. If these fringe areas are such civilised places, offering ready hospitality to the royal refugees from England, then surely the kingdom as a whole must share their admirable qualities. There would be nothing here to offend the Lovels, who held a lordship in the heart of that kingdom.

Perhaps we may venture one further thought. Chrétien assigned the leading role in his romance to a monarch, William of England, who appears to be entirely fictitious: he certainly seems to have nothing in common with the two Williams who had earlier occupied the English throne. Why, then, did he so name him? His supposed patrons owed a double allegiance: firstly to the king of England for their lands in Somerset, but also to another king in the north, of whom Chrétien knew only what he could glean from the circles in which he moved. But it was commonly agreed that, whatever his faults, this monarch was a man of genuine piety and was moreover (since 1186) the husband of a similarly pious queen. How fitting it would be if, in choosing the name of his leading player, the poet should have had in mind a historical King William, not though the Conqueror or his son, but William, king of the Scots.

Whatever the circumstances of its composition, *Guillaume d'Angleterre* seems to show that by the end of the twelfth century Scotland was enjoying beyond its frontiers a reputation for civilised living at least on a par with that on Plantagenet soil; and even the more lowly members of its society were worthy of high positions at the English court. The last romance we shall consider was apparently written in north-eastern France perhaps half a century later and has some surprises in store for us. It dates, then, from a time when not William the Lion but his son Alexander II, or just possibly Alexander III, was on the Scottish throne. Yet it bears witness to his legacy of a stable, civilised and prosperous kingdom and may, moreover, add a gloss or two to aspects of his family history. Read in this way it could be taken as a retrospective tribute to his achievements and even, as we shall see, to those of his brother Earl David as it sketches for its Continental public a picture of Scotland that would not be out of place in a modern tourist brochure.

The romance in question is *La Manekine*,* and its author names himself as Philippe de Rémi, saying that this is his first venture into verse. It is a long and involved story, full of pious sentiment and demonstrating how God may work miracles for those who apply themselves to a life of Christian devotion. Like *Guillaume d'Angleterre*, it has been tailored from old cloth, some perhaps of Scottish provenance; but we shall leave the discussion of sources until later. As for the poet himself, he has long been accepted as a member of the well-documented Beaumanoir family from Rémi, a village near Compiègne in the Beauvaisis. He was originally identified with Philippe, lord of Beaumanoir and one of the most celebrated of medieval French jurists; but although this remains the most common opinion, a case has more recently been made for the work's attribution to his father, also Philippe and known for his legal expertise. If *La Manekine* was by the elder Philippe, it would date from the 1230s or 1240s, not the 1270s as earlier proposed. We shall return to this question; but first let me summarise the plot of the romance with especial emphasis on the Scottish scenes.

There was once a king of Hungary, whose marriage to the daughter of the king of Armenia remained childless for ten years. Then they had their only child, a wise and beautiful girl named Joïe. Before the queen's premature death, she made her husband promise that should he marry again in order to have a male heir, he would only take a wife who was her equal in every respect. Joïe grew up to resemble her mother in her pious charity as well as physical appearance. Then the barons called on the king to remarry and have a son since, for the honour of the realm, they would not wish to be ruled by a woman after his death. Knowing of his pledge, they scoured the earth for a model bride, but without success. A duke then proposed that the king should marry Joïe, his daughter, and they would take the sin upon themselves. Overcoming his scruples and driven by an incestuous passion, the king

---

* Ed. Hermann Suchier in *Œuvres poétiques de Philippe de Remi, Sire de Beaumanoir*, Vol. I. Recent studies of *La Manekine* are by Marie-Madeleine Castellani, *Du Conte populaire à l'exemplum* ... and M. Shepherd, *Tradition and Re-Creation* ...

consented and told Joïe of his decision. Horrified, the princess rushed
to find a kitchen knife and, cutting off her right hand, flung it into the
river below the castle, where it was swallowed by a passing sturgeon.
She then reminded her father that any wife of his should be sound
of limb, at which he flew into a violent rage. He had her flung into
a dungeon with orders that she be burnt on a pyre two days later. His
seneschal did indeed have a pyre built and lit; and the news spread
that Joïe had perished. But, overcome by pity, the good man had in
fact taken her to the sea, where she was cast adrift in a rudderless boat
with a week's provisions. Praying devoutly to God and the Virgin, she
began her voyage, which was to last eight days.

On the ninth she spies land; it is Scotland. By the shore the townsfolk
of Berwick are celebrating the first Sunday of Lent with dancing and
games. The provost, who is present to make sure they keep the peace,
glances out to sea and notices the crewless boat approaching. When it
arrives at the shore and only Joïe is found aboard, he asks her name
and where she has come from. The princess requests his help, but will
say no more. He does not press her, but declares she shall be taken
to his lord the king, a handsome youth whose mother will take good
care of her. When he conducts her to his own house in the town she
is no more forthcoming. That night she is well looked after by his two
daughters; then at daybreak he mounts her on a palfrey and escorts her
straight to Dundee, where the king is holding court with his mother
and many fair ladies-in-waiting.

The king is at table with twenty-three of his barons when the provost
enters with Joïe and presents her to him, explaining her arrival and
suggesting she remain with the dowager queen. The good-natured king
enquires courteously about her circumstances, but elicits no response
other than tears. Sensitive to her grief, he sends her to be cared for
by his mother. Next day the provost returns to Berwick, leaving the
princess at court, where she inspires great affection. Yet still she will
not disclose so much as her name. Finding this an inconvenience, the
king himself decides that she shall be known as 'la Manekine', which
means 'the handless one'. She soon regains her full beauty, and for her
blameless charm is loved by all, not least the young king.

Whenever he is in Dundee, he seeks Joïe's company to enjoy a game
of chess, at which she is unbeatable, or of backgammon or some other
pastime. After a long excursus on the nature of love we learn that they
have both come to feel its pangs, though without admitting or even at

first realising it. For a year they suffer sleepless nights as they wrestle
with their feelings. He thinks of marriage but fears the disapproval of
his subjects; she puts his behaviour down to courtly politeness and in
any case would never become his mistress and risk the resentment of
his mother. Eventually the dowager queen, who is now revealed as a
wicked and treacherous woman, realises the situation and sends for
Joïe. She forbids her to keep company with her son in future, on pain
of burning. Having protested her innocence, Joïe resolves to tell the
king of his mother's threat.

The young man's reaction is an ardent declaration of his love,
followed by the offer to marry her and make her queen of Scotland
and of Ireland and Cornwall too. Diffidently she accepts his proposal.
The king tells her that his barons had often advised him to send to
England for one of the royal princesses; but now he will have no other
than her. Hand in hand they proceed to the great hall, where the ladies
present fear the queen mother's reaction. She, however, is sleeping in
her chamber and is not informed. Without more ado the king sends for
his chaplain, who conducts a private wedding ceremony with none but
the royal household present. Only then is the dowager queen informed
and invited to the marriage feast. Her fury and refusal to attend are
predictable.

The marriage festivities and coronation are arranged for Whitsun,
which is a fortnight away; and the king sends a summons throughout
Scotland, Ireland and Cornwall, commanding all his knights and their
ladies to attend. Every day, at Joïe's insistence, he pleads with his
mother to be reconciled with her, but in vain. So he goes ahead with
his preparations for the great feast. Tents are erected in the broad
meadowland beside the river; and there the great company assembles.
The poet now indulges in a conventional description of springtime,
with its nightingales, green flowery fields, running streams, fruit in the
orchards, and roses that were invoked by lovers and made into chaplets
by the ladies. There the country lads and lasses hurried for the dancing,
interrupted only when they went to the woods to collect lilies of the
valley for their garlands. On the eve of the feast the court gathered in
Dundee; and many a bullock, piglet and bear were butchered. All the
pavilions thronged with the nobility of the realm, dukes, counts and
knights with their ladies. In the evening after supper they went out into
the meadow, which was lit as bright as day with great torches. There
was no lack of wine and meat for one and all. There they revelled and

danced the night away until, at the approach of dawn, they rested a little to be fresh for the morning.

The new queen rose early to don her coronation robes which shone with gold and jewels, all described in detail. The gold crown she wore was less lustrous than her fair hair. With the king she attended the service before returning for the sumptuous banquet to the pavilions whose floors were strewn with lilies of the valley, violets and many other small flowers. After the trumpeters had sounded the call, the royal couple took their seats, followed by the rest of the nobility, segregated from the commoners. When they had all eaten their fill of rich meats, fish and fowl, the minstrels arrived, performing on a variety of instruments including harps and bagpipes before the dancing resumed with the silk-clad ladies adding their singing to the general gaiety.

The wicked dowager queen had no part in all of this: consumed with grief, she had left for a city named Perth, seven leagues (about twenty miles) away. Meanwhile, in Dundee the celebrations continued, with the participants only pausing to change their clothes from time to time. Despite her missing hand, Joïe was the centre of attention and admired by all. The revelries went on for three full days before the guests departed, laden with rich gifts by the royal couple, who remained behind to enjoy their love, with nothing but the dowager's opposition to cloud their happiness. Again the king begged her to accept Joïe as queen, saying that if she refused she must receive York as her dower and withdraw there. She made her choice and left at once for York.

About the following Easter, Joïe, whose piety and generosity had won the hearts of all her subjects, became pregnant. The king was overjoyed and decided the time had come for him to go to France and establish his chivalric reputation by fighting in tournaments. Joïe, though still fearing what the dowager might do, reluctantly agreed. So he had his ship made ready and provisioned at Berwick; and they rode there together to bid their tearful farewells. The king ordered his seneschal and two of his knights to look after the queen and protect her from his mother, and also to let him have news of the birth should he not have returned from France. He then set sail, richly supplied with money and equipment; and after a night at sea he landed at Damme, near Bruges. Travelling by way of Ghent, where he met the count of Flanders, Lille and Royes, he arrived at Ressons in the Beauvaisis, where a tournament had been arranged. There he jousted with the count of Flanders to great acclaim, bearing heraldic arms of gold alone, whereas his normal ones showed three gold lions rampant bordered with sable. From Ressons he went to further tournaments at Épernay and other places in France.

Having spent three days in Berwick, Joïe had returned to Dundee, 'for that was her favourite residence in Scotland'. She was escorted there by the good provost of Berwick together with the seneschal and two knights. And it was in Dundee that, while sadly missing her absent husband, she gave birth to a handsome son, John. The seneschal wrote the glad news in a letter, which he sealed and gave to a messenger to take to the king in France. Two days' journey took the bearer to York, where he lodged at the dowager's residence. Learning of his mission, she plied him with strong wine and then, as he lay in a drunken stupor, replaced the letter with another that told of the birth of a shaggy, four-footed monster.

This was the message that reached the king at Creil, in Flanders. He broke the seal and looked at the contents, for in his youth he had been taught to read both French and Latin as well as to write. Horrified, he asked his companions' advice. They persuaded him that, as Lent was now approaching, he should attend those tournaments he had undertaken and then return, having sent word that the infant was to be cared for until his arrival. He himself wrote a letter to his seneschal and the two knights to that effect; and entrusted it to the original messenger. As before, the man broke his journey at York; and as before the dowager substituted a forged letter for the original. This one carried the order that Joïe and her offspring were to be burnt without delay.

The messenger made his way back to Dundee, where the seneschal and knights were dismayed by the letter's contents; but they agreed that the king's orders must be obeyed. The news quickly spread throughout the kingdom, to the horror of one and all; but at first it was kept from the queen. Anxious to have word of her husband, she asked the seneschal if he had heard anything, at which the honest man burst into tears and told her that the king's love had turned to hate and that she was to be burnt within three days. At this she fell in a swoon; then, when she came round, she followed a bitter lament with the plea that the child at least should be spared. Moved to pity, the seneschal conferred again with the knights; and they resolved to take Joïe and the babe and set them adrift on the sea, having burnt two effigies in their place.

A good craftsman was ordered to make two life-like images under a vow of secrecy; then the three guardians left for Berwick with the queen and her son. After riding for two days, they arrived there at night and, having explained matters to the sympathetic provost, placed Joïe and the infant in the very boat in which she had first arrived at the port. Commending them to the Virgin, they then set them adrift. Turning two days' journey into one, they made their way back to Dundee. A pyre was built beside the castle and, amid universal grief, the mock burning was carried out before the local people who, suspecting no deception, were loud in their grief. The entire Scottish people laid the blame for the tragedy on their king. But when the news reached the dowager queen, she was delighted.

At Lent the king leaves Creil, north of Paris, with his friend the count of Flanders and makes his way to Damme, where he embarks. His seneschal has meanwhile arrived with a number of barons at Berwick to await his arrival; and there he arrives three days later. The lords ride to the shore to meet him. His first concern is for Joïe; but when he asks about her and the whole sorry story comes out, he resolves to search for her over land and sea. Having his suspicion that this was his mother's doing confirmed by the messenger, he sends for masons and orders the building of a tower on a cliff by the sea, remote from any town. It is to be round, with walls fifteen feet thick or more and no entry at ground level but just one high window; and it must be completed in thirty days. In it, despite a sense of pity, he has his mother imprisoned after she has been brought from York by the seneschal; and there she was to spend the rest of her days living on bread and water. Leaving the dowager to her grim fate, the king prepares to leave on his quest in the company of the seneschal and the others who had cast Joïe adrift.

For twelve days her craft carried her over the sea until it entered a river near Rome and was boarded by fisherman. They sold its occupants to a widowed senator of the city; and he and his daughters cared for them for seven years, in the course of which Joïe was never seen to smile. In Scotland the king had gone to Berwick with all his barons, whom he ordered to guard his people and his land during his absence. Then, having provisioned his ship, he put to sea with his seneschal and ten other knights. He scoured all known lands for seven years before arriving in Rome, where he decided to spend Easter. His seneschal arranged for the travellers to be lodged with the senator, who told Joïe and his daughters that the king of Scotland and Ireland would be staying with them. This much alarmed the queen, who expected to be put to death should her husband see her. It happened, however, that the king noticed their son John playing with the ring he had given Joïe at her coronation. Full explanations and a joyful reunion were not long delayed.

The king of Hungary now returns to the scene. After seven years he has repented his treatment of his daughter and, having learned of her escape from her native land, has come to Rome to seek absolution from Pope Urban. In St Peter's, Joïe overhears her father's confession and makes herself known to him. The general rejoicing reaches its climax when two clerks, replenishing the fonts at St Peter's, find in the fountain there Joïe's missing hand. They take it to the pope, who miraculously restores it to its owner. A divine voice tells them to go to the fountain, where they discover the great sturgeon in which it had remained intact for so long. The Easter celebrations are concluded in grand style.

The kings and their companies leave together for Hungary. The barons of that country do homage to the king of Scotland, and Joïe inherits Armenia from her mother. The daughters of the hospitable senator, who had made the journey with them, are married to the seneschals of Scotland and Hungary, after which a visit is made to Armenia, where homage is paid to the Scottish king. When he has spent six months in Hungary and six more in Armenia, he decides that, as another Easter approaches, the time has come for him to return with his wife and son to his own kingdom. So he sends the two seneschals to Berwick to announce his imminent arrival.

At Berwick the Scottish seneschal is recognised by the provost; and the happy news spreads quickly throughout the realm. By the time the king, Joïe and the young prince sail into Berwick bringing with them Joïe's father, all the magnates of Scotland, Ireland and Cornwall are there to greet them. Their reception much impresses the king of Hungary, who feels honoured that the lord of such a domain should have taken to wife his own daughter, and without being aware of her origins. For eight days they hold high festival in Berwick, after which the entire royal party rides through the kingdom, staying in each town in turn. Joïe asks for news of the dowager queen, whom she would gladly have restored to her position; but she is told that the source of their troubles had died the previous year.

Having concluded their royal progress, 'they came to live in Dundee; for that was Joïe's favourite residence in Scotland. So they often chose to stay there, but went elsewhere when they wished, since they had many residences'. In this way the loving couple spent many happy years as king and queen. God granted them five children, two daughters and three sons, with the girls eventually becoming queens themselves and the boys kings. After a life of piety, they came to a good end. With that assurance the poet draws his moral conclusion to the effect that we should never despair, so long as we put our trust in God.

This rather wordy poem raises for us a number of interesting and related questions. All the evidence points to its having been composed in the north-east French-speaking area, but whether by Philippe de Rémi the younger or by his father is unclear. It could therefore date from either half of the thirteenth century. If the pope, named as Urban, was Philippe's contemporary, he would have been Urban IV (1261–4); otherwise he could have been Urban III (1185–7), who had been involved with William the Lion in the St Andrews controversy; and even Urban II (1088–9) has been proposed. Then there is the question of the source of Philippe's knowledge of Scotland. He is credited with another romance, a courtly tale of a young Frenchman who entered the service of a count of Oxford and wooed and eventually won his daughter. It contains some apparent knowledge of the English scene, being mainly located in Oxford, London and Dover. So it is likely that Philippe had at some time crossed the Channel. Could he even have ventured beyond the Scottish border?

It may have been in England that he came across his source story, since what is probably its earliest known form is localised in Northumbria. The tale is included in the *Vita Offae Primi*, a Latin prose text purporting to record the life of the eighth-century King Offa and perhaps dating from the early 1200s.* Offa was hunting in a forest one day when he became separated from his companions. Hearing lamentations among the trees, he found they came from a beautiful maiden in royal apparel who, when questioned, told her story. Her father, a prince of York, had sought to commit incest with her; and when she refused, he ordered that she be taken into the wilderness, slain, and left for the wild beasts there. Her intended executioners, however, instead of killing her had simply left her alone to fend for herself. The king took her with him; and they passed the night with a hermit, who then led them back to the king's people, to some of whom the girl's welfare was entrusted.

---

* The relevant section of the *Vita Offae Primi*, formerly attributed to Matthew Paris, is printed on pp. 71–84 of *Originals and Analogues of some of Chaucer's Canterbury Tales*, ed. Furnivall, Brock & Clouston.

Several years later, the king's nobles advised him that it was time for him to marry. After some hesitation, he remembered the girl he had rescued from the forest; and as all those who knew her spoke highly and with affection of her virtues, he took her as his wife. They soon had a number of children, thus securing the future of his kingdom, which he continued to govern in peace. Britain was at that time divided between various kings, who were often at war with each other. One of them, the ruler of Northumbria, finding himself harassed by the Scots as well by some of his own subjects, appealed for help to Offa, promising to marry a daughter of his and then pay him homage for his lands.

A pact was concluded, and Offa headed north with a strong army of his knights. He quickly crushed the barbarous enemy and advanced into their own country. In the course of the expedition, he sent a despatch back home under royal seal. The messenger to whom he entrusted it travelled by way of York and lodged at the court of the prince whose daughter Offa had married. Learning of the messenger's mission, he had the despatch replaced with a letter telling that the expedition had suffered reverses sent by God on account of Offa's improper marriage to a dissolute and wicked woman. She was therefore to be taken to a wild place with her children; and there, with their hands and feet cut off, they were to be left to perish. Offa's magnates, despite their distress, felt obliged to obey; but though the children were dismembered, they spared the mother before abandoning her with the dead infants. A passing hermit heard her cries and came upon the tragic scene. He gathered the children's severed limbs; and they, as a result of his fervent prayers, were miraculously restored. He took them to his dwelling and took care of them to the best of his ability.

Offa, returning home in triumph, was distressed by his wife's absence, the reason for which was eventually disclosed to him. In order to relieve his resulting grief, he was persuaded to resume his favourite pastime of hunting. By chance his party came to the hermitage in the forest, where he told the holy man his story, only to learn that his family was in good health and in an adjacent room. The hermit declined a rich reward, asking only that Offa should found a monastery to the glory of God.

It seems safe to assume that this or something very similar was Philippe de Rémi's main source for *La Manekine*. It contains the essential events of the story: a king's marriage to the victim of a father's incestuous advances; their separation as the result of a malicious forgery perpetrated at York; the queen's exile with her offspring; a miraculous outcome involving the restoration of severed limbs by a holy man. Here, then, was a pseudo-historical moral tale of wonder in the hagiographic tradition, but without any apparent contemporary reference. Localised entirely in Britain, it contained only a brief reference to Scotland, which it portrayed as a barbarous and hostile country quickly subdued by an English king.

Although we cannot be sure, it is likely that Philippe came across this story on English soil. For some reason, and no doubt taking his cue from the brief account of Offa's Scottish expedition, he decided to make that country the scene of the main action. To do this, he substituted for Offa the unnamed ruler of Scotland and cut out all reference to England. He then gave the whole story a grandiose setting by painting it into a broad European canvas. Thus he had the deception perpetrated while the king was absent, not campaigning in Britain but doing the round of tournaments in Philippe's own land of France. The final miracle was to take place in Rome, the centre of Christendom; and the holy man who performed it with divine aid would be the pope himself. As for the heroine, she was made a native of the distant kingdom of Hungary, despite the implausibility of her drifting boat carrying her from there to the Scottish shore. Why then, one may ask, did Philippe choose Hungary as her starting point?

It would appear that his first decision was to focus the plot on Scotland and its king. To give it an authentic ring, he would then supply some local colour by incorporating a few topical ingredients. As he evidently had some knowledge of Scottish history as well as geography, though how he came by it we are left to guess, he was aware that reputedly the most pious and beloved of Scottish queens was Margaret, who, when he was writing, was on the point of being canonised if not already a saint. His choice of her as a model was even more appropriate because she came from the old Anglo-Saxon royal line; and she had been born in Hungary. It will be remembered that she had sought refuge in Scotland with her brother Edgar Atheling as well as her mother and sister. And it may be significant that according to Ailred of Rievaulx, who had spent some time in the household of Margaret's son David I, Edgar's intention had been to sail with the family party to Hungary, the land of his own birth; but they had been driven by a storm to Scotland. Philippe's account of Joïe's arrival in the latter kingdom would therefore appear to be patterned on that of the pious Margaret. And this justifies us in looking again at his romance with an eye to any other possible echoes of Scottish affairs, past or present.

We do not have far to search for a prototype for the young king of Scotland. William the Lion's son came to the throne as Alexander II when he was only sixteen, having been knighted by King John two years previously. In the romance the royal household had often pressed their lord to send to England for one of the royal princesses as a bride. King William had felt a similar urgency to arrange a suitable marriage for his son so that his line might be continued. Even before his birth the Scottish barons, like those of the fictional king of Hungary, had viewed with distaste the prospect of being ruled by a woman; and now that a male heir had appeared, it was vital that he should ensure the succession by taking a worthy wife. So as early perhaps as 1209, at Norham, William had broached with King John the possibility of Alexander's marriage to an English princess; and when in the following year John's daughter Joanna was born, she became William's target. To secure the match he seems to have pursued negotiations with the English monarch in which Queen Ermengarde played some part; and it is likely that an agreement was reached by the time of Alexander's knighting in 1212.

The marriage did in fact take place in 1221, after John's death but while Joanna was still a young girl. She herself died childless in 1238. So if, as seems very probable, Philippe de Rémi had Alexander in mind when he first introduced us to his own young Scottish king, Joanna would fit the part of the projected English bride. Although as such she was given no further role in the romance, we may well wonder if Philippe did not consciously use the first syllable of her name when he christened his heroine Joïe. Be that as it may, it is surely more than chance that his fictional situation matched history in having a young king under pressure from his household, including the dowager queen, to take as a bride an English princess.

Like the king in the story, Alexander still had little experience of active chivalry when he came to the throne. They would both, though, have received a sound schooling; and the former's proficiency in writing and in being able to read Latin as well as French was probably shared by Alexander. Philippe's account of how his king decided to complete his education in the chivalric sphere by leaving for a season of tourneying in France does not, however, correspond to Alexander's apprenticeship in arms, which took place on home territory. It does, on the other hand, forcibly remind us of King William's activities when, at the beginning of his reign, he followed Henry II to the Continent to establish his chivalric reputation and, according to Wyntoun, showed his prowess in tournaments and joustings. Henry in the meantime was courting the friendship of the count of Flanders, whilst in the romance the king enjoys the companionship of a count of that province. Moreover, the whole north-eastern region traversed by the fictional king had close links with Scotland during the twelfth and thirteenth centuries in both the commercial and the social spheres. It was, for instance, the homeland of the Balliol family as of Philippe himself; and Balliols are known to have held lands in Angus as well as Galloway.

In describing the jousting activities of the Scottish king Philippe adds the apparently gratuitous comment that his real armorial bearings were three lions rampant. Popular tradition has long associated the heraldic lion with all the Scottish kings, whilst the unsubstantiated claim has been made that it was King William's use of it that gave rise to his being styled 'the Lion'. In fact it is first found on a seal of Alexander II. There, however, we find only a single beast; and one wonders if Philippe could have been thinking of the three lions guardant of the English royal arms when he specified those of the king of Scotland.

It seems, nevertheless, reasonable to conclude that Philippe did have some knowledge of Scottish affairs and past history on which he was able to draw to create a plausible setting for his tale. Whether he acquired this during a visit to the country or gleaned it at second hand is another matter. The main evidence arguing for a personal visit is found in the relevant geography. In particular, there is nothing to fault in his siting of Dundee with its castle and riverside meadows or in his presentation of Berwick as a bustling harbour town; and, allowing for a little poetic licence, the impression he leaves of the distance between the two places does not strain our credulity. The one precise measurement he gives, namely the seven leagues or about twenty miles from Dundee to Perth, is surprisingly accurate.

The longer journeys described take us by well established routes. When the messenger is sent from Dundee to France, he travels overland to York, then takes ship at an unnamed port and disembarks at Gravelines, between Calais and Dunkirk; then for his return journey he makes a crossing from Damme, near Bruges. That is where the king himself disembarked after leaving Berwick and spending a night at sea and later took ship on his way back to Scotland. Philippe was not only acquainted with these much-travelled routes but also seems familiar with the whole business of sea travel as he details the preparation of the royal ship at Berwick, its provisioning and loading with equipment including horses and money to finance his expedition. More cursory is his description of the final royal progress through Scotland, with the party breaking its journey at the major, though unnamed, towns.

It is easy to believe that Philippe had himself once travelled to Scotland, perhaps as a page with some nobleman who had affairs to attend to in the kingdom. The evidence, though, is more scanty and less detailed than that we examined in *Fergus*, and so we cannot be certain. We would dearly like to know the reason for his special interest in Dundee. Could he perhaps have spent some time there in the days of its great patron Earl David, who literally put it on the map (it is one of the few places north of the Forth to appear in thirteenth-century examples)? Might he even have been present at some royal occasion there which left him with a favourable impression of Tayside hospitality? His account of the celebrations by the river was conceivably based on personal experience, although it certainly contains a good deal of conventional description. The attendant musicians plausibly include harpists and pipers; but on the other hand Philippe has graced the merrymaking peasants with French names common to their class. There are other social activities mentioned which he might also have observed for himself on Scottish soil: the popular festivities at Berwick on the first Sunday of Lent, and the private enjoyment at court of games of chess and backgammon. But again, these pastimes have nothing distinctively Scottish about them.

Where, then, has our discussion of *La Manekine* led us? It is only too easy to invent a set of circumstances that would explain the poet's sympathetic treatment of Scottish characters and locations. We could imagine a young Philippe de Rémi, in the early years of the thirteenth century, crossing with some noble party from his native land to Scotland, landing at Berwick, and proceeding to visit one of the royal courts held in Angus, perhaps during its residence in Dundee. Then when, much later, he turned his hand to telling for his fellow-Frenchmen the story of the handless queen, he drew on his distant memories of an enjoyable youthful experience. The presumption would be that this was the elder Philippe rather than his more famous son, the legist Philippe de Beaumanoir. Although the evidence we have collected might seem to favour such a hypothesis, it can only be advanced with extreme caution.

What we can say, and with some assurance, is that the poet, in order to give some credibility to a wildly implausible tale, situated its central action not in a Scotland of legend and fantasy, but in the Scotland of history, the real if here somewhat idealised kingdom as it had been shaped by William the Lion and his family. His vision was of a land of peace, prosperity and deep Christian values, a civilised kingdom respected and even admired in the furthest corners of Europe. We might say that, in a sense, he provides an outsider's retrospective view of a country which for him was still bathed in the afterglow of a golden age, when it had been presided over by a just and pious monarch and his equally devout queen.

Conclusion

Patrick Fraser Tytler, the Edinburgh historian, opened his multi-volumed work in the 1840s with the declaration: 'I have commenced the History of Scotland at the accession of Alexander the Third, because it is at this period that our national annals become particularly interesting to the general reader'. I hope I may have persuaded the friend I mentioned in my Foreword of the inadequacy not only of his own schooling in Scottish history but also of the view of it held by this Victorian scholar. Far from beginning with Bannockburn or even with Alexander III, the story of the kingdom was already rich with incident and, indeed, had passed through one of its most stirring and significant phases. By the time William the Lion left the scene, Scotland's reputation in the lands to the south was no longer of a wild and barbarous place beyond the fringe of the civilised world: it had secured its position within the European family of states and had come to be respected and even admired in some quarters as a realm where chivalry flourished and the Christian faith was fostered and which, far from being a stranger to the new courtly culture, itself played some part in extending it.

William, of course, had in no sense created the Scottish kingdom, which can be thought of as having existed in some form for over three hundred years before his accession. By his day we might think of it as a well-established family enterprise, brought under new management by Malcolm Canmore a century earlier and then put on a modern footing by his son David I. Yet external pressures apart, its ethnic diversity created tensions that called for careful handling: not only did its population contain three Celtic strands, namely the Picts, long reduced to a substratum, the languishing Britons of Strathclyde, and the more dominant Gaels, but there were also the Norse in the north and west, the English speakers by now firmly entrenched as far as the Highlands, and an increasing complement of Normans and French dominating the upper echelons of society.

From the time of Malcolm Canmore and his marriage to the saintly Margaret, English and Scottish affairs had become inextricably enmeshed. In this process other marriages had played their part: whereas Malcolm's wife came from the old Anglo-Saxon line, his sister's husband was the Conqueror's son Henry I, and his own son David I married the heiress to the earldom of Huntingdon; and William the Lion's mother was Ada de Warenne, who was related to both the Conqueror and the Capetian kings. One would like to believe the legend of a love-match between Malcolm and Margaret; but the fact remains that power politics played a greater role than amorous stirrings in such unions; and they were apt to produce territorial aspirations as well as royal progeny. Already the northern English counties were ripe for takeover in Scottish eyes, their strategic value being potentially greater than that of the earldom of Huntingdon.

So when William inherited the family business from his brother Malcolm IV it was a soundly based going concern. There were certain internal problems, it is true; but it enjoyed powerful if not altogether reliable connections, which seemed to hold out prospects for limited expansion. It had come to an important extent under French management organised on Continental lines and might have seemed poised to engage in multinational operations. William's first duty, however, was to consolidate the management structure of his kingdom; and this he did with considerable success, paying due attention to the religious institutions which were an integral part of the social fabric in its secular as well as spiritual aspects. His particular concern was to keep them in Scottish rather than English hands; and that too he achieved to the best of his ability.

Although there was an impulsive streak to his nature, he was on the whole wary of overseas commitments, as was shown in his attitude to the crusades. It was not that his piety was in doubt; but he preferred to put it to practical effect in providing for the religious foundations in his own country. The fall of Jerusalem in 1187 did not persuade him to raise forces for its recovery or even to respond positively to Henry II's request for a tithe to finance the crusade. Some Scots did obey the call, but on an individual basis; and although rather more made their way to the Holy Land after William's day, they never flocked there in large numbers.

If his reluctance to engage in overseas adventures could be put down to a native prudence, his obsession with the recovery of the northern English counties showed its limits. In 1174 he had put at risk the whole future of his kingdom by an expansionist gamble backed by unreliable associates and bad advice. This was his one serious misjudgment; and it took many years for his country and perhaps his own confidence to recover from the consequences. Nevertheless, he retained the loyalty of his principal barons, which is a token of the respect he enjoyed among his subjects; and he emerged from the experience a sadder but wiser and more mature man. Though he never gave up his ambition to regain the lost counties, he pursued it thereafter with more resignation than vigour, reserving the latter for the securing of his own border territories. In this way he made sure of leaving his kingdom on a sound footing for his son Alexander, independent and at peace. And so it was to remain, by and large, for the ensuing reigns of the two Alexanders. His own vision of a greater Scotland was, however, never to be realised.

We saw how one of his subjects, Guillaume le Clerc, waggishly encouraged us to cast William in the role of Scotland's King Arthur. The comparison may seem extravagant, yet it contains a grain of truth; and it is by no means impossible that the thought had occasionally crossed William's mind. We may surely give him the credit of aspiring to be, like his legendary counterpart, a model ruler: a 'lion of justice', as Fordun would have it, liberal in his dealings with his subjects and with Holy Church, staunch defender of his realm and jealous of its traditions. The courts of both monarchs were moreover centres of chivalry and civilised living, where the conduct of affairs of state did not exclude that of noble pastimes, and culture was held in high regard.

William had little in common with the all-conquering Arthur of Geoffrey of Monmouth's history; but it is in the romances that we find a closer parallel. For there the more usual picture we have of Arthur is of a worried man under constant threat from enemies within and without his realm and heavily reliant on the knights of his Round Table for defence and advice. Eventually he was brought low by treason, although tradition maintained that his destiny was to return to lead his people again in some future hour of need. More often than not he is depicted as a surprisingly passive figure, more so than William tended to be when the security of his kingdom was threatened. But the Scottish monarch, it seems, shared Arthur's attentiveness to the advice of his barons, whose loyalty appears never to have been seriously in doubt. We might think of his defeat and capture at Alnwick as corresponding to Arthur's demise on the legendary field of Camlann. But his return to his kingdom was not left as hopeful conjecture; for he was destined to die in his bed and not as a result of treason. And although his subjects were not buoyed by the hope of his future return, he had left a son to ensure the continuation of his dynasty.

A comparison of the two royal families reveals both similarities and differences, the latter being the more significant. The so-called Canmore dynasty, in contrast to the earlier Scottish lines, had maintained an admirable solidarity. King Arthur's family, leaving aside its legendary origins, had its internal problems. He had the unwavering support of Gawain, his renowned nephew and loyal counsellor, the flower of chivalry though prone to reckless philanderings. Mordred, his other nephew, was less prominent in the romances; but, working in the shadows, he made his inglorious mark as the agent of treason and seducer of Queen Guenevere. Arthur's wife, before she became the conscience-ridden victim of her infidelities, had performed her royal duties impeccably, dutiful towards her husband and sound in her advice as appropriate, admired and respected within the court and ready with hospitality for its visitors. As a widow, she sought consolation in religion.

For the historical king's family life we do not have the intimate details supplied by the romancers to flesh out their picture of Arthur. We know a good deal about his brother Earl David, enough to suggest a loyal relationship and David's value to him as his most eminent adviser. His queen Ermengarde, although sadly neglected in the records, seems also to have had some place in his counsels, especially perhaps towards the end of his life. Such marital infidelities as occurred were presumably on his part, not hers; but after his death she, like Guenevere, committed herself to religious works. It would be easy to imagine her similarly presiding over the domestic side of court life, promoting harmonious relationships and fostering an interest in cultural matters; but this is not the stuff of which chronicles are made, and any other evidence has long since vanished.

It may seem an idle exercise to look for these Arthurian parallels with the matter-of-fact career of the King of Scots. Yet it finds some justification in the apparent if partial equation made by that perceptive author of *Fergus* known to us as Guillaume le Clerc. That William himself may have found some inspiration in the stories of Arthur, as his Plantagenet neighbours certainly did, is more than likely. Chrétien de Troyes would have wished it so, for what better model, as he says in *Yvain*, can there be than 'Arthur, the good king of Britain, whose noble qualities teach us that we ourselves should be honourable and courtly'? Indeed, he 'was of such repute that he is spoken of near and far; and I agree with the people of Britain that his name will live on for ever. And through him are remembered those fine chosen knights who devoted all their efforts to honour'.* Yet this exemplary king, made more human through his frequent fallibility, was not merely a figure of myth for William's contemporaries. Shortly before his death, Henry II had initiated excavations at Glastonbury, the Avalon of legend; and there in 1191 the monks exhumed what they asserted were the bodies of Arthur and Guenevere. They also produced a sword which they claimed to be the king's famous weapon Excalibur; and this Richard I promptly put to diplomatic use when he presented it to his prospective ally Tancred of Sicily.

So King Arthur was still very much alive in people's minds during William's reign, and we can understand why Guillaume le Clerc, by a discreet play of associations, should make the flattering link between the two monarchs, real and fabled. But posterity did not take the poet's hint and, to its shame, has been all too slow in acknowledging its great debt to William the Lion for his many achievements. Had he lived in an earlier age when the growth of legend was less inhibited by the conscientious recorders of historical fact, he might well have come to enjoy a posthumous reputation as Scotland's very own King Arthur.

---

* Chrétien de Troyes, *Arthurian Romances*, tr. D.D.R. Owen, p. 281. For all his fine words, Chrétien then proceeds to show Arthur guilty of a social lapse which provokes the criticism of his courtiers.

The Perth Mirror-Case

In 1921 workmen were excavating the site for a new cinema in St John's Place, Perth, when about eight feet below ground level they unearthed by an old well a small pewter disc. Cut into it was a simple but enigmatic scene; and round its border was a message they could not decipher. Recognising the importance of their find, they handed it over to the city's museum, where it remains. Experts from the Victoria and Albert Museum were consulted and gave their opinion that it was probably French work of the early part of the thirteenth century; but for many years it attracted only sporadic attention. My own researches have convinced me of its significance in Scotland's cultural history of the period; and these I am pursuing under the expert guidance of Mark Hall of the Perth Museum and Art Gallery, while being largely responsible myself for such provisional conclusions as will be drawn.

Despite its modest size (barely two inches across), the disc, recently identified as a mirror-case, has much to tell us. It also poses many intriguing questions. Its maker, whoever he was, did not lack in skill and ingenuity. Within the border with its puzzling inscription he managed to portray at least four human figures, one on horseback, as well as a small animal below their feet. He grouped them on either side of what looks like a branching column. And, for our enlightenment, he provided three names: TRISTREM and ISOUDE beneath the figures and, above their heads, MARCU(I)S (I take the 'I' to be a casting flaw), so completing the celebrated love-triangle of legend. The spellings are characteristic of the forms found in Anglo-Norman; and some of the letters here and in the surrounding inscription, also in French, show insular features. While we are left to match the names to the figures as best we can, the maker was clearly intending to portray the characters more familiar to us as Tristan (or Tristram), his beloved Iseult, and King Mark, her jealous husband and Tristan's uncle.

Although of ultimately Celtic inspiration, with even Cornwall and Brittany adding some elements, the legend as we know it would have reached Scotland in one of the versions propagated by the writers of

French romance. The earliest surviving text is probably the substantial fragment by a poet called Thomas, who is believed to have composed it in England in about 1160.

The complete story told, with variations, how Tristan was sent to Ireland by his uncle Mark to fetch Iseult, the king's chosen bride, and bring her to his court at Tintagel. But on the ship taking them to Cornwall, they accidentally drank from a magic love potion that had been prepared for the bridal couple. Thus their destiny as lovers was sealed; and they pursued their illicit liaison through many furtive adventures before finally dying in each other's arms.

So runs the legend. But what part of it is portrayed on the Perth mirror-case? Previous suggestions have been flawed by the failure to take into account one important clue. The reason is that it lies not in what is in the scene as preserved, but what is missing from it. Above the name MARCUS at the top of the design and weakening both it and the whole object we see an irregular gap. Something must have been removed. But what? For an answer we have to turn to one of the best-known incidents in the legend, namely one of the lovers' secret trysts.

Tristan had enemies among his uncle's barons; and they got wind of clandestine nocturnal meetings he was having with Iseult at a fountain beneath a spreading tree. They reported this to Mark; and, reluctant as he was to believe their gossip, he was eventually persuaded to go to the spot and see for himself. Smuggled into the tree one night, he lay in wait in its branches. Sure enough, the lovers arrived independently at the fountain. But fortune was on their side; for in the moonlight they at once caught sight of the king's reflection in the water and were put on their guard. The conversation they struck up became all contrived innocence; and by the time they parted, Mark's suspicions had been allayed.

Ours, though, have been confirmed. That awkward gap above the king's name on the disc is just where he was depicted in medieval art. In fact, the scene of the 'tryst beneath the tree' was not only the most often reproduced but even the only one commonly used out of its narrative context. It is found decorating not just manuscripts but a variety of artefacts throughout Europe from Sicily to the British Isles. The Perth case, were it accurately datable, could be the earliest recorded example of the use of the scene in art and certainly has an important place in the whole of Tristan iconography. The original dating to the early thirteenth century has in fact been supported by an examination of the styles in dress and armour.

We have, then, identified the overall layout of the design as being based on the tryst episode. A comparison with other examples confirms that the craftsman has superimposed on the tree's trunk a stylised representation of the fountain with, at its foot, the basin or laver in which Mark's reflection was often depicted. The animal beneath it is the lovers' loyal hound, which was another standard feature. What, though, of the four human figures? Assuming Mark's disappearance from the tree and knowing that conventionally Iseult was placed to one side of the fountain and an unarmed Tristan to the other, two of the four would appear to be anonymous supernumeraries. In each of the known illustrations of the scene one finds variations from the norm; but the designer of our case, whether the craftsman himself or his model, has departed from it to a puzzling degree. There are, however, two small features that have guided me towards an explanation entirely to his credit: the first two figures from the left appear to be crowned, and the third is holding aloft what seems to be a goblet.

The most plausible interpretation would then be that the cloaked persons to the left are Queen Iseult with her husband King Mark, whilst between them and the tree stands Iseult's attendant Brangain, wearing a shorter dress and holding up the fateful love potion, which she had passed to the lovers in error. If so, the designer, having taken the tryst scene as his basic model, would have broken with tradition in order to widen the perspective from a single episode to the broad sweep of the whole legend. Reading the scene in symbolic terms, we now have the marriage (Iseult and Mark), the potion that was its undoing, the gallant Tristan (presented as the bold knight rather than the furtive lover), and at the base the lovers' loyal hound recalling their own fidelity. If this comes near the truth, whoever was responsible should be regarded not as a mere designer of fashionable trinkets, but as a true artist.

We turn to the border inscription with heightened expectations. Despite one or two dubious letters where the rim appears to have been at some stage broken and rejoined (probably when the present mirror fittings were added), the first and longest part offers little difficulty. In good thirteenth-century French it declares: '[Whoever] carries me will have no lack of joy.' There follow a few words and characters that may reinforce the fact, but await a satisfactory interpretation. What is clear is that this intriguing object was fashioned to serve as both a portable mirror and an amulet, a bringer of good fortune. More especially, its subject would seem to mark it out as a love-token.

Frustratingly, it still keeps half of its secrets from prying eyes. Having discovered something of its purpose and significance, we would dearly like to know its history. Was it, for instance, made in Perth or merely dumped there after its mutilation? It is tempting to see some lover feeling ill at ease with the sight of the spying cuckold and removing him before discarding the mirror itself. One of the Strathearn nobility, perhaps, whom we saw as practising something of a Tristan cult. On the other hand, there are some grounds for wondering whether or not this particular case ever left the workshop, owing to what we might call design problems.

In order to accommodate three figures to the left of the tree/fountain, the maker had needed to move this from its usual central position. That could have caused him difficulty with the spacing of the name MARCUS: one can, for instance, detect the 'ghost' of an original A above the goblet, as if changes had been made to the lettering on an original mould. Spotting this and other apparent defects, we might conjure up a situation in which this conscientious craftsman failed to produce for a patron an article he felt worthy of his skill; so he finally put it aside, having perhaps made use of it as an 'apprentice piece'. That would be a plausible reason for its being cast in nothing more precious than pewter.

If any of this speculation comes near the truth, the implication is that we are dealing with a local product. We know that Perth was well endowed with metal workers at this period, being a thriving trading centre and producing goods for export as well as home consumption. With its royal and ecclesiastical connections, its prosperity ensured the presence of a considerable number of French speakers, some resident, others passing through; so our mirror-case and others like it would find ready customers. I say 'and others like it' advisedly in view of two more recent discoveries.

Important in itself, the Perth artefact assumed an even greater significance when two more mirror-cases came to light. That in itself was not surprising, for these miniature accessories were produced and traded in vast quantities throughout Europe and as far afield as Egypt during the thirteenth and fourteenth centuries. What did both open up and complicate our field of research was the discovery that these further cases, one found at Billingsgate and the other in Regensburg, not only carry a Tristan motif, but are unmistakably derived from a Perth-type model.

Together they show how an original design can suffer progressive deterioration at the hands of second-rate imitators. Neither has retained the peripheral inscription; and in the Regensburg case even the names of the characters have been lost in any recognisable form. Some of the figures have been distorted; and there is no trace of the spying Mark, the space where we would hope to find him being filled with crude geometric shapes. Both workmen were not merely clumsy, but apparently lacking in any understanding of their subject.

Our provisional conclusion is therefore that the Perth case in its present state, if not the archetype, must at least represent a very early stage in the development of a sophisticated work of art. We must also assume that archetype to have presided over quite an extensive family of derivatives. Although we cannot be certain, there is a real possibility that the original craftsman was based in Perth and, directly or indirectly, inspired inferior versions that were circulated on the Continent as well as in England.

Seen in a broader perpective, these Tristan-orientated keepsakes illustrate how legends could be adapted to serve particular purposes in art; and they reveal something of the working methods and problems faced by the medieval craftsmen in their production. For the purposes of the present study, they provide further compelling evidence for a flourishing Franco-Scottish culture at the time of William the Lion and his successors.

Chronology

5th c	Scots establish the kingdom of Dalriada after the Roman withdrawal.
8th–9th c	Scandinavian invasions and settlements.
c.843–58	Kenneth MacAlpin is king of the Picts and Gaels.
1057	Accession to the Scottish throne of Malcolm III 'Canmore', whose first wife Ingibiorg probably died by 1069.
1059	Malcolm visits the English court.
1066	Accession of William I 'the Conqueror' to the English throne.
1068	Edgar Atheling takes refuge at the Scottish court, bringing with him his sister Margaret.
c.1069	Malcolm marries Margaret.
1072	Malcolm and William the Conqueror meet at Abernethy.
1080	After invading Northumberland, Malcolm submits to the English at Falkirk.
1091	Following a further abortive invasion of England, Malcolm swears homage to William II 'Rufus'.
1093	13 November: Malcolm is slain near Alnwick after again invading England.
	16 November: Queen Margaret dies.
1094–7	Donald 'Bane', Duncan and Edgar dispute the Scottish throne.
1097–1107	Edgar's reign.
c.1100	*The Song of Roland* is composed, probably by a Norman.
1107–24	Alexander I's reign.
c.1113	His brother David marries Maud de Senlis and acquires the earldom of Huntingdon.
1113	David founds Selkirk Abbey (Tironensian).
1116	He visits the abbey of Tiron.
1124	His accession as David I.
1128	Selkirk Abbey is transferred to Kelso.
	Dunfermline priory (Queen Margaret's Benedictine foundation) is raised to abbey status.
	Holyrood Abbey (Augustinian) is founded by David.
1135	Death of Henry I, who is succeeded by Stephen.
1136	Melrose Abbey (Cistercian) is founded by David.
	Geoffrey of Monmouth completes his *History of the Kings of Britain*.

1138	David's designs on Northumbria are thwarted at the Battle of the Standard.
1138–9	Augustinian canons are settled at Jedburgh.
1139	David's son Henry, earl of Northumbria, marries Ada de Warenne.
c.1141	David and his son Henry are deprived by Stephen of the earldom of Huntingdon.
1143 (?)	Henry's son, the future William the Lion, is born.
1144	An Augustinian priory is founded at St Andrews.
1149	David knights Henry Plantagenet at Carlisle.
1152	Dryburgh Abbey (Premonstratensian) is founded by Hugh de Moreville.
	Henry, earl of Northumbria, dies.
	David has Malcolm, Henry's eldest son, designated as his heir, and he presents William at Newcastle upon Tyne as earl of Northumberland.
1153	24 May: David dies at Carlisle and is succeeded by Malcolm IV.
1154	Henry II succeeds to the English throne.
	Somerled's rebellion.
1156–8	Somerled captures the Western Isles from the King of Man.
1157	July: Malcolm meets Henry II at Chester. He recovers Huntingdon but loses Northumbria, Cumberland and Westmorland.
1158	William is knighted by Henry at Carlisle (?).
1159	At Roxburgh Malcolm perhaps plans his departure for the Continent with William in support of Henry II.
	16 June: they cross the Channel to join Henry at Poitiers and proceed to Périgueux, where Malcolm is knighted by Henry. One tradition says Malcolm then knighted William.
	They participate in the abortive siege of Toulouse, then return with Henry to Normandy and probably attend his Christmas court at Falaise.
1160	Malcolm returns with William to Scotland and is besieged by rebel earls in Perth.
	Their sister Margaret marries Conan of Brittany.
1163	1 July: Malcolm, accompanied by William, pays homage to Henry II and/or the Young Henry at Woodstock. Their brother David remains as hostage in England.
1164	Malcolm founds Coupar Angus Abbey (Cistercian).
	Somerled is slain near Renfrew. The event is commemorated in a Latin poem by a Glasgow clerk.
1165	9 December: Malcolm dies at Jedburgh, probably in the presence of William, who attends his funeral at Dunfermline.

Christmas Eve: William is inaugurated king at Scone.

1166   March (?): he negotiates with Henry II at Windsor, then follows him to Normandy, where he may have participated in tournaments and been present at the siege of Fougères.

August or September: he meets Henry at Mont-Saint-Michel before returning to Scotland.

1167   William travels widely attending to his affairs in Scotland and England. On the Continent Henry II is in conflict with Louis VII.

1168   William is said to have offered Louis support against Henry.

1169   Henry and Louis reach an accord.

1170   5 April: on Henry's return to England, he holds a council at Windsor attended by William and his brother David.

31 May: David is knighted by Henry.

14 June: at Westminster Young Henry is crowned as king presumptive. William and David pledge him allegiance.

29 December: Becket is murdered at Canterbury.

1171–2 Back in Scotland, William's detailed movements are unknown.

1172   Becket is canonised.

1173   The Young King and his brothers rebel against Henry II and seek William's help in exchange for territories in northern England. William offers Henry his loyalty in exchange for Northumbria, but Henry refuses.

August: William musters his army and unsuccessfully besieges Wark, Alnwick and Newcastle upon Tyne, but takes Warkworth. He proceeds by way of Prudhoe to Carlisle, which he fails to capture before retreating to Roxburgh.

The English invade Lothian and burn Berwick. A winter truce is agreed.

1174   Earl David campaigns against Henry in England.

After Easter William again besieges Wark. His troops ravage Northumbria, but Wark does not fall, and he returns to Roxburgh.

May: Jocelyn, abbot of Melrose, is elected bishop of Glasgow (consecrated 1175).

June–July: William returns to Carlisle, which does not surrender, although he takes Appleby and Brough. Failing to seize Prudhoe, he marches on Alnwick.

13 July: William is captured at Alnwick and taken to Newcastle upon Tyne, then Richmond.

On Henry's return to England, David capitulates at Leicester but probably escapes to Scotland.

26 July (31 July, Howden): William is brought before Henry in Northampton, then taken as a captive to Falaise by way of Portsmouth and Caen.

August: revolt in Galloway by Uhtred and Gilbert, who then murders his brother.

30 September: the Young King and his brothers submit to Henry.

1 December: Treaty of Falaise (confirmed at Valognes 8 December).

11 December: William is released and leaves Normandy for Scotland.

1175   10 August: in York William and David swear allegiance to Henry II and the Young King. The terms of the Treaty of Falaise are confirmed, including the transfer of Roxburgh, Berwick and Edinburgh castles.

William leads an army into Galloway. Gilbert is pardoned.

1176   25 January: William is summoned with his leading bishops to Northampton to determine the allegiance of the Scottish church. The pope, Alexander III, despatches his legate to examine the question.

9 October: William escorts Gilbert to Henry's court at Feckenham (Worcestershire); Gilbert pays homage and makes amends for his fratricide.

1177   Saladin threatens the Christians in Palestine.

1 July: William is summoned to Henry's council in Winchester and probably accompanies him to Normandy for a brief period.

1 August: the papal legate meets the Scottish prelates at Holyrood.

1178   William probably spends Lent at Aberdeen.

Summer (?): he confers on his brother David the earldom of Lennox and other properties including Dundee.

Their mother Ada de Warenne dies.

William founds Arbroath Abbey (Tironensian) in honour of Saint Thomas Becket.

Summer: Richard, bishop of St Andrews, dies, and a long dispute over his succession ensues.

1179   William, with David, takes a large army into Ross and establishes strongholds at Redcastle and Dunskeath.

John 'the Scot' is elected bishop of St Andrews, but William appoints Hugh. John seeks papal support in Rome.

1 November: Louis VII has his son Philip crowned as his successor.

1180
Christmas: William attends Henry II's court at Nottingham.

30 March: with David, he holds a judicial court at Haddington to settle a dispute between Melrose abbey and his constable Richard de Moreville.

A papal legate arrives in Scotland and has John consecrated bishop at Holyrood. William banishes John, who takes refuge in Normandy.

September: Louis VII dies and is succeeded by Philip 'Augustus'.

1181
Spring: summoned by Henry, William travels with David to Normandy to confer on the St Andrews dispute. Henry's proposed compromise is rejected by the pope.

July: Henry confers at Gisors with Philip. William and the Young King are present.

Donald MacWilliam invades Scotland and seizes territory there.

26 July: William crosses with Henry from Cherbourg to Portsmouth, whence they make a pilgrimage to Saint Thomas' shrine at Canterbury.

August: William attends Henry's council at Nottingham.

As he returns to Scotland, he is confronted at Redden on Tweed by the bishop of Durham and the bishop-elect John. Having refused to accept John, he is excommunicated by Roger, the archbishop of York, and Scotland is placed under interdict. The deaths of the pope (30 August) and the archbishop (November) ease the situation.

1182
March: Scottish bishops persuade Pope Lucius III to retract the excommunication and interdict and review the election problem. Lucius sends William his Golden Rose and has legates go to Scotland for further discussions.

1183
Spring: on varying advice from his legates and cardinals, Lucius awards the St Andrews diocese to Hugh and Dunkeld to John.

11 June: the Young King dies.

William bestows his illegitimate daughter Isabel on Robert Bruce (de Brus).

1184
He bestows Ada, also illegitimate, on Patrick, earl of Dunbar.

Summer: he attends the English court in the hope of marrying Henry's granddaughter Matilda of Saxony; but papal assent is refused on grounds of consanguinity.

The Earl of Huntingdon dies.

William abandons an attempt to curb Gilbert's aggressions in Galloway.

Christmas: his brother David attends Henry's court at Windsor.

1185   January: Gilbert dies. Roland (Uhtred's son) then overruns much of Galloway, seizing the lands of Gilbert's son Duncan.

18 March (?): William and David are summoned to Henry's court at Clerkenwell. The earldom of Huntingdon is restored to William, who invests David with it.

William returns to Scotland, probably by way of Northamptonshire.

November: Pope Lucius III dies, and the St Andrews dispute is revived.

At about this time William Malveisin first appears in the records as king's clerk.

1186   25 May: William, with David, attends the court at Oxford, where Henry proposes his marriage to Ermengarde de Beaumont.

Early summer: William and David meet Henry at Carlisle to resolve the Galloway problem. Roland makes peace.

July: Pope Urban III intervenes in the St Andrews dispute. Hugh proves recalcitrant.

19 August: Henry's son Geoffrey, count of Brittany, is killed in France.

5 September: William's marriage to Ermengarde is celebrated at Woodstock. Edinburgh Castle is returned to become part of Ermengarde's dowry.

9 September: William is with Henry at Marlborough.

November: sixty rebels from the north are killed on a raid at Coupar Angus.

1187   March: William's clerk, Richard, is elected bishop of Moray and consecrated in St Andrews by Hugh.

March: a son, Arthur, is born to Constance of Brittany, Geoffrey's widow and William's niece.

July: William launches from Inverness a campaign against Donald MacWilliam, who is killed by troops under Roland of Galloway.

October: Jerusalem falls to Saladin. Prince Richard takes the cross, followed by Henry and Philip Augustus.

Pope Urban III dies. The Scottish prelates depose Hugh from the St Andrews see and excommunicate him.

1188   16 January: the new pope, Clement III, confirms Hugh's deposition and recommends the election of John.

February (?): Henry sends the bishop of Durham to seek payment of the 'Saladin tithe'. William meets him by the Tweed and demands in return the restoration of his castles. The negotiations prove abortive.

John, back in Scotland, resigns his claim to the St Andrews see and receives that of Dunkeld.

August: Hugh, pardoned by the pope, dies of the plague in Rome.

On the Continent Henry and Philip resume their hostilities.

1189   13 April: William presides in Perth over his cousin Roger's election to the St Andrews see.

6 July: having accepted terms from Philip, Henry dies at Chinon.

3 September: Earl David acts as sword-bearer at Richard's coronation in Westminster.

2 December: William pays homage to Richard at Canterbury and pledges a large sum in exchange for the restoration of Berwick and Edinburgh castles.

Late 1189 or early 1190: he holds a council at Musselburgh to arrange the levy.

1190   Late June: Richard leaves for the crusade.

26 August: David, having been confirmed by Richard in the earldom of Huntingdon, marries the heiress of the earl of Chester.

William's support for Arthur of Brittany as Richard's successor may have been enlisted.

1191   At Haddington William bestows his daughter Isabel, widow of Robert Bruce, on Robert de Ros, lord of Wark.

1192   William obtains a papal bull declaring the Scottish church subject only to Rome.

December: Richard is captured as he returns from the crusade.

1193   William marries his illegitimate daughter Margaret to Eustace de Vesci, lord of Alnwick.

John leagues against the captive Richard, to whose ransom William contributes.

William Malveisin is archdeacon of Lothian.

1194   February: Richard is released, returning to England on 13 March. Earl David helps to subdue the rebels.

2 April: William joins Richard at Clipstone (Nottinghamshire) and travels with him by way of Worksop, Southwell, Melton Mowbray, Rutland and Geddington to Northampton by 9 April and thence, after a quarrel with the bishop of Durham now earl of Northumbria, to Silverstone. He fails to recover Northumberland, Cumberland and Westmorland from Richard.

17 April: at Winchester Richard issues a charter specifying the

rights and privileges due to William and his successors when visiting the English court.

On the same day William acts as sword-bearer at Richard's second coronation.

19 April: the bishop of Durham surrenders Northumbria; but William's bid for the earldom fails.

22 April: William leaves Winchester for Scotland.

May: Richard leaves England for the last time.

1195   William issues his second coinage.

Summer (?): he is ill while at Clackmannan. He plans to marry his eldest daughter Margaret to Otto of Saxony, but some barons object.

Earl David founds the Tironensian abbey of Lindores (?).

1196   William pursues his marriage project with Richard, but no action is taken.

1196(?)   William counters a threat from Harald, earl of Orkney and Caithness. Taking an army into Caithness, he forces Harald to submit and promise hostages, including his son.

May: William is visited at Elgin by Earl David (?).

1197(?)   Having failed to deliver the stipulated hostages to William at Nairn, Harald is imprisoned in Edinburgh (or Roxburgh) until his son is produced. A dispute over Harald's title to Caithness ensues.

1198   24 August: William's heir, Alexander, is born at Haddington.

1198 or 1199   William gives the earldom of Caithness to the king of Man.

1199   6 April: Richard, who has been feuding with Philip Augustus, dies at Châlus.

25 May: John is crowned at Westminster, Arthur being under Philip's influence.

William, seeking restitution of the northern English counties, refuses John's summons to Northampton for discussions.

John leaves for Normandy and is followed by Earl David.

July (?): William spends a night of vigil at Queen Margaret's tomb at Dunfermline.

October: after the deaths of Bishop Jocelyn and the chancellor Hugh of Roxburgh, William Malveisin is elected to the Glasgow see and made chancellor.

William spends Christmas at Forfar.

1200   25–28 March: he declines John's summons to his council at York.

John returns to the Continent, with Earl David in his service.

23 September: Malveisin is consecrated bishop of Glasgow at Lyons.

8 October: John and his second wife Isabella of Angoulême are crowned at Westminster. Earl David and others are sent to escort William to his forthcoming court at Lincoln.

October: at Château Gaillard John issues a charter in favour of the burgesses of Dundee.

22 November: William pays homage to John at Lincoln. Earl David and Roland of Galloway are present. John defers a decision until the following Whitsun on William's plea for the restoration of the northern English counties. William returns to Scotland.

19 December: Roland of Galloway dies at Northampton.

Christmas is spent by William at Lanark.

His daughter Ada and sister Margaret die in the course of the year.

1201   February: John inspects his northern English fortresses.

May: he defers until Michaelmas a decision on William's plea for the 'lost counties'.

12 October: at William's council at Musselburgh the Scottish magnates swear allegiance to his son Alexander.

The papal legate John of Salerno holds a council in Perth.

William sends an army to counter Earl Harald's attempt to regain Caithness.

1202   Harald is brought to terms.

John of Salerno leaves Scotland having failed to resolve a dispute between Melrose and Kelso.

Philip Augustus opens hostilities against John.

August: Arthur of Brittany is captured by John at Mirebeau.

Earl David is at Le Mans after a visit to Scotland.

Bishop Roger of St Andrews dies and is succeeded by William Malveisin.

1203   Arthur of Brittany is murdered.

Earl David is in Normandy as John loses the struggle against Philip.

December: John returns to England.

1204   May: at Selkirk William settles the dispute between Melrose and Kelso.

He seems to have spent much of the year south of the Forth and to have resumed negotiations with John over the 'lost counties'.

1205   May: at Lanark he announces the founding of a new borough at Ayr.

October: he is at Stirling with Earl David, who perhaps pays homage to Alexander at this time.

November: John arranges to meet William at York.

1206   9–12 February: Earl David is sent to Scotland while the kings confer in York, where William is said to have effected a miraculous cure.

John issues a charter in favour of Arbroath Abbey.

William spends much of his time north of the Tay.

1207   Spring: the kings confer again in York without agreement. A further meeting planned for November does not take place.

Malveisin pays an extended business visit to Rome.

1208   John's strengthening of his defences at Tweedmouth causes tension with the Scots.

Earl David's influence at the English court wanes, whilst Malveisin's grows.

July: William and David are at Selkirk.

Following a dispute between John and Pope Innocent III over the Canterbury succession, England and Wales are placed under an interdict.

1209   Early: William is seriously ill at Traquair. On his recovery, John requests a meeting.

April: William goes to Alnwick and then, with John, to Norham, where their talks end in discord.

24 May: William holds a council at Stirling with Earl David present. An embassy to John led by Malveisin is met with threats.

From Forfar William sends a further embassy, but John's own envoys arrive to meet William in Edinburgh.

Malveisin reports to William at Traquair as John leads his army north.

William, at Melrose, decides to sue for peace.

July–August: he meets John at Norham and accepts humiliating terms.

6 August: the Treaty of Norham is sealed.

Michaelmas (or 1210?): William and Earl David escape from floods at Perth and hold a council at Stirling.

October (?): John, still in dispute with the pope, is excommunicated. Two of his bishops take refuge in Scotland.

Earl David's daughter Margaret is married to Alan of Galloway.

1210   July: John's daughter Joanna is born.

The Norham terms provoke unrest among certain Scottish barons.

Duncan of Galloway returns to John some fugitives from the Irish rebellion.

Earl David's daughter Isabel is married to Robert Bruce IV of Annandale.

William spends Christmas in Moray and is then detained by illness at Kintore.

1211 Summer: William fights an indecisive campaign in the north against Guthred MacWilliam.

1212 2 February: William meets John at Durham. With Queen Ermengarde and Alexander they adjourn to Norham.

8 March: having left Norham with John, Alexander is knighted by him at Westminster. John will arrange a suitable marriage for him.

Alexander returns to Scotland, perhaps with a force sent by John to help William against Guthred.

Summer: Guthred is betrayed, brought before Alexander at Kincardine, and beheaded.

Late June: John travels to Carlisle, Hexham and Durham. A reported meeting with William is unlikely.

William warns John of impending treason (?).

Queen Ermengarde plays an increasingly prominent role in affairs of state.

1213 Early: John may have sought a meeting with William and Alexander, though none took place.

May: John makes his peace with the pope.

William's charters suggest his current preoccupation with religious matters.

1214 Summer: William travels to Moray and makes a pact with Earl John of Caithness.

Ailing, he returns by short stages to Stirling.

4 December: he dies at Stirling, probably in the presence of Queen Ermengarde, Alexander and Earl David.

6 December: Alexander II is invested as king by Bishop Malveisin at Scone.

10 December: William is buried in Arbroath Abbey.

1219 Earl David dies in Northamptonshire.

1234 Queen Ermengarde dies and is buried in Balmerino Abbey (Cistercian), which she had recently founded.

1237 By the Treaty of York Alexander abandons the Scottish claim to the 'lost counties'.

1238 Bishop Malveisin dies near St Andrews.

1249 Alexander dies near Oban.

Purser, John, *Scotland's Music*, Edinburgh & London, 1992.

Ritchie, R.L. Graeme. *The Normans in Scotland*, Edinburgh, 1954.

– *Chrétien de Troyes and Scotland*, Oxford, 1952.

Sargent-Baur, Barbara Nelson, & Robert Francis Cook, *Aucassin et Nicolete: a Critical Bibliography*, London, 1981.

Shepherd, M., *Tradition and Re-Creation in Thirteenth-Century Romance: 'La Manekine' and 'Jehan et Blonde' by Philippe de Rémi*, Amsterdam & Atlanta, GA, 1990.

*Stringer, K.J., *Earl David of Huntingdon 1152–1219: A Study in Anglo-Scottish History*, Edinburgh University Press, 1985.

*Watt, D.E.R., *A Biographical Dictionary of Scottish Graduates to A.D. 1410*, Oxford, 1977.

Index

(Some minor literary names are omitted, and references to the Chronology are not included.)

58, 64–6, 71–2, 76, 84,
91
John, king of England, 33, 44, 58–9,
69–70, 74, 80, 82, 84, 88–113, 134,
149–50, 179
John, earl of Orkney and Caithness,
111
John (the Scot), bishop of St Andrews
and of Dunkeld, 62–4, 66–7, 73, 76
John, bishop of Dunkeld, 107
John of Salisbury, 19, 29, 41
Joïe, queen of Scotland in *La
Manekine*, 169–76, 178–9
Jordan Fantosme, *see* Fantosme
Judas, 108
Julius Caesar, 152

Kay, King Arthur's seneschal, 119,
122, 134, 139, 145
Kempston (Bedfordshire), 36, 40
Kenneth I MacAlpin, king of Picts
and Scots, 1
Kentigern, Saint (= Mungo), 4, 24, 30,
130, 132
Life of, 27, 155
Kerrera, Isle of (Argyll), 113
Kincardine (Mearns), 108
Kinghorn (Fife), 36
Kintore (Aberdeenshire), 98, 105
Kintyre (Argyll), 1, 14

Lac, fictional king, 156
Lacy, Hugh de, earl of Ulster, 104
lais (from *làed*), 27–8
Lammermuir, 123
Lanark, 36, 92, 96
Lancaster, county of, 83
Lancelot, knight of King Arthur, 122
Langton, Stephen, archbishop of
Canterbury, 100
Lateran council, 58
Lauderdale, 117, 128
Laudine of Landuc, fictional
heroine, 28
Laudunet, fictional duke, 28
Layamon, 24
Leicester, 53

earl of, 49, 76
Le Mans, 35, 68, 77, 94, 150
Lennox, earldom of, 49, 60, 70
Leopold, duke of Austria, 81
Leuchars (Fife), 105
Leudonus, fictional king, 27
Liddel Castle (Roxburghshire), 119,
123, 126, 135–7
Liddesdale, lordship of, 134–5, 137
Lille, 172
Limoges, 18, 42, 44, 68, 87
Lincoln, 92, 99
bishop of, *see* Grosseteste, Robert
Lindisfarne (Northumberland), 4
Lindores Abbey (Fife), 60, 81, 113, 143
Linlithgow, 36
Loch Lomond, 25
Lochmaben (Dumfriesshire), 36
Lombard, Master, 41
London, 53, 91, 166, 176
Longchamp, William, bishop of
Ely, 80, 82
Loth (Lot), King, 25, 158
Lothian, 3, 8, 13, 25, 28, 85–6, 91,
102, 119–23, 127, 129, 135–7, 141–2,
146–9, 155–6
East Lothian, 37
Midlothian, 37, 69
West Lothian, 37
Louis VII, king of France, 18, 32–3,
41–6, 54, 59, 71
Lovel, family of, 167–8
Lovel, fictional prince of England,
164–7
Lucius III, Pope, 64, 66–9, 71
Lucy, Richard de, 48–9, 51
Lulach, Macbeth's stepson, 2
Lyons, 91

Macbeth, king of Scotland, 2, 4, 21
MacHeth, family of, 73
Malcolm, earl of Ross, 16, 60–1, 86
MacWilliam, family of, 73, 98
Donald, 61, 64, 74–5, 106, 161
Guthred, 97, 106, 108, 112, 161
Magna Carta, 113
Mainard, provost of St Andrews, 115